Filipino, it transcends the specific context and offers invaluable insights for all, especially for the faithful in the Majority World. Read this book. Reflect deeply on its content. Thank God for your roots. And be part of God's transforming work in the Philippines and beyond.

Al Tizon, PhD
Affiliate Associate Professor of Missional and Global Leadership,
North Park Theological Seminary, Chicago, USA

Faith and Bayan is a testament to the power of solidarity in the midst of crisis. While the pandemic may have affected faith communities around the country, the contributors all agree that Christian engagement must carry on. In their view, faith is ultimately inseparable from the concerns of the everyday Filipino. And because faith is ultimately about taking risks (*pagtataya*), Christians are therefore called to be prophetic. For many Christians, however, this calling is neither fashionable nor comforting. Therein lies what being Christian demands today: commitment in the midst of crisis. In their own ways, the contributors to *Faith and Bayan* are showing the way. By doing so, they are telling the rest of us that we are not alone.

Jayeel Cornelio, PhD
Associate Dean for Research and Creative Work
Ateneo de Manila University, Philippines

There's plenty of reason to despair and to feel hopeless of our current sociopolitical situation. The darkness around us is deep. If there's a ray of light amid our deep darkness, it's that the Spirit has inspired a new generation of Filipino evangelical theologians and biblical scholars to challenge and shake the traditional image of evangelicalism. Instead of an obsession about salvation for the next life, which by default continues to support the status quo, this new generation is calling for active participation in the work of social transformation as central and constitutive of God's salvific plan. This is a breath of new life into our toxic and life-destroying political climate! Let's welcome and celebrate this exciting development!

Eleazar Fernandez, PhD
President Union Theological Seminary
Cavite, Philippines

I believe the message of this book is that to be a good Christian is to be a good citizen. It rightly debunks a current but mistaken notion of the separation of church and state in the Philippine constitution. If one actually reads the constitutional provision, it is addressed to the state not to interfere with the beliefs of people and should not establish its own church. It has no provision prohibiting the church to make critical statements about the government. In fact, it is not only the right, but the duty of the church to make moral statements about the actuations of government with political consequences. In some chapters of the book, this may be expressed as "dissent," "protest" or "critique." This is the prophetic expression of faith in contemporary times. A definition of "prophet" is to announce the good news and denounce the bad news. And the duty of the prophet is to stand up and speak out. I congratulate the authors of the book who in their articles are doing just this.

Sr. Mary John Mananzan, OSB
Former President, St. Scholastica's College, Manila, Philippines;
Chairperson Emerita, GABRIELA

Does the *pananampalataya ng simbahan* (faith of the church) have anything to do with the *pagsasamantala sa bayan* (exploitation of the nation)? "As long as our freedom to worship is not impaired, we should not get involved, in issues of society" seems to be the prevailing answer of many Christians, especially for those who identify themselves as evangelicals.

Faith and Bayan: Evangelical Christian Engagement in the Philippine Context presents a product of a soul-searching discernment, wrestling with the Scripture, and grappling with what our *kababayans* (those belonging to us) are facing on a daily basis. Will evangelicals just remain silent, and be isolated and insulated inside their sanctuaries, "singing like never before," as the first chapter quotes? This book answers with an emphatic no!

The book with its clear prophetic voice from the evangelical theologians, thinkers, and writers, is a timely and a welcome contribution that provokes, challenges, and moves Christians to be engaged and have *pagmamalasakit* – a deep concern for the life and common good of our land, people, and nation.

I heartily recommend this book to all discerning Christians who would refuse to relegate the Christian faith into individual piety that is devoid of social and political content, and who have the heart to work and witness as salt and light for the common good for our land, people, and nation.

Bishop Reuel Norman O. Marigza
General Secretary of the National Council of Churches in the Philippines

In a world of tweets, posts, and rambling blogs, I find myself constantly longing for thoughtful scholarship on the crucial matters of our time. *Faith and Bayan* is such a volume. Masterfully put-together by the editors, this book gathers scholars who grapple with Christian social engagement in the context of our love for and sense of rootedness in our *bayan*. Though this volume is decidedly

Faith and Bayan

Faith and Bayan

Evangelical Christian Engagement in the Philippine Context

Edited by

Lorenzo C. Bautista, Aldrin M. Peñamora, and Federico G. Villanueva

GLOBAL LIBRARY

© 2022 Lorenzo C. Bautista, Aldrin M. Peñamora, and Federico G. Villanueva

Published 2022 by Langham Global Library
An imprint of Langham Publishing
www.langhampublishing.org

Langham Publishing and its imprints are a ministry of Langham Partnership

Langham Partnership
PO Box 296, Carlisle, Cumbria, CA3 9WZ, UK
www.langham.org

ISBNs:
978-1-83973-277-5 Print
978-1-83973-658-2 ePub
978-1-83973-659-9 Mobi
978-1-83973-660-5 PDF

Lorenzo C. Bautista, Aldrin M. Peñamora, and Federico G. Villanueva hereby assert their moral right to be identified as the Author of the General Editor's part in the Work in accordance with sections 77 and 78 of the Copyright, Designs and Patents Act 1988.

All rights reserved. No part of this publication may be reproduced, stored in a retrieval system or transmitted, in any form or by any means, electronic, mechanical, photocopying, recording or otherwise, without the prior written permission of the publisher or the Copyright Licensing Agency.

Requests to reuse content from Langham Publishing are processed through PLSclear. Please visit www.plsclear.com to complete your request.

Scripture quotations marked (ESV) are from The Holy Bible, English Standard Version® (ESV®), copyright © 2001 by Crossway, a publishing ministry of Good News Publishers. Used by permission. All rights reserved.

Scripture quotations marked (GNT) are from the Good News Translation in Today's English Version-Second Edition. Copyright © 1992 by American Bible Society. Used by Permission.

Scripture quotations marked (MBB) are taken from the Magandang Balita Biblia, Copyright © Philippine Bible Society 2012.

Scripture quotations marked (NIV) are taken from the Holy Bible, New International Version®, NIV®. Copyright © 1973, 1978, 1984, 2011 by Biblica, Inc.™ Used by permission of Zondervan.

Scripture quotations marked (NKJV) are taken from the New King James Version (NKJV). Copyright © 1982 by Thomas Nelson, Inc. Used by permission. All rights reserved.

Scripture quotations marked (NRSV) are from the New Revised Standard Version Bible, copyright © 1989 National Council of the Churches of Christ in the United States of America. Used by permission. All rights reserved.

British Library Cataloguing-in-Publication Data
A catalogue record for this book is available from the British Library

ISBN: 978-1-83973-277-5

Cover & Book Design: projectluz.com

Langham Partnership actively supports theological dialogue and an author's right to publish but does not necessarily endorse the views and opinions set forth here or in works referenced within this publication, nor can we guarantee technical and grammatical correctness. Langham Partnership does not accept any responsibility or liability to persons or property as a consequence of the reading, use or interpretation of its published content.

Para sa ating bayan
(For our nation)

Contents

Preface xiii

Introduction: Faith and Bayan 1

1 Worship and Justice 13
   Federico G. Villanueva

2 "Act Justly, Love Mercy, Walk Humbly with God": Perspectives on Power and Politics from the Old Testament Prophetic Tradition 29
   Annelle G. Sabanal

3 Romans 13 and the Limits of Submission 49
   Junette B. Galagala-Nacion

4 Why the Church Needs to Learn How to Complain and Not Just "Trust and Obey" 77
   Federico G. Villanueva

5 Duterte, Democracy, and Dissent 99
   Roberto G. Barredo

6 Their Blood Cries Out from the Ground: An Ethic of *Malasakit* and the War on Drugs 115
   Aldrin M. Peñamora

7 "Your Kingdom Come, Your Will be Done": Disclosing the Ethics of the New Testament's Parousia 133
   Christopher D. Sabanal

8 Shepherding a Coalition for Justice 157
   Carlo Diño

Epilogue 175

Preface

This book was conceived, developed, and completed while the coronavirus wreaked havoc the world over. The initial idea for the book came from one of the editors, Aldrin Peñamora, who suggested that we organize Filipino evangelical scholars to address the tyranny and injustices of the Duterte administration that many Filipinos, including evangelical leaders, have sadly supported. None of us were able to meet face to face. The pre-editorial meetings, the first meeting of the writers on 22 June 2020, as well as the succeeding meetings were all held online. But this did not prevent us from becoming creative. Since we were not able to meet in person, we took advantage of the situation. Thus, for two months, from the first week of October until 7 December 2020, we conducted a webinar. Every Tuesday night, from 7:30 to 9:00, the webinar was shown live on Facebook. The livestream was also shared on other web pages, such as KapeTheo, Truth or Dare, CrossCurrents Philippines, Lapis Seesaw Channel, Parish of the Holy Sacrifice, Bawat Isa Mahalaga, Coalition for Justice, Ang Kristiyanong Blog, and South East Asia Alliance of Christian Leaders.

We were encouraged by the results of the webinars, as we were able to get a good number of viewers for our livestream as well as of those who watched the replay. The responses in the chat messages helped the writers later in the development of their respective chapters. What a very good way to write a book! We are thankful to Christopher and Annelle Sabanal, who provided the backbone for the webinar programs. Christopher handled the technical side while Annelle did the emceeing. We also would like to thank Angeline D. Rodriguez, who not only helped with the emceeing, but also designed the posters for each of the webinars.

This book has benefited not only from the comments and questions from the viewers but also from the responses of the responders. The latter come from various traditions and backgrounds, demonstrating the interdisciplinary and ecumenical spirit with which this book came about. We would like to thank the following for serving as responders for the book:

- Bishop Broderick S. Pabillo, DD
- Bishop Noel A. Pantoja

- Dr. Abigail R. Teh
- Dr. Lizette Tapia-Rachel
- Dr. Ferdinand A. Anno
- Dr. Zosimo E. Lee
- Sr. Mary John Mananzan, O.S.B., PhD
- Fr. Daniel Franklin E. Pilario, C.M., PhD
- Dr. Reimund R. Bieringer
- Dr. Melba P. Maggay
- Bishop Pablo Virgilio S. David, DD

The book would not have been possible without the help and support of various organizations, foremost of which is Langham Publishing, who sponsored the webinars and supported the whole process of the writing of the book. OMF Literature (Manila) also kindly sponsored some of the sessions in the webinar along with the Justice, Peace, and Reconciliation Commission of the Philippine Council of Evangelical Churches.

We thank each of the writers of this book for their great efforts and perseverance in completing their task:

- Dr. Roberto G. Barredo
- Ptr. Carlo Diño
- Prof. Junette B. Galagala-Nacion
- Dr. Aldrin M. Peñamora
- Dr. Annelle G. Sabanal
- Dr. Christopher D. Sabanal
- Dr. Federico G. Villanueva

The webinar was a success and an important part of the writing process, but it was only the beginning. The hard part was the writing of the book itself, which was done in the continuing isolation of the pandemic. In 2021, we had the worst COVID-19 surge in the Philippines. There was not one among us who did not have either a loved one, a friend, or a colleague who did not have COVID-19, or worse, died. The father of Rico Villanueva died 11 April 2021. Several members of our group also got infected. The current political situation did not help either as the killings in the "war on drugs" have continued and even increased according to some reports. While many of our people are struggling with how to survive, with the rate of unemployment at its peak, we hear of reports of corruption. It has not been easy to write during this time as many of us have felt helpless, powerless. But one of the things that kept us going is the writing of this book. We believe that this book makes an important contribution toward our *bayan*.

Lorenzo Bautista, Aldrin Peñamora, and Federico Villanueva (editors)

Introduction

Faith and Bayan

Evangelical Christian Engagement in the Philippine Context

As reflected in the title, this book is about the relationship between "faith" and "*bayan.*" The particle "and" in "faith *and* bayan" is central, literally and figuratively. "Faith," if it is to be true to the teachings of the Bible, has to be related to "bayan." This is the underlying conviction of the book. The different chapters in the book argue this point, demonstrating what the relationship between "faith" and "bayan" might look like. But before we proceed, it is necessary to explain what we mean by the words "faith" and "bayan."

Bayan

Bayan is a Tagalog word which has two categories of meaning: (1) as a place and (2) as a people. "Bayan" comes from the word *balayan*, which is a combination of the noun *balay* (house) and the suffix *an*.[1] Together, *balayan* means a group of houses or the place on which these are built.[2] "Bayan" stems from the concept of place. It could refer to a city, a town, or even the whole country. The Philippines is referred to as "ang bayan kong Pilipinas" (my "country" the Philippines) in the famous Filipino song "Bayan ko." But bayan does not just refer to a "place." The concept of rootedness is strong in the concept of bayan.

---

1. Mary Jane Rodriguez-Tatel, *Ang Dalumat ng Bayan sa Kamalayan at Kasaysayang Pilipino* (Quezon City: Bagong Kasaysayan, 2006), 3.

2. Rodriguez-Tatel, *Ang Dalumat ng Bayan*, 3: "kalipunan ng mga balay/bahay o lugar na pinagtayuan nito."

We refer to our bayan as our "lupang tinubuan" (literally, "land out of which we sprout") or "bayang sinilangan" (the place where we were born). Even Filipinos who have lived abroad for a long time still long for the time when they can go back to their own bayan. We are always reminded by the famous Filipino saying: "Ang hindi marunong tumanaw sa pinanggalingan, hindi makararating sa paroroonan" (Those who do not know how to look back to where they have come from will not reach their destination).

Unfortunately, some Filipino Christians do not know how to look back to where they have come from. They tend to forget their roots, their "lupang tinubuan." They think that when they become Christians, their identity as Filipinos is no longer important. And they give up any notion of engagement with their bayan. But the Bible speaks of "a great multitude . . . from every nation, from all tribes and peoples and languages" which will gather before the throne at the end of the age (Rev 7:9).[3] Note the presence of people from "all tribes" and the word "languages." This means that the identity of each nation, tribe, and people remains until the end. We will not face the Lord as "universal," rootless Christians. The word "peoples" in the Tagalog translation of the Greek word, *laon*, is "bayan" (MBB). This is an apt translation of the word since bayan also refers to people. In Tagalog, citizens are referred to as *mamamayan* and *taumbayan*. The leader of the community is called *punong-bayan*. At the end of the age, when all the peoples of the earth gather before the Great Throne of God, we don't want to miss our own bayan. Revelation 7:9 also mentions "languages." We'd like to hear our own languages being spoken before the presence of God. People from "all tribes . . . and languages" will stand there. We don't want to miss hearing Tagalog, Ilokano, Bisaya, and so on! Surely, Christians from other countries of the world would want to hear their own languages spoken there as well.

Our hope is that the things we will be discussing in this book will find relevance in other contexts. For some of the questions and problems we encounter in our own Philippine context may be similar to those which our brothers and sisters in other countries, particularly those from the Majority World, are facing. As we will mention below, our encounter with Christianity came through colonization – an experience which we share with many peoples in Asia, Africa, and Latin America.

---

3. Unless otherwise indicated, all quotations are from the ESV.

Faith

Our understanding of "faith" is shaped by our own history, culture, and experience. Faith is closely linked to our own context. There is no such thing as a universal, perspective-free faith. Each culture, context, and people makes its own contribution to our understanding of "faith." Culture is reflected in our language. For instance, in Tagalog, the word for "faith" is very long, occupying more space when written and taking a longer time when spoken. In contrast to the English word, which consists of only one syllable and five letters ("faith"), the Tagalog word consists of seven syllables and fifteen letters – *pananampalataya*. It is as if the word itself is forcing us to slow down, take our time, and consider carefully its meaning. If the importance of a word is judged by its length, then surely *pananampalataya* is a vital word.

The word *pananampalataya* can be divided into two words: "*pagnamnam* (tasting) and *pagtatataya* (taking risk)."[4] *Pananampalataya* is about experience, which is implied in the word *pagnamnam* (taste). As the psalmist declares, "Oh, taste and see that the LORD is good!" (Ps 34:8). Faith is founded on a genuine relationship with Jesus Christ, the founder of Christianity. Only those who have encountered the Lord can express faith.

But it is not enough that one has encountered the Lord. One has to make a commitment. Faith, in the Filipino sense of the word, involves taking risk (*pagtataya*). Faith is not easy. It's not simply praying to receive Christ. Some of our politicians, including some of our past presidents, have prayed to receive Christ. But they were also some of the most corrupt leaders. Faith is not simply believing. For "even the demons believe – and shudder!" (Jas 2:19). Jesus warns those who want to follow him that they must be prepared to "count the cost" (Luke 14:28). The Tagalog word *pananampalataya* gives an opportunity to those uttering it to think first before committing.

How We Received the Faith: The Philippine Experience

Given our historical experience, there is a need for us to think over and evaluate the faith we have received. The Christian faith was introduced to us by Catholic missionaries when they came to our bayan together with the Spanish colonizers. This put the Catholic missionaries in a very complicated position. How could the missionaries claim to be bringing the message of Jesus, who offered his life for others, when they were coming with those who

---

4. R. L. Rebustillo, "*Bahala Na*: In Search of an 'Ordinary Theology' for the Filipino Diaspora," *International Journal of Practical Theology* 22, no. 2 (2018): 240.

saw us and treated us as less than human? Jesus came to set us free, but our colonizers came to make us their slaves.

Thus, the message of the gospel was compromised from the start, resulting in what Jaime Bulatao called "split-level Christianity."[5] It's true that the majority of the population adopted Christianity. But Christianity did not penetrate deep enough to transform their *loob* (inner being). Jesus remained as someone who was outside (*taga-labas*). An example of "split-level Christianity" is the practice of doing "under the table" transactions (a bribe or *lagay*, as we call it). On top of the table is the Sto. Niño (statue of the baby Jesus). Filipinos don't see any problem holding these two conflicting attitudes.

Probably, one of the biggest failures in Philippine evangelization during the time of the Spanish colonization was the lack of good role models whom the people could emulate. Not only was the cross used as an instrument for conquest, but those who were supposed to bring the message of the gospel were not good witnesses. According to Karl Gaspar, "what finally was a source of scandal for the natives was their [friars'] witness in the way they lived their lives."[6] This longing for someone to follow and imitate is expressed in the *pasyon* – the influential Filipino document which narrates the story of Jesus and his suffering. The main purpose of telling the story of Jesus is to imitate him. According to the *Casaysayan ng Pasiong Mahal*, one of the reasons why Jesus came down to earth was in order for us to have someone to imitate:[7]

At caya nag asal duc-ha	This is why they acted poor,
nag-anyong tauong mababa,	appeared as humble folk:
yao,i, tiquis na guinaua	they made such a sacrifice
nang may cunang halimba	so that people on earth
ang tauong hamac sa lupa.	May have a source of good example.

At the end of the *pasyon*, the author warns the readers not to imitate wicked teachers. Instead, they should imitate Jesus:[8]

---

5. Jaime C. Bulatao, "Split-Level Christianity," in *Phenomena and Their Interpretation: Landmark Essays, 1957–1989* (Manila: Ateneo de Manila University Press, 1992), 22–31.

6. Karl M. Gaspar, CSsR, *Handumanan (Remembrance): Digging for the Indigenous Wellspring* (Quezon City: Episcopal Commission on Indigenous Peoples and Claretian Communications Foundations, 2021), 378.

7. René B. Javellana, *Casaysayan Nang Pasiong Mahal Ni Jesucristong Panginoon Natin: Na Sucat Ipag-Alab Nang Puso Nang Sinomang Babasa* (Quezon City: Ateneo de Manila University Press, 1988), 52 (stanza 232). For the English translation, see p. 164.

8. Javellana, *Casaysayan Nang Pasiong Mahal*, 128. English translation on p. 233 (emphasis mine).

Talicdan nangang totoo	Turn away completely
ang manga dangal sa mundo,	from the honors of the world
tumulad cay Jesucristo,	*imitate* Jesus Christ
nang tayo,i, houag mabuyo	so that we will not be trapped
sa aral nang manga lilo.	by the deceivers' teaching.

But how could they imitate Jesus without embodied demonstrations of his life? Although there were Spanish missionaries who tried to live out a life of Christlikeness, on the whole our people did not have good models, for even those supposedly "good models" were co-opted by the whole business of colonization.

Evangelical Christians may think that with the coming of the Protestant Americans the situation changed. Those of us who have been converted to the "born again" type of Christianity might say that finally the right kind of faith arrived. But like their predecessors, the American Protestant missionaries came with the American colonizers. The introduction of evangelical Christianity was also fraught with contradictions from the very start. Why were we being colonized again? This must have been what crossed the minds of our parents at the end of the nineteenth century. Just when they thought they had finally won the long-awaited (more than three hundred years!) freedom, they realized they had simply changed masters. Even the lament of the psalmist, "How long, O LORD?" (Ps 13:1), could hardly contain the pain, the frustrations, the anger, our parents must have felt at that point. After the Spanish colonizers, it was the turn of the supposedly Protestant Christians. But that was the situation when the Christian message was brought to us by the American missionaries under the guise of "benevolent assimilation."

Today, as we look at our bayan, we feel what our poet Balagtas wrote during the time of the Spanish colonization, when he described our bayan as *sawi* (unfortunate, a failure): "Sa loob at labas ng bayan kong sawi . . ." (in and out of my unfortunate/hopeless country). While we may no longer be under direct foreign control, colonization continues. The difference is that it is our own *kababayan* (one belonging to us) who has become our colonizer. We write this book under a president who has explicitly compared himself to Hitler.[9] The majority of our people feel it's dangerous to say anything against the Duterte

---

9. Felipe Villamor, "Duterte, Citing Hitler, Says He Wants to Kill 3 Million Addicts in Philippines," *New York Times* online, 30 September 2016, accessed 31 August 2021, https://nyti.ms/2VaFweI.

administration.[10] Duterte's so-called "war on drugs" has resulted in thousands of deaths. Even in the midst of the pandemic, the killings have continued. And while many of our people are struggling to survive, investigations into massive, unprecedented corruption are being conducted. We write this introduction in the midst of the pandemic. According to one report, the Philippines ranks "last in infection control, vaccination and mobility" among 121 countries.[11]

Introducing the Chapters of the Book

How do we engage with our bayan in this situation? How do we live out our calling as Christians when the very lives of our people are at stake, when the future of our bayan is on the line? We cannot afford to be silent. If there is a time when the relationship between "faith" and "bayan" is needed, it is now. Our bayan needs our faith.

But some may say, is not our faith already tied in with our bayan? The Philippines is often referred to as "the only Christian nation in Asia." If in the Bible, Christians are referred to as "bayang pag-aari ng Diyos" (God's own people; 1 Pet 2:9 MBB), some Filipino Christians claim that the Philippines is "bayan ng Diyos" (people of God).[12] But while this has led to some advocacy for the common good, it has also resulted in the rejection of values other Filipinos consider important.[13]

While some may "claim" the Philippines for God, others view "faith" as only "spiritual," concerned with issues within the church and which affect only a person's "spiritual" well-being. One Christian leader, for example, commented that we should not meddle with politics. He explains that even if President Duterte curses a lot, that's not a concern for us, since that is outside the church's spiritual sphere.[14] He adds that our concern should be within the church. In

---

10. Sofia Tomacruz, "Majority of Filipinos Think It's Dangerous to Publish Anything Critical of Duterte Admin," Rappler, 3 August 2019, accessed 27 October 2021, https://www.rappler.com/nation/majority-filipinos-think-dangerous-publish-things-critical-duterte-admin-sws.

11. Zacarian Gavin H. Sarao, "PH Ranks Last out of 121 Countries in Global COVID-19 Recovery Index – Nikkei," Inquirer.net, 6 October 2021, accessed 23 October 2021, https://newsinfo.inquirer.net/1498167/ph-ranks-last-out-of-121-countries-in-global-covid-19-recovery-index-nikkei.

12. Jayeel Cornelio, "Claiming the Nation: Theological Nationalism in the Philippines," in *What Does Theology Do, Actually? Observing Theology and the Transcultural*, eds. M. Robinson and I. Inderst (Leipzig: Evangelische Verlagsanstalt, 2020), 158.

13. Cornelio, "Claiming the Nation," 160.

14. In a personal conversation with one of the editors.

the first chapter of this book, Villanueva quotes a social media post which is basically saying that so long as the government does not prohibit worship in the church, there is no need to comment on anything the government is doing. Even if thousands of poor people are already being killed in the "war on drugs," what is important is that we can still "worship." Such a view of "faith" needs serious correction. The issue is not whether we can worship or not, but whether our worship is acceptable to God. The question is, how can we worship God if we do not care about issues of justice? This is the theme of the first chapter.

The Bible is clear: we are called to be the "salt" and "light" of the earth" (Matt 5:13–14). We are to be concerned with what happens not just inside the church, but in the world. For did not our Lord teach us to pray, "Your kingdom come, your will be done, *on earth* as it is in heaven" (Matt 6:10, emphasis added)? We cannot truly pray this prayer unless we really long for God's will to be done on earth. Such a longing finds expression in actions which contribute toward the realization of what we are praying for.

Unfortunately, in view of our bayan's experience of colonization, an overemphasis on the doctrine of divine sovereignty as taught in some Christian circles has led to the weakening of the view of the role of human agency and participation in the social and political spheres. While we are not against the doctrine of divine sovereignty, this should be taught in the light of our own experience of colonization. Being under foreign power for so long has led to the weakening of human resolve. Thus, it is possible that divine sovereignty, when taught without reflection, can further contribute to the degrading of the Filipino Christian's resolve. It is common to hear Filipinos say, "kung may awa ang Diyos" (if God has mercy). We are always at the mercy of our tormentors and conquerors, so we tend to depend only on "mercy." We often hear people, when confronted with difficult situations, including injustices, say, "ipasa-Diyos mo na lang" (just leave it to God). This was actually what people said to a mother whose son was unjustly killed in the "war on drugs."[15] One of the editors of this book remembers delivering a couple of sermons against the injustices of this so-called "war." But after all his efforts, one of the leaders in the church had only one response: "trust God." Indeed, some pastors believe God sent President Duterte as a "righteous intervention."[16] Our problem with

---

15. Aileen Paguntalan-Mijares, "Rebuilding Lives amid the Ruins of Duterte's War on Drugs," *Journal of Human Rights and Peace Studies* 6, no. 2 (2020): 256.

16. Jayeel Cornelio and Ia Marañon, "A 'Righteous Intervention': Megachurch Christianity and Duterte's War on Drugs in the Philippines," *International Journal of Asian Christianity* 2, no. 2 (2019): 211–30.

this is that the "war on drugs" is far from being "just" or "righteous." And if it is an intervention, it surely is not divine, and it is a big failure. The president himself admitted that the drug problem has got worse.[17]

But why do so many Christians, including pastors and priests, support Duterte? One of the common explanations is Romans 13. In a debate on social media between two theologians, when asked about his basis for defending Duterte one theologian simply said, "Romans 13." Romans 13 has been used before to justify the oppression of others, such as by America's pro-slavery advocates, leading to the Civil War, and supporters of Hitler and his Nazi regime. Now, many evangelical Filipinos are using the same text to support a president who has compared his actions to those of Hitler and has cursed God on public television. Because Romans 13 is such an important passage, we have devoted one chapter to it (see chapter 3 by Junette Galagala).

One of the problems with the use of Romans 13 is that it is treated as if it is the only passage in the Bible. Other relevant passages concerning how we should relate to government are ignored, such as those in other parts of the New Testament (e.g. Rev 13) and the prophetic teachings in the Old Testament, which find their climax in Jesus. That is why in this book, we not only offer a more comprehensive treatment of Romans 13 in its New Testament context, but also consider the Old Testament. In chapter 2, Annelle Sabanal explores the prophetic literature to highlight relevant themes. Her chapter provides the much-needed foundation for any discussion of Romans 13. Those who might ignore the prophetic literature need to be reminded that Jesus saw himself as continuing the ministry of the prophets. The church can do no less than be like its master.

Unfortunately, the image of Jesus introduced to us by our colonizers was one that promoted a passive response. Jesus, we were taught, was patient, so we needed to just bear our sufferings. Here is the line of argument which our colonizers used, according to Jose Mario Francisco: "Mapagtiis si Kristo, kung kaya't dapat ding tiisin ng indio ang kanyang aping kalagayan" (Christ is patient, so the *indio* should bear his pitiful condition).[18] Francisco explains: "Kinasangkapan ng mga Kastila at ng kanilang alipures ang larawan ni Kristo upang mapanatili ang dayuhang kapangyarihan" (The Spanish and their

---

17. CNN Philippines, "'Things Have Worsened,' Duterte Says of Drug Problem," 26 March 2019, accessed 27 October 2021, https://cnnphilippines.com/news/2019/3/26/duterte-drug-problem-worsened.html.

18. Jose Mario C. Francisco, "Panitikan at Kristiyanismong Pilipino: Ang Nagbabagong Larawan Ni Kristo," *Philippine Studies* 25 (1977): 196.

compatriots used the image of the Christ to maintain foreign power).[19] Even today, we hear of some megachurch pastors pointing to Jesus as the "silent one," in order to maintain the status quo. But Jesus is far from just being a "silent one." Yes he did become silent, but that was after he had done his part, rebuking the leaders of his time for their injustice (see Matt 23:23). Jesus did not merely remain passive. He also complained to the leaders, and even to God himself. On the cross, he asked God, "Why have you forsaken me?" As Villanueva argues, complaint should be a part of the Christian life (see chapter 4, "Complaint against God").

One of the important contributions of the message of the prophets and of our Lord Jesus is the place of dissent in the life of faith. Prophets speak against unjust kings or rulers. Annelle Sabanal points out that while the prophets also know how to speak positive words of encouragement, they are better known for their criticisms of leaders (see chapter 2). They are more defined by their critical distance from worldly rulers. It is this critical distance which engenders dissent.

Dissent is an important part or essence of democracy. This is one of the main differences between the context and historical situation of Paul and our time today. Today, every Christian has the right and responsibility to express what he or she thinks is right. When Jesus commanded his disciples to let their "light shine before others, so that they may see your good works" (Matt 5:16), what will be considered good work in a democratic society in situations of injustice is not passive submission but active engagement, which includes dissent. We often hear these days of young Christians leaving the church because they no longer see the relevance of what is being taught there right where they are living their lives. In chapter 5, Roberto Barredo provides a creative presentation of the place of dissent in democracy, as exemplified by key concepts from the political thinker Claude Lefort, in engagement with the Scripture centered on the biblical institutions of the king, Torah, and the prophets.

Dissent is often viewed negatively in our society. But in the Bible, one of the reasons why people complain and lament is because they care. Our Tagalog word for utmost care or concern is *malasakit*. This word comes from the root word *sakit* (pain). We speak out because we feel and are concerned about the pain others are experiencing. One of the subtle arguments behind the "war on drugs" is *pagmamalasakit* (deep concern). According to this view propounded by President Duterte himself and his associates, drug users must

---

19. Francisco, "Panitikan at Kristiyanismong Pilipino," 196.

be exterminated for the sake of the good of our bayan. Yet as Aldrin Peñamora points out, the "war on drugs" is the very opposite of *pagmamalasakit*. If anything, it exemplifies *walang pagmamalasakit* (no care or concern at all) in its blatant disregard for human life and for God's image in the alleged drug addicts who are brutally slain. It is for this reason that a genuine ethic of *pagmamalasakit*, an ethic that follows the "way of Jesus," needs to be cultivated for the sake of the oppressed such as the victims of the drug war (see chapter 6).

Yet the sad reality is that, despite being aware that killings of mostly poor people are being committed in the "war on drugs," many Christians don't seem to care. Instead of doing anything to fight it, they simply shrug their shoulders and say, "These are end times indeed!" When you have killings, the pandemic, reports of wars in other countries, and so many other uncertainties, you'd wish for the second coming of Christ to fully inaugurate God's kingdom. You'd wish for this present world to end.

This is another common response to what is happening to our bayan. Everything that is happening is seen as among the signs of the second coming. Many Christians argue that because we cannot do anything about our present troubles, all we can do is to pray and wait for the second coming of our Lord. This is related to the overemphasis on the belief in trust in God, which has as a corollary human inability and powerlessness in the face of events which are apocalyptic in nature. But, as we will see in chapter 7, the end-times teaching in the New Testament is not confined to the second coming. The focus is not only on our Lord. We have an important role to play. As Christopher Sabanal demonstrates in his chapter, there is not one end-time teaching, but several. And in each of these, we see the struggles of the followers of Jesus in making sense of Christ's delayed coming. But in these struggles, the importance of human action, creativity, and perseverance is displayed. The second coming is rightly about the coming of Jesus, but it is equally about the active engagement of his followers. In the end, when the different teachings about the end times are considered, the result is a very rich tapestry of human ingenuity amid uncertainties.

Following on from these first seven chapters, we will be in a position to ask, "What does it look like to engage with the social and political concerns of our bayan?" The final chapter, by Carlo Diño (chapter 8), provides a narrative of an actual example of engagement through the initiatives of the Coalition for Justice. Here we will see one important social exemplification of involvement by evangelicals in the public square – *social protest*. While this form of involvement is but one of the many possible expressions of our concern for our bayan that arises through faith, it is a crucial course of publicly expressing the church's prophetic calling. This is especially the case during times when the authorities fail dismally to promote the good of the bayan and defend the rights of its oppressed. Such is the situation we live in under the current Duterte administration that we can no longer afford to be silent. By not being silent but instead speaking up in this book against the evils of our time, we hope we are able to provide a model for how our faith ought to engage with our bayan.

Bibliography

Bulatao, Jaime C. "Split-Level Christianity." In *Phenomena and Their Interpretation: Landmark Essays, 1957–1989*, 22–31. Manila: Ateneo de Manila University Press, 1992.

CNN Philippines. "'Things Have Worsened,' Duterte Says of Drug Problem." 26 March 2019. Accessed 27 October 2021. https://cnnphilippines.com/news/2019/3/26/duterte-drug-problem-worsened.html.

Cornelio, Jayeel. "Claiming the Nation: Theological Nationalism in the Philippines." In *What Does Theology Do, Actually? Observing Theology and the Transcultural*, edited by M. Robinson and I. Inderst, 149–165. Leipzig: Evangelische Verlagsanstalt, 2020.

Cornelio, Jayeel, and Ia Marañon. "A 'Righteous Intervention': Megachurch Christianity and Duterte's War on Drugs in the Philippines." *International Journal of Asian Christianity* 2, no. 2 (2019): 211–30.

Francisco, Jose Mario C. "Panitikan at Kristiyanismong Pilipino: Ang Nagbabagong Larawan ni Kristo." *Philippine Studies* 25, no. 2 (1977): 186–214.

Gaspar, Karl M., CSsR. *Handumanan (Remembrance): Digging for the Indigenous Wellspring*. Quezon City: Episcopal Commission on Indigenous Peoples and Claretian Communications Foundations, 2021.

Javellana, René B. *Casaysayan Nang Pasiong Mahal Ni Jesucristong Panginoon Natin: Na Sucat Ipag-Alab Nang Puso Nang Sinomang Babasa*. Quezon City: Ateneo de Manila University Press, 1988.

Paguntalan-Mijares, Aileen. "Rebuilding Lives amid the Ruins of Duterte's War on Drugs." *Journal of Human Rights and Peace Studies* 6, no. 2 (2020): 255–82.

Rebustillo, R. L. "*Bahala Na*: In Search of an 'Ordinary Theology' for the Filipino Diaspora." *International Journal of Practical Theology* 22, no. 2 (2018): 234–52.

Rodriguez-Tatel, Mary Jane. *Ang Dalumat ng Bayan sa Kamalayan at Kasaysayang Pilipino*. Quezon City: Bagong Kasaysayan, 2006.

Sarao, Zacarian Gavin H. "PH Ranks Last out of 121 Countries in Global COVID-19 Recovery Index – Nikkei." Inquirer.net, 6 October 2021. Accessed 23 October 2021. https://newsinfo.inquirer.net/1498167/ph-ranks-last-out-of-121-countries-in-global-covid-19-recovery-index-nikkei.

Tomacruz, Sofia. "Majority of Filipinos Think It's Dangerous to Publish Anything Critical of Duterte Admin." Rappler, 3 August 2019. Accessed 27 October

2021. https://www.rappler.com/nation/majority-filipinos-think-dangerous-publish-things-critical-duterte-admin-sws.

Villamor, Felipe. "Duterte, Citing Hitler, Says He Wants to Kill 3 Million Addicts in Philippines." *New York Times* online, 30 September 2016. Accessed 31 August 2021. https://nyti.ms/2VaFweI.

1

Worship and Justice

Federico G. Villanueva

I once saw a post on social media which said: "Protest for what? Against the government? Kung sinisikil na ang pag worship sa Lord yes I will protest . . . Kung ang bansa natin ay bawal mag gather to worship iba usapan na yun. Pero kung makikisawsaw lang sa gulo ng politika I'm busy in my own personal problem." ("If worship is already being prohibited, yes I will protest . . . If in our nation we are no longer allowed to gather to worship, that is different. But if I will just meddle with politics, I'm busy with my own personal problem.")

The post sees worship as important. Worship is mentioned twice:

> Kung sinisikil na ang pag worship sa Lord [If worship to the Lord is already being prohibited]

> Kung ang bansa natin ay bawal mag gather to worship. [If in our nation, we are no longer allowed to gather to worship]

It's saying: You can mess with other things, but not worship.

But the post reflects a particular view of worship, one which understands it in terms of "church" worship. What is important is that we are able to gather together to worship. Things outside – for example, politics – are not part of worship. I often encounter this view.

I remember before the lockdown, I was invited to a church to preach. It was the week when twenty-two Filipino fishermen were left floating in the sea after a Chinese vessel hit their boat. I was hoping there would be something in the church worship that would mention, or at least allude to, the event, maybe in the pastoral prayer or in the worship songs. But there was nothing in the entire worship service about what had happened to those fishermen.

The very first song we sang in the worship service was Matt Redman's song "10,000 Reasons." The chorus goes as follows:

> Bless the Lord, O my soul . . .
> Worship his holy name
> Sing like never before, O my soul . . .

I was in the front row of the church. As I stood with the congregation, I was struggling to join in the singing. How could I "sing like never before" after what had happened to our *kababayan* (fellow Filipinos)?

This is also the question that I would like to ask in this chapter: How can we worship if we do not care about what is happening outside our churches? Will our worship be acceptable to God if we do not care about issues of justice?

My answer to the second part of that question is a resounding "no!" In this chapter, I provide three main reasons why this is so. We cannot worship God if we do not practice justice, because

- the God we worship is the great king whose throne is founded on righteousness and justice;
- "righteousness and justice" are among the requirements for entrance into God's holy presence;
- Jesus protested against the oppression and injustice in the temple.

We will elaborate on each of these points in this chapter.

The God We Worship Is the Great King Whose Throne Is Founded on Righteousness and Justice

First of all, let us briefly define what we mean by "worship."

What Is Worship?

The Bible does not provide one specific definition of worship.[1] But, broadly, worship may be understood as a response to and communion with God.[2] The

---

1. W. McConnell, "Worship," in *Dictionary of the Old Testament Wisdom, Poetry and Writings*, eds. Tremper Longman III and Peter Enns (Downers Grove, IL: InterVarsity Press, 2008), 929.

2. Sigmund Mowinckel, *The Psalms in Israel's Worship*, trans. D. R. Ap-Thomas, vol. 1, 2 vols. (Grand Rapids, MI; Dearborn, MI: Eerdmans ; Dove Publishers, 2004), defines worship, or what is called "cult," as "the socially established and regulated holy acts and words in which the encounter and communion of the Deity with the congregation is established, developed, and brought to its ultimate goal. In other words: a relation in which a religion becomes a vitalizing

primary purpose of all the rituals of worship (for example, the sacrifices in the Old Testament) "was to establish a relationship with YHWH and maintain his presence."[3] "Relationship" is a key word in connection with worship. In this relationship, the focus is God. The song "Heart of Worship" goes in the right direction when it says that worship is "all about you, Jesus."[4] Unfortunately, the songwriter did not develop this theme. In a "me, me, me generation" and a Western individualistic culture, it is easy to fall into the temptation of thinking that this is all about "me."

But when you think about Jesus, what image comes to your mind? Is it not of one who gave his life for others? The one we worship is a God whose focus is not on himself but on others. As we often hear in the Lord's Supper, "This is my body which is given *for you*." Jesus devoted his life to others, particularly the marginalized. At the beginning of his ministry, Jesus made it clear what the focus of his mission would be: "to proclaim good news to the poor . . . to set at liberty those who are oppressed" (Luke 4:18).[5] This quotation from Isaiah orients Jesus's whole ministry as one that is focused on the "good news to the poor."[6] On his return as the King and Judge, one of the things he will look for in his followers is how they treated the least of their brothers and sisters – "The King will reply, 'Truly I tell you, whatever you did for one of the least of these brothers and sisters of mine, you did for me'" (Matt 25:40 NIV).

The word "least" is crucial. God shows special care for the least and most vulnerable. He "watches over the sojourners; he upholds the widow and the fatherless" (Ps 146:9) This verse mentions three groups of people – the sojourner, widow, and the fatherless/orphan.[7] What's so special about this trio? It's not that God cares only for these people and no longer cares about the rich.

---

function as a communion of God and congregation, and of the members of the congregations amongst themselves" (p. 15). He adds: "The cult is . . . the visible and audible expression of the relation between the congregation and the deity" (p. 16).

3. Bohdan Hrobon, *Ethical Dimension of Cult in the Book of Isaiah*, BZAW (Berlin: De Gruyter, 2010), 17.

4. The song was composed by Matt Redman.

5. This verse is a quotation from Isa 61:1–2 and 58:6. Its position at the beginning of Jesus's ministry "serves a 'programmatic' purpose for much of Jesus' ministry." J. Daniel Hays, "'Sell Everything You Have and Give to the Poor': The Old Testament Prophetic Theme of Justice as the Connecting Motif of Luke 18:1 – 19:10," *Journal of the Evangelical Theological Society* 55, no. 1 (March 2012): 45. All Scripture quotations in this chapter are from the ESV unless stated otherwise.

6. Bryan R. Dyer, "Good News to the Poor: Social Upheaval, Strong Warnings, and Sincere Giving in Luke-Acts," in *The Bible and Social Justice*, eds. Cynthia Long Westfall and Bryan R. Dyer, McMaster New Testament Series (Eugene, OR: Pickwick, 2016), 75.

7. The trio are also mentioned in Deut 10:18; Jer 7:5–7; Zech 7:9–10, among other verses.

Rather, it's that these three groups are the ones who really need help. "The worst problem" of this trio is "powerlessness and its consequences: lack of status, lack of respect, making one an easy mark for the powerful and unscrupulous."[8]

The sojourner is "the one who doesn't belong."[9] In a society that "depended so heavily on human muscle power for subsistence, a family without one adult male . . . would find it difficult to survive."[10] The orphans have no one to take care of them; they are also unable to help themselves, either.

That is why God gives special attention to them. This is reflected in the key biblical term "righteousness and justice."

"Righteousness and Justice"

The words, "righteousness" and "justice" in Hebrew can mean different things when used individually.[11] But they are often used together as a pair.[12] And when they are, the term becomes the equivalent of what we call "social justice."[13] According to Weinfeld, the term "righteousness and justice" "refers primarily to the improvement of the conditions of the poor."[14] As Annelle Sabanal points out in her chapter in this volume, the term is "almost always . . . associated with a Hebrew verb that denotes action."

Social justice is a matter that is very important to God. We usually get angry when the things or people we consider important to us are violated. In

---

8. Donald E. Gowan, "Wealth and Poverty in the Old Testament: The Case of the Widow, the Orphan, and the Sojourner," *Interpretation* 41, no. 4 (1987): 344.

9. Gowan, "Wealth and Poverty," 344.

10. Gowan, 343.

11. Justice (*mishpat*) can mean "judgments" (in a judicial sense) and "justice" (fairness). See B. Johnson, "מִשְׁפָּט שָׁפַט שָׁפוֹט," TDOT 9: 93–94. Righteousness (*tsedaqah*) is usually translated as "righteousness" but it can also mean "justice" or "salvation/acts of deliverance." See Gerhard von Rad, *Old Testament Theology* (New York: Harper, 1962), 372–73.

12. Ernst Jenni with Claus Westermann, eds., *Theological Lexicon of the Old Testament*, 3 vols. (Peabody, MA: Hendrickson, 1997), 1729.

13. Walter J. Houston, *Contending for Justice: Ideologies and Theologies of Social Justice in the Old Testament* (London: Continuum, 2009), 61, writes: "This pairing . . . has been shown to refer to what we call social justice, or negatively put the elimination and avoidance of oppression and exploitation, which of course is obvious from the context in Amos in any case."

14. Moshe Weinfeld, "'Justice and Righteousness': *Mshpt Wtsdqh* the Expression and Its Meaning," in *Justice and Righteousness: Biblical Themes and Their Influence*, ed. Henning Graf Reventlow (Sheffield: Sheffield Academic Press, 1992), 237. Dyer, "Good News," 69, notes that justice in the prophets is "closely connected to the care for the orphan, widow."

Psalm 82, God gets angry because the "weak and the fatherless" are deprived of justice (Ps 82:3).[15] That is why he demands:

> Defend the weak and the fatherless;
>   uphold the cause of the poor and the oppressed.
> Rescue the weak and the needy;
>   deliver them from the hand of the wicked. (vv. 3–4 NIV)

This text, along with Zechariah 7:9–10, presents the essence of social justice: "Administer true justice; show mercy and compassion to one another. Do not oppress the widow or the fatherless, the foreigner or the poor" (NIV).

Righteousness and Justice as the Foundation of God's Throne

The book of Psalms declares twice that "righteousness and justice are the foundation" of God's throne (89:14; 97:2b). By saying this, the Bible is telling us that the care of the poor and most vulnerable is of utmost importance to God. The word "foundation" is crucial.[16] We know that in any building, the foundation is the most important part, for a simple reason: the foundation carries the weight of the entire building; the entire building sits on top of it!

When there is justice the world is "established." As Psalm 96:10 declares:

> The LORD reigns!
>   . . . the world is established; it shall never be moved [*mut*];
>   he will judge the peoples with equity.

In the structure of the verse above, the first and third lines are parallel. God's reign is characterized by justice. And when this is in place, "the world is established."

But when the "weak and the fatherless" are oppressed, "all the foundations of the earth are shaken" (Ps 82:3–5). The word "shaken" (*mut*) is used in both Psalm 96:10 and 82:5. The former declares that when there is equity/justice, the world will never be moved (*mut*). But when the poor are exploited and harassed, not only is the world shaken, but "all" of its "foundations" are shaken.

---

15. In Ps 82, God complains about the gods. See Daniel O. McClellan, "The Gods-Complaint: Psalm 82 as a Psalm of Complaint," *Journal of Biblical Literature* 137, no. 4 (2018): 833–51. For a discussion of Ps 82 as an expression of God's anger over injustice in connection with the Lord's Prayer, see Villanueva, "What's the Father Like 'in Heaven'? The Lord's Prayer and Psalm 82" (forthcoming).

16. For the background in the ancient Near East for throne as the foundation, see Erich Zenger and Frank-Lothar Hossfeld, *Psalms 3: A Commentary on Psalms 101–150*, ed. Klaus Baltzer, trans. Linda M. Maloney (Minneapolis: Fortress, 2011), 472–73.

Notice the word "all" in Psalm 82:5. In Tagalog, "Kapag ang 'mahina at ulila' hindi nabigyan ng 'katarungan,' 'lahat ng saligan ng lupa ay nayayanig'" (Awit 82:3, 5, ABB). That is how critical "righteousness and justice" is.

I remember the last time we had an earthquake in Manila. I was in an office on the seventh floor of a building. The day started as usual. There were many things to do. I was also thinking about some future plans. But suddenly, as I was sitting, I noticed that the ground was shaking, then my table was moving. I felt dizzy. Just like that, I forgot about everything else. I felt as if it was the end of the world. Gone were all my plans. I forgot all the things I had planned to do that day. I just prayed to the Lord and offered him everything.

That's how it is when the foundations are shaken, when righteousness and justice are ignored. Unfortunately, it appears that that is not how it is with many evangelical Christians today. Even though we see injustices being committed right before our very eyes, even though many people have already been killed in the "war on drugs," many don't seem to care. What is so unjust about the war on drugs is that it is directed against the poor, those who are most vulnerable. The tragedy is that it has produced more widows and orphans. In its 2018 report, the Philippine Department of Social Welfare and Development said that 18,000 children had been orphaned as a result of Duterte's war on drugs.[17] Yet many Christians don't seem to care, and some are even supportive of this policy.

When we go to church, it's as if we are transported to a different world. People sing praises to the Lord "like never before." Most of the songs are songs of praise. The prayers are always positive. Even the sermons are about victory. Karl Marx was right: for many Christians, religion has become like the "opium of the people." Worship has become like a drug, an escape. We need to go to worship so that somehow we might have "hope." But hope becomes denial, for we end up ignoring the problem before our very eyes. Worship becomes about "me" and "my God."

But can we worship God without paying attention to issues of justice? No! Because justice is of utmost importance to God. God is "the protector of the weak par excellence."[18]

The God we worship is the "King" who "in his might loves justice" (Ps 99:4). He is the "LORD" who "works righteousness and justice for all who are oppressed" (Ps 103:6). And he expects those who worship him to do the same.

---

17. Shallah Montero and Sol Juvida, "Children of the Drug War Speak Out," ABS-CBN News, 19 March 2018, accessed 3 September 2021, https://bit.ly/3zvDJ2F.

18. F. Charles Fensham, "Widow, Orphan, and the Poor in Ancient Near Eastern Legal and Wisdom Literature," *Journal of Near Eastern Studies* 21, no. 2 (April 1962): 137.

In Psalm 106:2, the psalmist asks: "Who can utter the mighty deeds of the LORD, or declare all his praise?" And in verse 3, we hear the answer: "Blessed are they who observe justice, who do righteousness at all times!" It is those who observe justice and do righteousness who can declare God's praise. That is why they are called "blessed." Not everyone can worship the Lord.

Righteousness and Justice Are among the Requirements for Entrance into God's Presence

The "question and answer" pattern in Psalm 106 is also a feature found in the so-called "entrance liturgies" (Pss 15 and 24).[19] The entrance liturgy reminds us that we cannot just barge in to the presence of God. "Not just anyone might worship God. Only the one who was prepared might enter the sanctuary . . . Only the one who had fulfilled the requirements of holiness was fit to serve God."[20] Psalms expert Hermann Gunkel explains that when a worshipper was about to enter the sanctuary, the worshipper would ask the priest: "Who shall dwell on your holy hill?" The priest would then recite the requirements found in Psalm 15:[21]

- "He who walks blamelessly and does what is right and speaks truth in his heart" (v. 2);
- "Who does not slander with his tongue" (v. 3);
- "In whose eyes a vile person is despised, but who honors those who fear the LORD" (v. 4);
- "Who does not put out his money at interest and does not take a bribe against the innocent" (v. 5ab).

Then, depending on the prerogative of the priest, he would add the blessing.

How about if we did this today, when we are able to meet at church? All the members would stand outside the church and ask: "Who shall dwell on your holy hill?" (Ps 15:1). And then the pastor would recite the answer from Psalm 15:2–5.

---

19. Peter C. Craigie, Joel F. Drinkard, and Page H. Kelley, *Jeremiah 1–25*, Word Biblical Commentary 26 (Irving, TX: Word, 1991), 120, note: "During the pilgrimage festivals in the temple, the pilgrims were greeted at the temple gates by a servant of the institution, who asked them to examine their moral lives prior to passing through the gates and participating in the worship."

20. John D. W. Watts, "Elements of Old Testament Worship," *Journal of Bible and Religion* 26, no. 3 (July 1958): 217.

21. Hermann Gunkel, *The Psalms: A Form-Critical Introduction* (Philadelphia: Fortress, 1967), 22.

Would there be anyone there who would qualify? Would the pastor qualify? Two of the requirements in Psalm 15 pertain to justice and righteousness:

- "In whose eyes a vile person is despised, but who honors those who fear the LORD" (v. 4);
- "Who does not put out his money at interest and does not take a bribe against the innocent" (v. 5).

The second of these is directly connected to the experiences of the poor. It is usually poor people who are forced to borrow money and are prone to abuse and exploitation. That is why God prohibited the charging of interest among his people: "If you lend money to any of my people with you who is poor, you shall not be like a moneylender to him, and you shall not exact interest from him" (Exod 22:25). In the preceding context, the trio group (sojourner, widow, fatherless) are mentioned: "You shall not wrong a sojourner or oppress him . . . You shall not mistreat any widow or fatherless child" (Exod 22:21–22). Clearly, the requirement not to put out one's money at interest is directed against those who will abuse the vulnerable. God adds a warning against those who will take advantage of the poor: "If you do mistreat them, and they cry out to me, I will surely hear their cry, and my wrath will burn, and I will kill you with the sword, and your wives shall become widows and your children fatherless" (Exod 22:23–24).

God hates oppressors.[22] He will never allow the oppressor to enter his sanctuary. The first requirement connected to justice in Psalm 15 makes this clear: "in whose eyes a vile person is despised" (Ps 15:4). Those who will be allowed to enter God's presence are those who "despise" the "vile person." If God will not allow those who do not despise the vile person to enter his sanctuary, how much more so the vile person him- or herself? The word "vile" here is translated from the Hebrew word *ma'as*, which means "rejected" (*nim'as*).[23]

In Jeremiah 6:30, the word "rejected" (*nim'as*) is used twice: "Rejected silver they are called, for the LORD has rejected them." The context in Jeremiah

---

22. Jayeel Cornelio and Rico Villanueva, "Praying with Harry Roque," Rappler, 8 September 2020, https://www.rappler.com/voices/thought-leaders/opinion-praying-with-harry-roque. See response from Gilbert Foliente, "Prophets, Priests, and Politics: A Theological Reflection on God's Redemptive Power and the Church's Calling," Victory, 29 September 2020, https://victory.org.ph/prophets-priests-politics-a-theological-reflection-on-gods-redemptive-power-and-the-churchs-calling/?fbclid=IwAR0kBDkjfTt90RNLP3naU8FFEX1Ri5u8FToqY0eQcoKh0AqUPQT_AmIRa3U.

23. Ang problema sa atin, yung ni-reject na ni Lord, iniimbita pa natin sa prayer meeting (The problem with us is that we even invite into our midst those whom God has already rejected). And if you say anything against those who are oppressing the poor, some Christians will even despise you or reject you.

7 explains why they were rejected. The setting is similar to the one in the entrance liturgy. In Jeremiah 7, the people were entering the "gates to worship the LORD" (v. 2). Like the priests in Psalm 15, God asked Jeremiah to "stand in the gate of the LORD's house" (v. 2) to declare a message to the people of Judah. But instead of proclaiming God's blessing on the worshippers, Jeremiah was to deliver God's rebuke.

Apparently, the people had been oppressing the sojourner, the fatherless, and the widow – the famous trio.[24] That is why God commanded Jeremiah to proclaim to the people: "Amend your ways" (v. 3; cf. v. 5). God warns them that they will be allowed to remain in the land only if they stop their oppressive actions and violence: "For if you truly . . . execute justice one with another, if you do not oppress the sojourner, the fatherless, or the widow, or shed innocent blood in this place . . ." (vv. 5—6).

The problem with the people was that they did not see anything wrong with going to the temple to worship even if they had not been practicing justice. The temple was believed to be where God dwelled.[25] But there came the notion that because they had the temple, they were already secure.[26] The situation was similar to what our national hero José Rizal observed of some Catholic Christians during his time:

> To them a just and good Christian is one who frequents the church, who attends the most processions, who lights the most candles and gives luxurious dresses to the images, without taking into account whether the money used in these works (pious, yes, but not at all necessary) has been acquired at the cost of the hunger and tears of many unfortunate men.[27]

Interestingly, Rizal mentions the "orphan and the widow":

---

24. Craigie, Drinkard, and Kelley, *Jeremiah 1–25*, 121, write: "The substance of the prophet's remarks indicates that the practices he describes were rampant in the land."

25. Baruch A. Levine, "On the Presence of God in Biblical Religion," in *Religions in Antiquity; Essays in Memory of Erwin Ramsdell Goodenough*, ed. Jacob Neusner (Leiden: Brill, 1968), 81.

26. Levine, "Presence of God," 81, notes: "the Jerusalem temple and its attending cult produce certain reflexes in the religious attitudes of the people. One such reflex is the notion that God's presence in the Jerusalem temple guarantees the security of the city and its residents, an idea extended to include the whole people of Israel and its land."

27. José Rizal, "The Religiosity of the Filipino People," translated by Dr. Encarnación Alzona, The Filipino Mind, 12 November 2009, accessed 6 July 2020, https://www.thefilipinomind.com/2005/10/religiosity-of-filipino-people-dr.html.

> you can rob the orphan and the widow, or take away the honor of a man who has no other patrimony; you can call him the most injurious and basest names; you can make him pay with bitter tears his sad fate and your enviable situation; in short, even maltreat him, slap him, and kill his mortal life. You can do all this and even more, and no one will say that you are a bad Christian so long as you hear mass, you confess, you take communion, and attend all processions, praying all day and fasting on fast days marked on the calendar.[28]

I'm afraid Protestants and we evangelical, born-again Christians are no different. Some of us may say, "We are not doing anything wrong. We don't murder or take advantage of the poor." But "sin" in the Bible does not mean only sins of commission. There are also sins of omission. When we do not do what we know is right, that too is sin (Jas 4:17).[29] When we don't care if justice and righteousness are being violated, then there is something seriously wrong with our Christianity. As José Miranda remarked: "Frankly I do not see how there can be an authentic compassion for the oppressed without there being at the same time indignation against the oppressor."[30]

Jesus himself became indignant when he saw oppression and injustice in the temple. He quoted the words of Jeremiah when he went into the temple.

Jesus Protested against Injustice and Demanded That Those Who Follow Him Practice Justice and Righteousness

The Gospel of Mark tells us that upon entering the temple, Jesus "began to drive out those who sold and those who bought in the temple, and he overturned the tables of the money-changers and the seats of those who sold pigeons. And he would not allow anyone to carry anything through the temple" (11:15–16). And then he told them: "Is it not written, 'My house shall be called a house of prayer for all the nations'? But you have made it a den of robbers" (v. 17). The latter part of this verse is a quotation from Jeremiah 7:11.

Jesus was obviously angry. His actions showed that something really important, something "foundational," had been violated. The temple had to be disrupted. It could not be business as usual. Worship as it was being done

---

28. Rizal, "Religiosity of the Filipino People."

29. There is such a thing as "indirect oppression." Sandra Van Opstal, *The Mission of Worship*, Urbana Onward (Downers Grove, IL: IVP Books, 2012), 31.

30. José Porfirio Miranda, *Marx and the Bible* (Maryknoll, NY: Orbis, 1974), 47.

at that point had to stop. And even though his actions lasted only for a while, the meaning of his actions stands.

What was it that Jesus found wrong?

Jesus's action is a "prophetic pronouncement against the temple."[31] Jesus uttered a similar message to that of Jeremiah.[32] Unless they changed, destruction was coming. The reason for the judgment was the people's failure to live up to what it means to be God's people and to "enact justice within her society, not least within the Temple system itself."[33] From the perspective of the "poorer classes," the temple symbolized "the oppression they suffered at the hands of the elite."[34] The poor were required by law to pay the temple tax, which financed the temple. Most of the people at that time were poor, and this proved to be another burden. There was also evidence of oppression within the temple which greatly affected the poor. For example, according to Leviticus, the dove was the poor person's sacrifice (Lev 5:7; 12:8), but according to sources, the price of the dove "had been raised to one gold denar, a price some twenty-five times the proper charge (m. Ker. 1:7)."[35] This explains why the temple had a "record of debts." Maraming mahirap ang nabaon sa utang (Many were buried in debts). In fact, as N. T. Wright points out, "when the revolutionaries took over the temple, the first thing they did was to burn the record of debts."[36]

Jesus's actions reinforce the message of the entrance liturgies.[37] Those who would enter the temple should have been living out the requirements

---

31. Craig A. Evans, "Jesus and the 'Cave of Robbers': Toward a Jewish Context for the Temple Action," *Bulletin for Biblical Research* 3 (1993): 107. Evans thinks the text in Jer 7 is key (p. 108).

32. Mark F. Whitters, "Jesus in the Footsteps of Jeremiah," *The Catholic Biblical Quarterly* 68, no. 2 (April 2006): 229–47, argues that the author of Matthew used the book of Jeremiah as guide. There are two things that Jesus and Jeremiah have in common: (1) both are rejected by their own people; (2) both prophesied destruction (p. 230).

33. N. T. Wright, *Jesus and the Victory of God* (London: SPCK, 1996), 417.

34. Wright, *Victory of God*, 412. Jesus came from a poor background. According to Wolfgang Stegeman, "Background III: The Social and Political Climate in Which Jesus of Nazareth Preached," in *Handbook for the Study of the Historical Jesus*, eds. Stanley E. Porter and Tom Holmén (Leiden: Brill, 2011), 2313, "there was an economic and political crisis in Jewish Palestine in the time of Jesus," and he describes the Jesus movement as a "poverty movement by and for poor Jewish men and women."

35. Craig A. Evans, "Jesus' Action in the Temple and Evidence of Corruption in the First-Century Temple," in *Jesus and His Contemporaries: Comparative Studies*, AGJU 25 (Leiden: Brill, 1995), 331.

36. Wright, *Victory of God*, 412.

37. Jesus's entrance into the temple recalls the entrance liturgies. According to Craig A. Evans, "Praise and Prophecy in the Psalter and in the New Testament," in *The Book of Psalms: Composition and Reception*, eds. Patrick D. Miller and Peter W. Flint (Leiden: Brill, 2005), 554,

of justice and righteousness. They ought to have cared for the poor and not oppressed them. But that was not what was happening. The poor became poorer and the rich, richer. Josephus writes about the "opulence of the Temple and the incredible wealth of its treasury."[38] The high priests' families "possessed extraordinary wealth," and widows of high priests were "beneficiaries of extremely generous pensions."[39]

Jesus's actions exemplify the meaning of "righteousness and justice." It means caring about and fighting for the rights of the poor and vulnerable.[40] Through his actions, Jesus is teaching us that it is not enough to do acts of compassion like those we do in our churches; we also need to have "a sense of advocacy."[41] As Stott put it: "It is always good to feed the hungry; it is better if possible to eradicate the causes of hunger. So if we truly love our neighbors, and want to serve them, our service may oblige us to take (or solicit) political action on their behalf."[42]

Justice and righteousness involve protesting against oppressive governments and leaders. One common misconception about Jesus is that he protested only against the religious leaders, not against the government. But the high priest was also the government during Jesus's time.[43] The temple had "great political power."[44] Rome ruled through the high priest because it was "the best way to guarantee tranquility and taxation."[45]

Jesus shows us that the issue of justice and righteousness is of utmost importance. It is a matter worth protesting about and dying for. Jesus knew what the consequences of his actions would be and yet he still did them. Scholars agree that it was what Jesus did that day in the temple which eventually

---

the "Psalter becomes especially important for Jesus when he enters the city of Jerusalem. This is hardly surprising, given the role played by the Psalter in pilgrimages to Jerusalem and the temple . . . for worship in Jerusalem."

38. Evans, "Jesus' Action in the Temple," 321.

39. Evans, "Jesus' Action in the Temple," 322.

40. Weinfeld, "Justice and Righteousness," 235–36.

41. Harold T. Lewis, "Theology, Ministry, and Praxis: A Forty-Year Retrospective," *Anglican Theological Review* 93, no. 4 (2011): 620.

42. John R. W. Stott, *Issues Facing Christians Today*, ed. R. McCloughry, 4th ed. (Grand Rapids, MI: Zondervan, 2006), 36. He adds: "If travelers on the Jerusalem–Jericho road were habitually beaten up, and habitually cared for by 'Good Samaritans,' the need for better laws to eliminate armed robbery might well be overlooked. If road accidents keep occurring at a particular crossroads, it is not more ambulances that are needed but the installation of traffic lights to prevent accidents" (p. 36).

43. E. P. Sanders, *The Historical Figure of Jesus* (New York: Penguin, 1993), 25.

44. Evans, "Jesus' Action in the Temple," 322.

45. Evans, 323.

led to his death.[46] It is not true that Jesus was silent in the face of oppression and injustice. He protested. He even called the religious leaders a "brood of vipers." He uttered seven "woes" against them. He was obviously not silent. He did become silent when he was arrested – but that was not until after he had spoken out against those who were unjust. The problem with some Christians is that they are already silent even without having done or spoken out about anything first.

One of the reasons why many Filipino Christians do not experience persecution is because they do not engage with issues of justice. Their understanding of worship is limited to the confines of the church. They never say anything to defend the poor and the oppressed. They know that if they did so, they would be red-tagged. But Jesus shows us that justice is not a matter for discussion only. It is a matter worth dying for, protesting for. The issue of righteousness and justice is foundational.

Jesus taught about the importance of a foundation in Matthew 7:24–27:

> Everyone then who hears these words of mine and does them will be like a wise man who built his house on the rock. And the rain fell, and the floods came, and the winds blew and beat on that house, but it did not fall, because it had been founded on the rock. And everyone who hears these words of mine and does not do them will be like a foolish man who built his house on the sand. And the rain fell, and the floods came, and the winds blew and beat against that house, and it fell, and great was the fall of it.[47]

This is the time of shaking of foundations. If our foundation is not firm and sure, it will fall.

Bibliography

Ådna, Jostein. "Jesus and the Temple." In *Handbook for the Study of the Historical Jesus*, edited by Stanley E. Porter and Tom Holmén, 2635–2675. Leiden: Brill, 2011.

---

46. Jostein Ådna, "Jesus and the Temple," in *Handbook for the Study of the Historical Jesus*, eds. Stanley E. Porter and Tom Holmén (Leiden: Brill, 2011), 2671.

47. George A. Kennedy, *New Testament Interpretation through Rhetorical Criticism*, Studies in Religion (Chapel Hill: University of North Carolina Press, 1984), 63, comments that the "tone is somewhat mitigated by the final appeal, the similes of the wise and foolish to the builders of houses on rock or on sand; but even here it must be noted that the dire simile is put last, and it is with the fall of the house that Jesus leaves his audience."

Cornelio, Jayeel, and Rico Villanueva. "Praying with Harry Roque." Rappler, 8 September 2020. https://www.rappler.com/voices/thought-leaders/opinion-praying-with-harry-roque.

Craigie, Peter C., Joel F. Drinkard, and Page H. Kelley. *Jeremiah 1–25*. Word Biblical Commentary 26. Irving, TX: Word, 1991.

Dyer, Bryan R. "Good News to the Poor: Social Upheaval, Strong Warnings, and Sincere Giving in Luke-Acts." In *The Bible and Social Justice*, edited by Cynthia Long Westfall and Bryan R. Dyer, 68–76. McMaster New Testament Series. Eugene, OR: Pickwick, 2016.

Evans, Craig A. "Jesus' Action in the Temple and Evidence of Corruption in the First-Century Temple." In *Jesus and His Contemporaries: Comparative Studies*, 319–44. AGJU 25. Leiden: Brill, 1995.

———. "Jesus and the 'Cave of Robbers': Toward a Jewish Context for the Temple Action." *Bulletin for Biblical Research* 3 (1993): 93–110.

———. "Praise and Prophecy in the Psalter and in the New Testament." In *The Book of Psalms: Composition and Reception*, edited by Patrick D. Miller and Peter W. Flint, 551–79. Leiden: Brill, 2005.

Fensham, F. Charles. "Widow, Orphan, and the Poor in Ancient Near Eastern Legal and Wisdom Literature." *Journal of Near Eastern Studies* 21, no. 2 (April 1962): 129–39.

Foliente, Gilbert. "Prophets, Priests, and Politics: A Theological Reflection on God's Redemptive Power and the Church's Calling." Victory, 29 September 2020. https://victory.org.ph/prophets-priests-politics-a-theological-reflection-on-gods-redemptive-power-and-the-churchs-calling/?fbclid=IwAR0kBDkjfTt90RNLP3naU8FFEX1Ri5u8FToqY0eQcoKh0AqUPQT_AmIRa3U.

Gowan, Donald E. "Wealth and Poverty in the Old Testament: The Case of the Widow, the Orphan, and the Sojourner." *Interpretation* 41, no. 4 (1987): 341–53.

Gunkel, Hermann. *The Psalms: A Form-Critical Introduction*. Philadelphia: Fortress, 1967.

Hays, J. Daniel. "'Sell Everything You Have and Give to the Poor': The Old Testament Prophetic Theme of Justice as the Connecting Motif of Luke 18:1 – 19:10." *Journal of the Evangelical Theological Society* 55, no. 1 (March 2012): 43–63.

Houston, Walter J. *Contending for Justice: Ideologies and Theologies of Social Justice in the Old Testament*. London: Continuum, 2009.

Hrobon, Bohdan. *Ethical Dimension of Cult in the Book of Isaiah*. BZAW. Berlin: De Gruyter, 2010.

Jenni, Ernst, with Claus Westermann, eds. *Theological Lexicon of the Old Testament*. 3 vols. Peabody, MA: Hendrickson, 1997.

Johnson, B. "מִשְׁפָּט שָׁפַט שְׁפוֹט." *TDOT* 9: 86–98.

Kennedy, George A. *New Testament Interpretation through Rhetorical Criticism*. Studies in Religion. Chapel Hill: University of North Carolina Press, 1984.

Levine, Baruch A. "On the Presence of God in Biblical Religion." In *Religions in Antiquity; Essays in Memory of Erwin Ramsdell Goodenough*, edited by Jacob Neusner, 71–87. Leiden: Brill, 1968.
Lewis, Harold T. "Theology, Ministry, and Praxis: A Forty-Year Retrospective." *Anglican Theological Review* 93, no. 4 (2011): 619–27.
McClellan, Daniel O. "The Gods-Complaint: Psalm 82 as a Psalm of Complaint." *Journal of Biblical Literature* 137, no. 4 (2018): 833–51.
McConnell, W. "Worship." In *Dictionary of the Old Testament Wisdom, Poetry and Writings*, edited by Tremper Longman III and Peter Enns, 929–35. Downers Grove, IL: InterVarsity Press, 2008.
Miranda, José Porfirio. *Marx and the Bible*. Maryknoll, NY: Orbis, 1974.
Montero, Shallah, and Sol Juvida. "Children of the Drug War Speak Out." ABS-CBN News, 19 March 2018. Accessed 3 September 2021. https://bit.ly/3zvDJ2F.
Mowinckel, Sigmund. *The Psalms in Israel's Worship*. Translated by D. R. Ap-Thomas. Vol. 1. 2 vols. Grand Rapids, MI; Dearborn, MI: Eerdmans ; Dove Publishers, 2004.
Rad, Gerhard von. *Old Testament Theology*. New York: Harper, 1962.
Rizal, José. "The Religiosity of the Filipino People." Translated by Dr. Encarnación Alzona. The Filipino Mind, 12 November 2009. Accessed 6 July 2020. https://www.thefilipinomind.com/2005/10/religiosity-of-filipino-people-dr.html.
Sanders, E. P. *The Historical Figure of Jesus*. New York: Penguin, 1993.
Stegeman, Wolfgang. "Background III: The Social and Political Climate in Which Jesus of Nazareth Preached." In *Handbook for the Study of the Historical Jesus*, edited by Stanley E. Porter and Tom Holmén, 2291–314. Leiden: Brill, 2011.
Stott, John R. W. *Issues Facing Christians Today*. Edited by R. McCloughry. 4th ed. Grand Rapids, MI: Zondervan, 2006.
Van Opstal, Sandra. *The Mission of Worship*. Urbana Onward. Downers Grove, IL: IVP Books, 2012.
Watts, John D. W. "Elements of Old Testament Worship." *Journal of Bible and Religion* 26, no. 3 (July 1958): 217–21.
Weinfeld, Moshe. "'Justice and Righteousness': *Mshpt Wtsdqh* the Expression and Its Meaning." In *Justice and Righteousness: Biblical Themes and Their Influence*, edited by Henning Graf Reventlow, 228–46. Sheffield: Sheffield Academic Press, 1992.
Whitters, Mark F. "Jesus in the Footsteps of Jeremiah." *The Catholic Biblical Quarterly* 68, no. 2 (April 2006): 229–47.
Wright, N. T. *Jesus and the Victory of God*. London: SPCK, 1996.
Zenger, Erich, and Frank-Lothar Hossfeld. *Psalms 3: A Commentary on Psalms 101–150*. Edited by Klaus Baltzer. Translated by Linda M. Maloney. Minneapolis: Fortress, 2011.

2

"Act Justly, Love Mercy, Walk Humbly with God"

Perspectives on Power and Politics from the Old Testament Prophetic Tradition

Annelle G. Sabanal

Current popular discourse on political theology in the Philippines seems narrowly constrained to the New Testament and only to a few passages such as Romans 13 (you may want to visit chapter 3 which deals in detail with the exegesis of Rom. 13) or 1 Timothy 2:2. Theological discussions usually revolve around how these particular passages are to be understood in relation to the high-ranking leaders of the country, while all other sociopolitical issues are relegated as secondary in the work of theologizing. This kind of theological exercise is done to the detriment of other parts of Scripture that may offer better insights for reflection given specific sociopolitical issues that we face in the country today.

Hence, this chapter takes a look at the much-neglected Old Testament of the Bible, and in particular its prophetic section, both the Former Prophets and the Latter Prophets, in order to point to an alternative source of material for political reflection and to expand our potential scriptural source for political theologizing. Furthermore, it highlights some theological themes related to politics from the prophetic material to show the range of possibilities of relevant insights from this part of the Bible that may be useful in the discussion of current sociopolitical issues in the Philippines today. One cannot emphasize enough the importance of these materials as a source of reflection for how Christians should consider their role in society with respect to politics, especially because Jesus himself lived out the prophetic mandate particularly in his interaction with the unjust rulers of his time (see below). If we claim to be followers of Jesus, then we "must live as Jesus did" (1 John 2:6 NIV).

The chapter will elaborate on the following themes in the prophetic material: prophets and prophecy, God and earthly rulers, justice and righteousness, prophecy and hope, worship in the prophets, and prophecy and the nations. It concludes by exploring the implications for the church today.

Who Are the Prophets and What Is Prophecy?

Modern-day understanding of prophets and prophecy has muddled our understanding of Old Testament prophets. Certain sectors of the Protestant community have co-opted the term "prophets" and taken it to mean people who are able to predict the future. Such understanding is then imposed on the Old Testament, causing a great deal of exegetical misunderstanding of the nature of Old Testament prophecy.

Prophets are characterized in many ways: as visionaries (sometimes mystics), great poets and literary figures, theologians or religious philosophers, social reformers or radicals, upholders of holiness, seers, intermediaries, and so on.[1] An Old Testament prophet would usually exhibit at least two or more of these qualities. Not one or even a combination of them would fully describe what an Old Testament prophet is. But however they are presented, what sets them apart from other groups of inspired biblical characters is their involvement not only in the religious affairs of their nation but in the political and social affairs of the state as well. Samuel was involved in the establishment of the monarchy; Nathan and Gad appear in connection with important events in the life of David; Elijah and Elisha were involved in key crises in the history of the northern kingdom; and the classical prophets such as Amos, Micah, Isaiah, and Jeremiah addressed their messages to specific individuals including kings and princes, groups and communities, and the nation as a whole. Their activities and sensibilities were always rooted in history, in actual space and time. Unlike

---

1. J. R. Porter, "The Origins of Prophecy in Israel," in *Israel's Prophetic Tradition: Essays in Honour of Peter Ackroyd*, eds. R. Coggins, A. Phillips, and M. Knibb (Cambridge: Cambridge University Press, 1984), 12–31; G. M. Tucker, "The Role of the Prophets and the Role of the Church," in *Prophecy in Israel: Search for an Identity*, ed. D. L. Petersen (Philadelphia: Fortress, 1987), 159–74.

our modern perception of prophets and prophecy, Old Testament prophets did not take flight to another realm of reality. They closely paid attention to, and did not operate detached from, the social, political, and religious events occurring during their time. They wisely discerned the implications of these events for the community. This kind of sensitivity to the world around them prompted them to utter messages consistent with the nature of God and the covenant in order to address ongoing and potential problems. They fearlessly called the leaders and the nation to accountability to God. Not infrequently, their words were a scathing rebuke of the civic and religious leaders of their community (Isa 1:21–26; 56; Jer 10:21; Ezek3 4; etc.). Their preaching of the reign of God consistently pointed to God's rule and action within and among human beings in ordinary space and time. The prophets perceive history as an interaction of Yahweh with humanity and the way this relationship is manifested in how people treat their fellow human beings. Within this perspective, prophets called their fellow human beings, leaders and citizens alike, to account.

The Old Testament prophets did speak about future events, but they did not do it in the same way as a fortune-teller or our modern-day conception of a prophet is expected to do. Instead, the concerns of the Old Testament prophets, even as they spoke of the future, were rooted within history and society as they knew it, and, with a few exceptions, an immediate future. But even their concern with the immediate future still bears relation to their contemporary concerns. As such, any prediction that a prophet might make that had reference to the immediate future served only as a response to the present situation. Thus, the prophet's message almost always had something to do with what was wrong at the time and what needed to be done to avert the impending doom or future calamity.

What kind of message did they proclaim? They proclaimed judgment and disaster to counter false hope. They also announced deliverance and hope when there was misguided despair. They spoke against the status quo in society and consistently expressed judgment on both active commissions of injustice or a passive silence in the face of it (Isa 5; 10:1–3; Jer 5:26–29; 22; Ezek 22:23–29). They persistently pointed out the injustices in society, especially those committed by leaders, and uttered scathing rebukes and judgment against them. Scholars say that this persistent message of doom against violators of justice and righteousness is what eventually distinguished true prophets from false ones.[2] As would be expected, this kind of negativity did not sit well with

---

2. C. H. Hayes, *Introduction to the Bible* (New Haven, CT: Yale University Press, 2012), 239–41.

the established interests. Hence, we see stories of prophets going into hiding, running for their lives, or being persecuted for their messages of doom. And when God finally executed his judgment against the community, the prophets willingly suffered with them and, in time, provided hope and energized the community in the midst of the tragedy and despair. They spoke on behalf of God by delivering his message and advocated on behalf of the people for God's mercy when they knew that God's judgment was at hand.

Their message was, however, not a new kind of message. It was anchored in a rich theological tradition that we find in other parts of the Old Testament. For example, while we do not see an explicit expression of the covenant formula as we read it in the Pentateuch, we find echoes of the covenant within the prophetic corpus. The admonition to love God with all of one's heart, soul, and might (cf. Deut 6:5) is expounded in the prophetic material through the insistence that loving God entails not just faithful fulfillment of the rigid demands of worship and the sacrificial system detailed in Leviticus, but also the outward care for the marginalized in society.

God, Prophets, and Earthly Rulers

Prophecy and kingship were closely connected in Israel and its neighbor countries in the ancient Near East. Recall that in the early narratives of the book of Samuel, kings are anointed by Yahweh through the prophets. Such is especially the case for the first two kings of Israel. This also tells us that, during the early period of the monarchy, prophets had ready access to kings.

Prophets not only anointed kings but also reprimanded them for their mistakes. Eventually, prophets also pronounced the kings' fall from power. In the narratives of the Former Prophets (i.e. Joshua to Kings), a common motif that runs through the stories is the prophets' opposition to kings – Samuel against Saul, Nathan against David, Elijah against Ahab, Micaiah against Ahab, and so on. Later on, in the books which we more prominently call the classical prophets (e.g. Isaiah, Jeremiah), we no longer see oracles affirming the kings or leaders except in those oracles that seem to foresee a coming messianic king. In these materials, most, if not all, of the oracles that pertain to kings and leaders are classified as judgment oracles that announce God's rejection of their leadership and their impending punishment. In a sense, prophets may be thought of as God's representatives in giving legitimacy to the authority that the kings and the community leaders of Israel held. They were king-makers and, more prominently, in the latter part of the monarchy, they were king-breakers. With their persistent criticism of abuses of power, opposition to official or royal policy, and call for reform and changes, one may think of them as God's watchdogs in the world of politics and in the exercise of power.

As already mentioned, not all prophets behaved in this way. We read accounts of prophets who were adjudged as false prophets, especially when they were co-opted by wielders of power. From the biblical perspective, a true prophet is someone who is determined to deliver God's word, even if it is opposed to the wishes of the king or the view of the majority. These prophets are willing to proclaim a message even if it is one of judgment or doom. They put their lives at risk to challenge and dismantle the dominant consciousness not just of the leaders but also of the citizenry. Interestingly, this kind of perceived negativity or propensity to criticize the powers that be and their fellow prophets employed by the kings is what would be regarded as one of the marks of a true prophet. Later tradition would single out some of these prophets, whose relationship with the royal institution was quite adversarial, as the ones who had spoken truthfully. It is their words that eventually made it into the prophetic collection.

Israel shared similar prophetic forms and themes with its neighbor states in the ancient Near East. Oracles categorized as prophecy and other literary materials from the ancient Near East also feature a close connection between the deity, the prophets, and kings. As in the Old Testament, these materials highlight the expectation that kings and leaders should exercise prudent and just leadership because they are the representatives of the deity's leadership over his subjects. However, one way in which Old Testament prophecy differs from prophecy in the ancient Near East is in the lack of stinging critique against abuses of the leaders in the latter.[3] One can, of course, make the unrealistic inference that this lack is due to the absence of injustice in all other states within the ancient Near East. But the more reasonable explanation is that the emphasis of the ancient Near Eastern prophetic oracles and other literary materials on kings and leaders is on their divine legitimation – that the kings are authorized

---

3. This lack in the prophetic oracles in the ANE is noted by J. W. Hilber, "Prophecy, Divination, and Magic in the Ancient Near East," in *Behind the Scenes of the Old Testament: Cultural, Social, and Historical Contexts*, eds. J. S. Greer, J. W. Hilber, and J. H. Walton (Grand Rapids, MI: Baker Academic, 2018), 371–72; and J. H. Walton, *Ancient Near Eastern Thought and the Old Testament* (Nottingham: Apollos, 2007), 252. For a sampling of prophetic oracles from the ANE, see H. Ringren, "Prophecy in the Ancient Near East," in *Israel's Prophetic Tradition: Essays in Honour of Peter Ackroyd*, eds. R. Coggins, A. Phillips, and M. Knibb (Cambridge: Cambridge University Press, 1984), 1–11. For a comparison of other literary materials from the ANE featuring themes of politics and justice vis-à-vis the king with the OT prophetic material, see A. Sabanal, "The Motif of 'Shepherd' and Politics in the Hebrew Prophets" (PhD diss., University of Edinburgh, 2017), 29–35.

and chosen by their gods.[4] The Old Testament departs from this literary and ideological tendency. Instead, it features copious judgment oracles and rebukes against the abuses of the kings and leaders of the community. This affirms the importance that the Old Testament puts on keeping the leaders of the community and the nation in check through the ministry of prophetic rebuke. It also highlights that the Old Testament is not naive regarding the evils of politics and the exercise of power. And instead of avoiding it, the prophets face it head-on by calling for accountability from those with privilege and power.

What is the theology that underpins this kind of prophetic perspective? The undergirding worldview behind this prophetic consciousness is the idea that God alone is the only true authority, and human authority and power are subordinate to it. Consequently, the goods of creation and the community are under the safekeeping and redemptive work of God. These two notions affirm the humane character of God's work in history as a manifestation of his divine rule. Essentially, the authority of leaders emanates from God, whether leaders are conscious of it or not. The king, or the earthly leader, is simply a vicegerent or an administrator of God. As God's administrator, the human king is the centralizing symbol of the community, the dispenser of Yahweh's justice, and the chief redistributor of material and symbolic goods within the community. In this sense, kingship is perceived in a positive light. Kings are perceived as the designated defenders of the cause of the poor, the oppressed, and the marginalized. Because of this role, kings need to be attentive to divine sanction. The nature of accountability demanded of the king is much greater than the accountability asked of an ordinary citizen. Every wrong or right thing the king does has a corresponding effect upon the people he leads. This is the reason why the kings and the leaders of Israel are usually referred to as "shepherds" of the people. Kings and leaders are accountable to God, who is the owner of the flock. In contrast, the flock is portrayed as helpless, delicate, and in need of dedicated guidance. Thus, the kings and the community leaders are expected to guide the flock and ensure their well-being.

However, many of the kings of Israel fell short of their mandate to deliver justice and material well-being to the community. Sometimes they were accused of active commission of injustice. Other times, they were accused of neglecting justice and being passive about injustice. Both behaviors are perceived as an affront to Yahweh. And when the kings failed or were failing to do their duty, the prophets did not hold back from criticizing them. Moreover,

---

4. Comparison of materials in Sabanal, "Motif of 'Shepherd,'" 29–35, yields the same observation.

it was not just the kings or the highest leaders of the land whom they criticized. They also criticized the princes, elders, the nobles of the community, and even their fellow prophets. Overall, the prophets uttered some of the most scornful words to be recorded in Scripture. According to their assessment of history, the kings' and the leaders' stance toward injustice was the reason why the entire nation had to go into exile.

But what frames the rhetoric on politics, power, and governance in the prophetic materials? The central aspect of the governance of God through the kings and leaders is justice and righteousness. We turn to this idea next.

Justice and Righteousness

Justice in the classical prophets is usually explored through oracles that condemn unjust acts. In this "negative rhetoric" about justice, we may be able to approximate the prophetic notion of justice, especially in the context of power and politics. Certainly, justice does not stand on its own as a concept, not just in the prophetic material but throughout the Old Testament. Justice almost always stands synonymously with the idea of "righteousness," whether explicitly or conceptually.[5] In the modern perspective, righteousness is usually understood in the modern sense of "being holy." It implies moral uprightness due to one's belief in God. It is often used of people who are active members of a faith community or church and who try to live uprightly. However, in the prophetic material, righteousness carries the notion of the right order of things following the standards of God's rightness.[6] Hence, righteousness means doing what is just, and justice implies doing what is right. Both concepts are always related to an act of "doing." Almost always, they are associated with a Hebrew verb that denotes action. Hence, justice and righteousness are not simply abstract concepts that an Israelite was supposed to know, but an ethical stance that one was supposed to do or act out.

The goal of doing justice and righteousness is shalom, or wholeness and harmony for the community. This sense of wholeness through justice is explored in the prophetic corpus when it contends with the reality that there are different hierarchies of power within the community. More often than not, the subject of the doing of justice (and righteousness) in the prophetic material

---

5. As in other parts of the Hebrew Bible, the notion of justice is multilayered. It has implications related to jurisprudence and legal decisions, the right of certain parties, the authority of a ruler, etc.

6. B. Johnson, "ṣāḏaq," *TDOT*, XII (2003): 245.

is someone (or a group of people) who has more power, while the object is someone who holds less power than the subject. Hence, the king is expected to exercise justice and righteousness over his subjects. His reign has to ensure the well-being of everyone in the community by ensuring that those who have less power and fewer resources do not suffer because of their lack. At the same time, the nobles, princes, and community leaders are expected to do the same on behalf of those who have less power and fewer resources than them.

Thus, the demand for accountability for doing justice and righteousness is not restricted to the king alone. It applies to other community leaders as well, and to anyone who holds power or privilege in the community. The higher up one is in the hierarchy of power, the greater the accountability that is demanded. The nature of Israel's social existence as described by the prophetic material is ordered such that the oppressed and vulnerable are expected to be protected by those who hold more power than they do. As in other parts of the Old Testament, the marginalized sector (orphans, widows, and strangers) of their community find special mention. It is the exercise of the human act of justice and righteousness that will guarantee that they are provided for in the biblical world where there exist different privileges because of different access to resources. Anyone with power is enjoined to fulfill the responsibility of taking care of the poor and marginalized. However, the king, or the most powerful leader in the community, is specially commissioned to make sure that this will indeed happen. The king not only dispenses justice himself, but restores it where persons responsible for it have denied it.

A king's reign may be established and upheld only with justice and righteousness. So, while the king derives his authority from God, the legitimacy of the continuity of the king's claim to power is dependent on his exercise of justice and his compassion for the poor and the marginalized. This idea harks back to the notion that God is the only true ruler and the king derives his mandate from him. God's rule is supposed to result in shalom for the community, and the human king is the agent by which this vision will become a reality. Hence, the king is supposed to mediate God's rule by ensuring that no member experiences any lack, especially the marginalized and the poor. While most of the kings of Israel failed in their divine mandate to take care of the marginalized and the oppressed, the prophetic corpus did not give up on politics. It also did not give up its hope for an ideal leader, but looked forward to a time when God's just and righteous rule would be embodied by a just and righteous leader. This idea is explored in different ways in the hope oracles of the prophetic material.

Regardless of one's position within the community, the exercise of justice from the prophetic standpoint is a notion that is not dependent on laws and stipulations but on the commitment of the individual to stand by it. This obligation arises not from external authority but from the personal commitment which is itself undertaken because the person is just.[7] Although it is a commitment that one is expected to undertake, it is also demanded of those who have more power and resources to wield. They have to be more just if the prophetic vision of a just society is to exist.

The Prophetic Theology of Hope

If there are passages in the prophetic corpus that have attracted frequent use in our churches today, they would be the passages that speak of hope, and understandably so. Verses such as Jeremiah 29:11 and Isaiah 41:10 are go-to passages for people seeking encouragement or those who seek to encourage others.

Certainly, prophets were not merely to point out the mistakes people made. They were there to plead on behalf of the people, especially those who, without any choice, had to suffer the judgment of God because of the wickedness of those who abused their power. Aside from pleading on behalf of those who deserved salvation, the prophets were also to bring hope and energy to the community, especially when despair seemed to be the only response. But what kind of hope do the prophets offer? How are we to understand the hope that passages like Jeremiah 29:11 advocate?

The hope espoused by the prophets, particularly that expressed in the oracles of hope and oracles of salvation, is best understood when read against the backdrop of the judgment oracles and the voice of lamentation and despair that interweaves with or surrounds them. From this vantage point, one realizes that the prophets do not offer easy consolation. Above all, the prophetic message of hope is not a passive call for one to simply sit idly while pinning one's hope on some promised future. It is not the same as the Filipino mindset implied in the popular expression "ipagpasa-Diyos mo na lang" – to just let go and give it to God while awaiting his redemptive act. Instead, alongside the declaration of hope are declarations to act, as we read in passages like Isaiah 56:1 and 61:1–4. In these passages, hope is expressed in the context of the call to continue doing justice and defending the cause of the oppressed. These hope passages insinuate that hope is not a passive stance. Hope becomes a reality

---

7. W. J. Houston, *Contending for Justice* (London: T&T Clark, 2006), 132.

when people strive for justice and righteousness while holding on to God's promises to bring about the completion of justice whereby he himself will punish the oppressors and those who sit idle while injustice happens.

At the same time, hope is not an easy antidote for discomfort or simply a quick and dismissive excuse for shallow disagreement with the current state of affairs. Take note that the hope oracles were written against the backdrop of the exile – an event that caused the feeling of abandonment, disorientation, and grief over loss, with no prospect of redemption. The destruction of the city and the temple and the deportation of the king and many of the people negated everything that made Israel feel secure. The words of the laments recorded in the prophetic corpus, the book of Lamentations, and the Psalms describe in great detail and express the resulting sense of loss and anguish that overcame the people as a result of the catastrophic events of the exile. Their complaints and bitter words exude abject despair and weariness (chapter 4 of this book explores the theme of "complaint against God"). They are words of people who are truly aware of what is at stake. One cannot be in this state unless one is truly invested in what has been lost or is about to be lost. The inclusion in the Old Testament of these oracles expressing utter brokenness is a recognition that the feeling of despair must be given its due, and that one has to have the courage to face the reality of abandonment and God's absence. It is in this context that the prophets are to declare and establish hope for the broken people. The element of participation in despair is an essential component in the experience of hope. It comes as no surprise, therefore, that hope is offered to the faithful prophet himself (Isa 61:10–11). His prophetic awareness must have allowed him a front-row experience of feelings of despair. But despite this, he remained the most ardent advocate of justice and righteousness. He tirelessly urged the people to turn from their wicked ways and instead go the way of the Lord (vv. 8–9).

When words of hope are uttered within the context of deep anguish, they do not become just easy relief or an expression of wishful thinking. The prophetic words of hope do not simply serve as a balm to pain but act as a direct riposte to the despair and brokenness that the people have to go through. This is highlighted in the contrasting ideas in the following phrases where the positive ideas dominate the negative: "darkness into light . . . rough places into level ground" (Isa 42:14–16 ESV); "power to the faint . . . strength to the powerless" (Isa 40:28–29, translation mine). Moreover, the prophetic tradition also takes extra care in framing the claims of hope so that it does not present it just as a continuation and repetition of what God has done in the past. Rather, hope is portrayed as a new action, an expression of a new resolve on the part of God to save the remnant of the community (cf. Isa 40; 42:14–16). It is framed not as some fanciful acts or a result of human interference, but as a new historical possibility that God himself is to bring about.

Aside from the prophet himself, the main recipients of the promise of hope and salvation are those who have been denied justice and become victims of oppression. These are usually the poor, the marginalized, the disempowered (Mic 4:6–7). In the days of salvation, God will finally bring about his own justice, and his shalom will reign. Those who have been oppressed and disempowered will be vindicated. The hope for this kind of justice and righteousness is most evident in the promises of a future redeemer who will bring about the ideals of God's rule (cf. Isa 42). Hope may therefore be seen as an expression of resistance to powers that seek to dominate and oppress. It is living out the belief that the authority of God is able to liberate one from oppression and that the good governance of God is possible. During the exile, there is no doubt that the Babylonian Empire preferred the Israelites to languish in hopelessness. But the utterances of hope in the prophetic corpus stand as an act of defiance against the power of empire and against any human power that seeks to exert absolute authority.

As is the case today, there were people during the prophetic period who had the wrong notion of hope. According to the prophet Amos, these were the people who were content to wait for the "day of the LORD" (Amos 5:18). We can surmise from the tone of the prophet that "the day of the LORD" was perceived as positive and predictable and something that every Israelite anticipated with eagerness. However, the prophet immediately turns this anticipation on its head, shattering the positive expectation that this day will be a day of jubilation and redemption for the Israelites. Interestingly, what follows the diatribe in Amos 5:18–20 is the expression of God's displeasure over the ritual sacrifices and worship that the Israelites offer. The prophet castigates them for feeling secure about their wealth, as if the judgment day is the farthest thing from their minds. He accuses them of performing these traditional worship practices while neglecting the needy (ch. 6). For Amos, the people's show of worship through their performance of the rituals and sacrifices is a very superficial manifestation of worship. He calls them instead to "let justice roll down like waters, and righteousness like an ever-flowing stream" (ESV). This view of hope, especially in relation to the notion of "the day of the LORD," is not limited to Amos. The other prophets see this day (cf. Isa 13:6, 9; Ezek 13:5; Joel 1:15; 2:1, 11; 2:31; 3:14; Obad 15; Zeph 1:7, 14; Mal 4:5) as a day of varying judgment for all the enemies of God, as well as for Israel and Judah.

In sum, hope should not be an excuse for complacency and apathy. It does not mean detachment from the concerns of the here and now while waiting for God to act. The promise of hope urges us to live our lives in active participation in God's work of justice; to grieve when God's righteousness cannot be felt; to resist with a firm belief that God will act in history to bring an end to injustice. The work of justice comes with a future certainty because God is the God of justice. It is an assurance that the work of justice is not a senseless act. On the contrary, it is an action that sees itself in a secure future.

Worship in the Prophets

Israel is primarily a worshipping community. Everything about its existence – its politics, social expressions, and relationships – may be said to be subsumed under the overarching category of worship. This is an idea that is evident in the prophetic material and dominates the entire Old Testament. In this worldview, there is no clear demarcation between what we in the modern world would classify as secular and sacred. All aspects of life are perceived as under the purview of God's jurisdiction. This holistic perspective toward life is underscored by the doxologies in the prophetic material that declare God's ultimate sovereignty over the created order, over all the earth, and over everything that happens in it (cf. Isa 66). The idea is also implicitly suggested by the prophetic concern for the different aspects of life such as politics, the economy, and the environment.

Given such a worldview, Israelites are therefore expected to order all aspects of their lives in a manner that subscribes to God's intention of worship. This holistic perspective toward life is the reason why we do not sense in the Old Testament, and even more so in the prophetic material, the kind of ordering or sense of hierarchy of the different aspects of life that we can discern from modern Christians that considers spiritual categories as primary and anything secular as secondary. This dichotomy between the spiritual and the secular results in a theological reduction of worship to something that carefully maintains boundaries between the two. It espouses the view that worship is first and foremost done within the context of the church (the worship service, participation in the ministry sanctioned by the church, etc.). However, the prophets do not see worship or life under God in this way. While there are some ethical principles that are held in higher esteem, life is seen as a connected whole and all aspects of it are subsumed under the category of worship of God.

This is not to say that the prophets rendered rituals obsolete. Certainly, as we may learn from the book of Leviticus, rituals have their proper place in the exercise of worship in Israel. Recent studies on the book, especially those that appreciate the contributions of the social sciences to the study of the biblical text, have pointed out how all kinds of living cultures engage in different kinds of rituals or symbolic actions that are meaningful to them. In the case of Israel, it is its worship rituals that allow the community to experience a symbolic contact with God even for that brief ritual moment.[8]

Although there is a predominant Protestant distaste for anything that is ritualistic, it cannot be denied that, similar to Israel, we in the evangelical community maintain our own sets of rituals. These are practices that have become consistent and repetitive and where part of their meaning derives from the repetition of the practice. Examples include practices such as coming together as a congregation to worship, tithing, holy communion, baptism, and being engaged in regular Bible studies. In the same way that the rituals of Leviticus convey a meaningful actualization of the worship of the Israelite community, so our own rituals convey not just our expression of worship but our corporate aspiration to be the embodiment of Christ and the rule of God here on earth.

However, the prophets remind us that anything that is routine may gradually lose depth, such that worshippers may lose sight of the meaning that underlies what they do. Moreover, prophets insinuate that rituals should not be an end in themselves. Many passages, including Isaiah 1:12–17 and Amos 5:21–24, decry any form of worship that is one-dimensional and lacking in a critical edge. The prophets also reject obsession over elements that may superficially denote worship of God or closeness to God, such as the land and the temple (Jer 7; 29; Ezek 33:23–29). For the prophets, what caused the exile was a failure of worship. However, the failure was not in the execution of the worship rituals that they were so accustomed to doing. Rather, they failed to account for the real meaning of worship – one which affirmed the two aspects of God's sovereignty which are his holiness and his justice (the relationship of worship and justice is explored in greater detail in chapter 1 of this book). The inseparability of these two aspects of worship is explored in passages such as those in Isaiah that insist that the failure to observe justice is what grieves the Holy One of Israel (Isa 1:4; 5:18–19, 24; 30:8–14; 37:23–25). For the prophets, worship without its ethical component expressed through justice is incomplete. To disregard justice is to disregard the very reason for which worship was instituted for Israel. In the prophetic material, God's holiness is made manifest through the performance of righteous and just acts by human beings.

---

8. See M. Douglas, *Purity and Danger* (London: Routledge, 2002).

Prophets and the Nations

Much of the Old Testament material reflects an inward-looking perspective. It comprises mainly reflections of Israel about itself, its history, what it has done wrong as a nation, what caused the nation to be exiled and to suffer under the rule of its more powerful neighbors, and so on. However, there are several places in the Old Testament where we can sense a more outward-looking perspective, that is, a look at other nations and, sometimes, an assessment of Israel's relationship with them. Examples beyond the prophetic material are the table of nations in Genesis 11, the narratives of Daniel and his friends, and the narrative of Esther. The latter two narratives are usually used as a source for reflection on how citizens should behave under the domination of another nation. From these, we can already see how the Old Testament shows God's positive interest in international political processes.

In the prophetic material, we see explicit claims for God's sovereignty over nations and their leaders in passages such as Micah 4:1–5; Isaiah 2:2, 4; 24; 45; 47; 49:7, 22–23; Jeremiah 1:10; 10:7; 12–16; 25:9; and Ezekiel 39:21. This is not surprising, especially as the prophetic material is set within a period of empire expansion of superpower nations. Most, if not all, of the prophetic materials are set within the time of exile or very close to it. During this period, Israel and Judah have had to deal with the aggressive and competing expansionistic agendas of the imperial powers Egypt, Assyria, Babylon, and Persia. Often, the fledgling nations of Judah and Israel are portrayed as caught in the middle of the competition among these superpowers. As with the Philippines, the geographical location of Israel may partly explain why it was under constant threat of the usually violent imperialistic advances of the superpowers. This historical reality explains the copious and diverse oracles expressing prophetic thoughts on the activities and relations of nations that may provide a source of reflection for similar issues in the modern context, such as the incursion of China into territories of its less powerful neighbors such as the Philippines, and our experience of subjugation during the colonial expansion of Western nations in recent history.

A significant body of material in the prophetic corpus that deals centrally with the theme of nations and can thus serve as a source for theological reflection on geopolitics is the material called the Oracles Against the Nations (OAN). They are found in the major prophetic collections (Isa 13–23; Jer 46–51; Ezek 25–32; Amos 1–2; Zeph 2) and are usually expressed in the genre of lawsuit, or *rib*. Often, Bible readers gloss over them because of their seemingly repetitive, formulaic content. However, they are interesting not just because they deal with the theme of the nations, but also because they portray the nations as having been dealt with by God without a mediating reference to Israel.

Passages from these sections of the prophetic material articulate the idea that the rule of God imposes upon nations a certain standard of human interaction that requires them to act humanely toward each other. God is portrayed as the guarantor of these relationships expressed through the demands, indictments, judgments, and sanctions imposed on the offending nations (Isa 47; Jer 30:11; Ezek 36:1–13; 38–39; Mic 7:16–17; etc.). Any violation of this standard is considered to be an act of self-sufficiency and arrogance toward God's rule.

Because these materials are predominantly expressed in a condemnatory tone against the nations, one might think that they simply serve a biased Yahwistic agenda or are used to justify an ideology that elevates Israel. However, the same demand to treat other nations humanely is also made of Israel. In fact, in different instances, Israel is reprimanded for its self-preoccupation. Such is the case in the series of OAN in Amos 1–2. In the first six of the seven oracles, the prophet denounces the other nations and declares punishment on them because of their inhumane treatment of others, Israelites and non-Israelites alike, during wars. The series of rebukes initially makes the reader think that the first two chapters of the book are merely a condemnation of other nations. One can imagine how the original Israelite listeners must have been drawn to these oracles, with their images of their enemies getting what they deserved. But in a surprising twist, the prophet then turns the indictment and directs the last accusation at Israel, charging them with something worse. If their enemies are being condemned for their brutal acts in times of war, Israel's atrocities are much worse, because their acts of brutality were committed even in times of peace! It can even be argued that the rhetorical progression of the OAN in Amos was merely a way for the prophet to use his long condemnatory diatribe against the nations as an object lesson for Israel.

Under the rule of God, Israel is therefore not exempt from a responsibility toward other nations. The geopolitical ethic expected from the other nations applies to Israel as well. In fact, it makes sense to conclude that, since Israel is portrayed as the model nation in many parts of the prophetic material, *more* is expected from Israel in its exercise of ethical sensibilities, especially in relation to foreigners and other nations.

This equitable expectation of the obligations and rights of nations implies that there is more in the relations of nations than simply the exertion of brute force or power, especially of the more powerful nations against the less powerful ones. In reality, the end goal of God's geopolitics is the rule of a shared shalom between the nations. The theology of the OAN suggests that there is a divine justice that calls nations to account and that this justice goes beyond the challenge of even the most powerful state. This is specifically suggested by the oracles against superpowers such as Babylon and Assyria (cf. Isa 13; 30:27–33; Jer 50–51). This is what it means when Isaiah describes God as judging the nations with righteousness, equity, and truth (Isa 2:4; cf. Ps 96:10, 13; 67:4).

The witness of the prophetic material and the entire Old Testament suggests that the presence of nations and superpowers is not necessarily wrong in itself nor shunned by God. In fact, they can be God's partners in his geopolitics. We see this in the affirmation of Cyrus and Persia in Isaiah 44–45 and elsewhere in the Old Testament. Power does not need to be in defiance of the political ethics of God. Whether nations are great or small, powerful or not, there is an expectation of cooperation among them – cooperation that does not tolerate barbarism and arrogance, but exudes human civility and mercy. This cooperation is supposed to be life-preserving, not only for the superpowers but also for the nations that are under the constant threat of imperial domination and subjugation. An abrogation of this expectation is a challenge to God's sovereign rule over the nations. Hence, we read of God's anger against the superpowers of Egypt, Assyria, and Babylon, powerful nations that vaunted their might against Israel and other less powerful nations. The rhetoric of the oracles against these superpowers demonstrates more than simple rage. It demonstrates that this aversion to self-aggrandizement and the unrestrained persecution of other nations lies at the very heart of God.

The prophetic perspective insinuates that powerful nations should exercise generosity and mercy defined by what is just and right. Such are the geopolitical ethics that define the sovereign power of God over the nations and which he, in turn, expects them to exercise. Thus, in a sense, the inclusion of the OAN in the prophetic material is an affirmative expression of this ethic and a show of resistance to any power that tries to subvert the sovereign will of God for the nations.

The Old Testament Prophets and the Church Today

Full awareness of the state of Philippine politics and their effects, especially on marginalized and impoverished communities, will make it difficult to read the message of the prophets and look away without being bothered and rebuked. While the institutions and structures they railed against may be different from ours, the societal and political issues they pointed to are very much the same as the issues we face today. The prophets responded to these issues with a message born out of a clear belief that God is the Lord and king of history and society. When they spoke of justice, righteousness, salvation, and judgment, they did so in concrete, specific, and tangible terms – rooted in experience within the realm of space and time. Unlike our common modern theological understanding of salvation that confines it to something otherworldly or spiritual, the prophets recognized the multidimensionality of salvation. Thus, they spoke of salvation using the language of shalom or wholeness of life and how this shalom bears on all aspects of experience such as war and peace, works of justice within the community, survival of the marginalized, and the role of the privileged. They stressed the importance of community and the interconnectedness of its many facets, especially of individuals with other individuals – about how one's mistakes and sins, especially those of the king, have grave consequences for the larger community.

To read the prophets seriously will undoubtedly cause some discomfort to people who feel at ease. The prophets have a way of unsettling the conscience. They were the biblical personalities who questioned structures and behaviors that usually make people feel very secure. Prophets shake us out of our complacency, and question our comfort zones and our orthodox assumptions of God and what it means to be God's worshipping people.

It is, therefore, not surprising that Jesus himself identified with the prophetic tradition, given his own teachings that upended worldviews, norms, and structures. Many of the passages attributed to him came from the prophets. The passage in Luke 4:18–19, which he quotes at the beginning of his ministry and which seems to summarize his mission, derives from Isaiah 61:

> The Spirit of the Lord is upon me,
>   because he has anointed me
>   to bring good news to the poor.
> He has sent me to proclaim release to the captives
>   and recovery of sight to the blind,
>   to let the oppressed go free,
> to proclaim the year of the Lord's favor. (NRSV)

Similarly, Matthew 23 depicts Christ aligning himself with the prophets in his scathing rebuke of the scribes and the Pharisees. At that time, they were the civic and religious leaders of their community. In his pronouncement of woes against them, particularly in verses 23–36, it is noticeable that the language of Jesus and the themes he speaks of find similarity with what we read in the prophetic material. For example, Jesus's stinging words "Woe to you, scribes and Pharisees, hypocrites! For you tithe mint, dill, and cumin, and have neglected the weightier matters of the law: justice and mercy and faith" (NRSV) echo Isaiah 1:11–17; 58:3–7; and Amos 5:14–24. Moreover, in verse 37, Jesus likens his impending death to the sufferings of the prophets when he says, "Jerusalem, Jerusalem, the city that kills the prophets and stones those who are sent to it!" (NRSV). Even his symbolic cleansing of the temple earlier in chapter 21 draws inspiration from the prophetic symbolic acts. These apparent parallels between the life of Jesus and the prophets should prompt anyone who claims to be a disciple and follower of Christ to pay close attention to the words and tradition that Jesus lived by.

Moreover, if the church considers itself to be the bearer of the new covenant with God and the continuation of the worshipping community that Israel was in the Old Testament, then it would do well to consider and be instructed by the prophetic heritage of holistic worship which includes an exercise of its prophetic witness. This is the worship that permeates all aspects of lived life. It is lived out by seeking the well-being not just of self but of others through active participation in the concrete works of justice and righteousness in society, and the exercise of prophetic rebuke, especially when justice and righteousness are being disregarded by wielders of power. Only in this way may the prophetic vision of God's rule be attained. The challenge of the prophets for concrete participation in the processes of the communities we live in is expressed well in the words of Micah 6:8:

> He has shown you, O mortal, what is good:
> > And what does the LORD require of you?
> To act justly and to love mercy
> > and to walk humbly with your God. (NIV)

Bibliography

Douglas, M. *Purity and Danger.* London: Routledge, 2002.
Hayes, C. H. *Introduction to the Bible.* New Haven, CT: Yale University Press, 2012.
Hilber, J. W. "Prophecy, Divination, and Magic in the Ancient Near East." In *Behind the Scenes of the Old Testament: Cultural, Social, and Historical Contexts*, edited by J. S. Greer, J. W. Hilber, and J. H. Walton, 368–74. Grand Rapids, MI: Baker Academic, 2018.
Houston, W. J. *Contending for Justice.* London: T&T Clark, 2006.
Johnson, B. "ṣāḏaq," *TDOT*, XII (2003): 239–64.
Porter, J. R. "The Origins of Prophecy in Israel." In *Israel's Prophetic Tradition: Essays in Honour of Peter Ackroyd*, edited by R. Coggins, A. Phillips, and M. Knibb, 12–31. Cambridge: Cambridge University Press, 1984.

Ringren, H. "Prophecy in the Ancient Near East." In *Israel's Prophetic Tradition: Essays in Honour of Peter Ackroyd*, edited by R. Coggins, A. Phillips, and M. Knibb, 1–11. Cambridge: Cambridge University Press, 1984.

Sabanal, A. "The Motif of 'Shepherd' and Politics in the Hebrew Prophets." PhD diss., University of Edinburgh, 2017.

Tucker, G. M. "The Role of the Prophets and the Role of the Church." In *Prophecy in Israel: Search for an Identity*, edited by D. L. Petersen, 159–74. Philadelphia: Fortress, 1987.

Walton, J. H. *Ancient Near Eastern Thought and the Old Testament.* Nottingham: Apollos, 2007.

3

Romans 13 and the Limits of Submission

Junette B. Galagala-Nacion

Introduction

What does the Bible say about Christians speaking truth to power, when that power is their own government itself?

Often, prayer and submission are supplied as the only components of Christian duty to human rulers, with Romans 13 as the reason behind the church's silence on issues concerning the government. Such silence comes in the face of massive disregard for human life and the weakening of structures that hold our government accountable.

In this chapter, I will read Romans 13 in its literary and historical contexts. Placing Romans 13 in the framework of unity and reconciliation within the church shows an appeal to humility amid diversity in light of Jewish-Gentile tensions. The Christian community in Rome needed to live prudently and ensure survival while providing good testimony to the gospel. The letter was also written during the earlier part of Nero's reign, when the empire was still benign toward Christians. This reading also sheds light on Paul's understanding of the function of human rulers and, as such, qualifies his statement on voluntary submission to governing authorities. Paul also possibly alluded to the tradition reflected in Mark 12:17 with regards to payment of taxes, and in Romans 1:4 likely contended against the imperial claim of divine sonship. Here we see the dominant ideology being propagated in the first century (the emperor as "son of God") being contested by Jesus as true ruler and source of peace.

Other passages that call for subjection to human rulers (1 Tim 2:1–4; Titus 3:1–2; and 1 Pet 2:13–17) had a similar need among their communities. They had to avoid persecution while living as good testimonies to the gospel. The contexts of these passages are similar – there was a need to survive persecution and to thrive as a religious minority. These communities also needed to provide a faithful witness to the gospel by upholding order in society; that is, living peacefully with gentile neighbors and submitting to government.

Finally, I will provide an overview of Revelation 13 as a counterpoint to Romans 13. Revelation 13 shows a government that embodies evil, as opposed to the more benign context of Romans 13 at the beginning of Nero's rule. Revelation 13 shows a different tone toward and response to human rulers as Rome did not govern as expected of rulers representing Pax Romana both in the political and the religious sense. As such, the call for believers was to endure persecution while resisting the oppressive empire.

Christians, therefore, have to consider their civic duty in terms of their context. In the modern participatory democracy of the Philippines, Christians need to fully embrace the obligations of citizens, and that includes keeping the powers of civic servants in check under the rule of law. Contrary to popular notions, holding our governments accountable does not mean upending the God-given order. It is actually upholding the divine mandate for human authority when understood according to its purpose. This is part of determining the shape of Christian testimony in our time.

Romans 13 in Context
Call for Unity between Jews and Gentiles

One major theme in Romans is the new terms of the relationship between Jews and Gentiles now that they are both under Christ. This is perhaps the overarching concept that holds the entire letter together. The first half of Romans discusses the accountability of all humanity, both Jews and Gentiles, for their sin. Both are under God's wrath. It sets out the distinctions between life under sin and life in Christ for both groups. They have different spiritual ancestry, with Jews being the primary receivers of the law and the first recipients of the grace of God. Despite this, those outside the law, the Gentiles, now have open access to God through faith. While Jews have the privilege of being the first to know God, Gentiles now have the opportunity to partake of God's kingdom as well.

Paul demonstrates how one man, Adam, became the instrument by which sin entered and led to disobedience and trespass. In a parallel manner, Christ became the means of redemption. In a series of rhetorical questions, Paul explains the implications of being united to Christ in his death and resurrection. Even as the law made sin multiply, grace became more abundant. So Paul asks, first, whether one should continue sinning in order that grace might abound. To this, he replies that, through the symbol of baptism, believers have been buried with Christ in death, which is death to sin. In the same way that Christ was raised, Christians are called to "walk in newness of life."[1]

Next, Paul asks whether believers have a license to sin since we are under grace and not the law. He replies that one is a slave of whomever one obeys. As believers are slaves to righteousness, their bodies should be presented for sanctification. So Paul explains that believers have been freed from enslavement to sin but are now under God instead. He provides the analogy of marriage, which is binding only while the married persons are alive. Similarly, believers have died to the law through Christ's death. The Jewish law is no longer binding. What is in place, though, is new life in the Spirit.

Third, Paul then argues that law is not sin but has become a means by which one becomes aware of sin at work in oneself. That is, because we realize that we should not desire things that belong to others, the sin within us produces covetousness instead. Paul continues that it was not something good – the law – that brought death to us, but the sin at work in us. He then segues into a monologue of sorts, presenting the struggles within his own body. While he is willing to do what is right, he is unable to do it, and ends up doing the evil which he does not want. He cries out because of his own wretchedness, pointing out that while with his mind he is a slave to God, his own body is a slave to sin.

The undercurrent in this first section – a recurring theme if you will – is that of a new life in the Spirit through Jesus. An important shift begins in Romans 8, where Paul brings the discussion of such a life to the fore. There is no condemnation in such a life, as Christ has fulfilled the requirement of the law and, as such, has set us free from sin and death. This life is also characterized by suffering, wherein the Spirit also intercedes for us. The chapter ends with a declaration that nothing in all creation can separate us from the love of God. Paul then segues into an outpouring of his sorrow for Israel. The nation received the benefits of faith – adoption, glory, covenants, law, worship, promise, patriarchs, and from them the Messiah – but has not totally come to faith. While God has not totally rejected Israel, their refusal became an opportunity for the Gentiles to be included as God's people.

---

1. Scripture quotations are taken from the NRSV unless indicated otherwise.

In Romans 12, Paul moves into a discussion of the life that should characterize those who follow Christ. This life is one that is transformed through the offering of one's body as a "living sacrifice," a reference that makes a contrast with the sacrificial system of the law. This chapter marks the second division of the letter. This section speaks of transformation, an offering of oneself that spreads into one's community. Such a transformation occurs through the renewing of the mind that enables one to discern God's will. Despite the differences between Jews and Gentiles, they are now members of one body. They have varying gifts and functions so they need to view each other in sober judgment – that is, not to think too highly of themselves.

Paul goes over various aspects of practical advice on living in community: considering the many gifts in one body and thinking of oneself soberly, not more highly than others (12:3–8), as expressed by living in harmony, not avenging oneself but "overcoming evil with good" (vv. 9–18). Romans 13 comes after a turning point in the discussion, after Paul painstakingly has argued his point about the same grace being available to Jews and Gentiles and the new life in the Spirit. This new life available through Christ is evidenced by transformed living. Chapter 13 closes with a discussion on honorable living, with Paul pointing out that it is love that fulfills the law.

The general tone of the subsequent text is consistent with the previous focus on a changed life that lives harmoniously in community. These later chapters contain Paul's advice on the matter of eating food considered unclean. Here, Paul comments that believers in Rome should neither judge nor put stumbling blocks before each other (14:1–12). Instead, they should consider those who are "weaker" in the faith and make room for these sensitive consciences even as they enjoy the freedoms in Christ. They should strive for "peace and . . . mutual upbuilding."

Thus, it is in this spirit of consideration and cooperation that the instruction to obey the government is given. So why did Paul place so much emphasis on harmony both inside the church and outside? To answer this we need to consider the circumstances surrounding the writing of Romans.

Jewish Political Tensions in Rome and the Church's Testimony

Among ancient writers, allegiance to the state was a common theme seen on "lists and discussions alongside proper treatment of parents, elders and friends."[2] The appropriate behavior of both government officials and citizens was among the topics "philosophers and moralists" wrote about.[3]

Paul's letter to the Roman Christians was written at a time of political tension. It was likely written in AD 56–57,[4] with the reigns of Claudius (AD 41–54) and Nero (AD 54–68) especially relevant.[5] At least three factors contributed to the tension in this period: (1) Emperor Claudius's expulsion of some Jewish Christians from Rome (49; Claudius died in 54); (2) the growing unrest in Judea (Jewish revolt in ten years); and (3) the imminent widespread martyrdom of Christians under Emperor Nero (in six to eight years).

First, Emperor Claudius expelled some Jewish Christians from Rome, a fact which is supported by Acts 18:2 (AD 49–50).[6] Commentators say that around a decade prior to the writing of Paul's letter, these Jewish Christians were expelled likely over debates over the Messiah's identity, and Paul was possibly avoiding the repetition of those arguments that led to civil disturbances.[7] In AD 54, the new emperor allowed the Jews to return; however, they came back to churches now devoid of Jewish leadership and dissociated from Judaism.[8] By the time the letter to the Romans was written, some of the expelled Christian Jews had returned into a now largely gentile community, and this was the cause of the tension discussed earlier.[9]

Another factor was the growing unrest in Judea which would blow up into the Jewish revolt in about a decade.[10] Third was the widespread imminent martyrdom of Christians under Emperor Nero. At the time of Paul's writing, Nero was still under the influence of benevolent mentors, but six to eight

---

2. Craig S. Keener, *The IVP Bible Background Commentary: New Testament*, 2nd ed. (Downers Grove, IL: InterVarsity Press, 2014), 450.

3. Keener, *Bible Background Commentary*, 450.

4. Robert Jewett, *Romans: A Commentary*, Hermeneia: A Critical and Historical Commentary on the Bible (Minneapolis: Fortress, 2006), 20.

5. Jewett, *Romans*, 47.

6. Jewett, 19.

7. Keener, *Bible Background Commentary*, 450. See also N. T. Wright and Michael Bird, *The New Testament in Its World* (London: SPCK, 2019), 829; Douglas Moo, *The Epistle to the Romans*, New International Commentary on the New Testament (Grand Rapids, MI: Eerdmans, 1996), 4.

8. Sylvia C. Keesmat, "Reading Romans in the Capital of the Empire," in *Reading Paul's Letter to the Romans*, ed. Jerry Sumney (Atlanta: SBL, 2012), 48.

9. James D. G. Dunn, *Romans 1–8*, Word Biblical Commentary 38A (Dallas: Word, 1988), xlviii.

10. Keener, *Bible Background Commentary*, 450.

years after the writing of the letter, Emperor Nero began killing Christians.[11] It was important, then, for Jewish people to pay attention to public opinion. At the time, Christianity was viewed as a smaller sect within Judaism and so Christians had to be particularly cautious against being viewed as subversive.[12]

And so Paul also culled from Israel's political wisdom that had withstood "oppression and dispersion." He advises "political quietism," and such a "political prudence" was common among the "earliest Christian communities," as evidenced by other Christian writings in the first century, such as 1 Peter 2:13–17.[13] Thus, Paul was likely concerned about the Christians' testimony – it was important that Christians were perceived as good citizens. Amid these tensions, they had to be "good neighbors (13:8–10), since 'love is the fulfilling of the law.'"[14]

Romans 13:1–7
Submission vs. Resistance to God-Ordained Institutions (vv. 1–2)

> [1] Let every person be subject to the governing authorities; for there is no authority except from God, and those authorities that exist have been instituted by God. [2] Therefore whoever resists authority resists what God has appointed, and those who resist will incur judgment.

The passage in question, Romans 13:1–7, commands *all persons* to be subject to governing authorities. As mentioned earlier, this section of the letter comes after Paul's urging for a changed life in the Spirit in Romans 12. Now the verb translated "be subject" (*hypotassesthō* from *hypotasso*) has the sense of "subjecting oneself to someone else," connoting voluntary submission.[15] In its active form, *hypotasso* means to "cause to be in compliance with requirements for order" and covers different kinds of relationships, including that with a "human authority figure or system."[16] So Paul's encouragement for the Roman congregation to willingly submit themselves to governing authorities is part

---

11. Keener, 450.
12. Keener, 450.
13. James D. G. Dunn, *Romans 9–16*, Word Biblical Commentary 38B (Dallas: Word, 1988), 759.
14. Wright and Bird, *New Testament in Its World*, 829.
15. Jewett, *Romans*, 788.
16. Frederick William Danker, *The Concise Greek-English Lexicon of the New Testament* (Chicago: University of Chicago Press, 2009), 367.

of the transformed life, one that does not conform to this world, even as they discern God's perfect will in specific circumstances.[17] This is not then an "authoritarian ethic of obedience" but one that necessitates "public discussion and spiritual insight."[18] The reason given for this submission is that it was God himself who put these authorities in place. Submission to the ruling authorities is not showing respect merely to human rulers but to the "crucified deity who stands behind them."[19] Paul even asserts that those who go against such authorities will incur judgment because to do so is to defy what God has appointed.

But what does "resist" here mean? In Romans 13:2, there are two words translated as "resist."

First is *antitassomenos* (v. 2a: "Therefore whoever resists the authorities"), from *antitásso*, which means "set opposite to, range in battle against."[20] Its middle form extends a military picture[21] and has the sense of resisting the very organization or arrangement of something or to oppose squarely "*in principle and in practice.*"[22] This is the same root used of God resisting the proud in James 4:6 and 1 Peter 5:5.[23]

The other word, *anthestēken* (v. 2b–c, "Therefore whoever resists authority *resists* what God has appointed, and those who *resist* will incur judgment"), is from *anthistémi*, which means to "take a position in opposition to."[24] It has the sense of holding one's ground, being firm in one's conviction, or remaining unmoved against a contrary position.[25] From both meanings, one gains a sense of sustained rejection, a total 180-degree opposition. The opposition here is one of "determined and established policy," leaning more toward "anarchy rather than single-issue protest."[26]

---

17. Jewett, *Romans*, 789.
18. Jewett, 789.
19. Jewett, 790.
20. Danker, *Greek-English Lexicon*, 37.
21. Danker, 37.
22. HELPS Word-studies, "498 *antitássomai*," Bible Hub, accessed 5 November 2020, https://biblehub.com/greek/498.htm. Emphasis original.
23. George V. Wigram, *The Englishman's Greek Concordance of the New Testament*, 9th ed. (Grand Rapids, MI: Zondervan, 1970), 57.
24. Danker, *Greek-English Lexicon*, 33.
25. HELPS Word-studies, "436 *anthistémi*," Bible Hub, accessed 5 November 2020, https://biblehub.com/greek/436.htm.
26. Dunn, *Romans 9–16*, 762.

Since Paul is saying that it was God who set up governments and rulers in place as a means of executing his will, those who resist government are effectively resisting God. "Judgment" here is from God and may be presumed to refer to the end times; however, Paul may have also thought of God's judgment coursing through human structures that are also divinely ordained.[27]

Why does Paul think this way? Note that while Nero was already emperor, he was not yet oppressing minorities such as Christians at this time.[28] He was also largely popular in Greece, where Paul was writing the letter; while some Jews in Palestine were already promoting resistance to Rome, Palestinian Jews were said to have sworn themselves to non-resistance.[29] They believed that it was God who had appointed all civil authorities,[30] and the Old Testament also teaches that it is God who is sovereign over earthly rulers.[31] Despite what the "Roman civic cult and administrative system" believed about their gods, they were still serving God from Paul's perspective.[32]

Most of the Jews in Rome supported such a view and it would only be a decade later that the Jewish revolt against Rome would erupt.[33]

Let's return to 13:1c: "those authorities that exist have been instituted by God" (*hupo theo tetagmenai*). Scholars say that the phrase "authorities . . . have been instituted by God" implies that government authority is (1) subject to the limitations of such a structure[34] and (2) proportionate to the submission being required.[35] This means, then, that those who have authority that is given by God are accountable for it and will be judged should they abuse it or call for submission that is greater than what God has ordained. Another consequence is that it is the limits ordained by God that determine how far a subject may submit. Thus, Paul's advice may be adjusted in view of the changes in "political systems and conditions" throughout history.[36]

---

27. Dunn, 762–63.
28. Keener, *Bible Background Commentary*, 450.
29. Keener, 450.
30. As seen in the OT (Isa 45:1; Jer 25:9; Dan 4:32). In Keener, 450.
31. Prov 16:10; 21:1. In Keener, 450.
32. Jewett, *Romans*, 791.
33. Keener, *Bible Background Commentary*, 450.
34. See Matt 8:9; Luke 7:8; Acts 15:2; 22:10; and 1 Clem. 20:2; 61:1–2. In Dunn, *Romans 9–16*, 761–62.
35. Dunn, 761–62.
36. Dunn, 762.

Qualifiers of the Role of Government (vv. 3–4)

> ³ For rulers are not a terror to good conduct, but to bad. Do you wish to have no fear of the authority? Then do what is good, and you will receive its approval; ⁴ for it is God's servant for your good. But if you do what is wrong, you should be afraid, for the authority does not bear the sword in vain! It is the servant of God to execute wrath on the wrongdoer.

Paul argues that the terror of rulers is not for those who do good but for those who do bad. He argues that doing good will lead to approval from authorities, hence there is no need to fear. Otherwise, one would have reason to fear the government because of the sword. Paul goes so far as to say that governments are God's instruments of wrath on those who do wrong.

"For *It Is God's Servant* for Your Good" (v. 4a)

The notion of God's sovereignty over the entire created order is elaborated in Romans 8:18–30 (in light of suffering as creation is also groaning for redemption) and 9:1–5 (Paul praises God who created all, both Jews and Gentiles). In 13:4a, commentators say that Paul was trying to remove the barriers between sacred and secular, "cult and everyday," "'chosen' and Gentile."[37] This agrees with the overall tone of the letter which seeks the unity of Jewish and gentile believers in Rome. Meanwhile, Dunn argues that by referring to authorities as "God's servant," Paul was broadening the concept of service that may be admissible to God.[38] The phrase "for your good" here refers to the Christian recipients but the emphasis is on their "status as residents of Rome" and their "civic well-being rather than spiritual."[39] This argument fits with the said concept of God being lord of all.

"It Is *the Servant of God* to Execute Wrath on the Wrongdoer" (v. 4d)

The Roman Empire in Paul's time held power over life and death[40] for those who did wrong. The "sword" is a reference to beheading, which was the typical means of execution at this time; to signify such authority swords were "carried in front of Roman officials."[41] It is even argued that this sword was not a

---

37. Dunn, 764.
38. Dunn, 764.
39. Dunn, 764.
40. Strong's Concordance, "μάχαιρα," in "3162. *machaira*," Bible Hub, accessed 5 November 2020, https://biblehub.com/greek/3162.htm.
41. Keener, *Bible Background Commentary*, 450.

ceremonial sword but "the military sword, the classic symbol for governmental coercion."[42] Such a reminder was especially effective in Rome because everyone there faced the empire's ultimate power. Roman citizens, when elsewhere, could appeal to higher courts and even up to the emperor.[43] But Rome was itself the seat of the empire, the highest authority to which one could go.

Keener points out that Paul's advice here is the typical moral admonishment of his time. He notes that the Roman Empire was responsible for many evil actions and dispensed justice based on social class. But in general terms, the Romans promoted "justice and toleration," so Christians did not yet have reason to fear them.[44]

Thus, rulers are supposed to be God's servants (1) for the good of the people (v. 4a) and (2) for the carrying out of punishment for those who do wrong (v. 4b). This arrangement, however, is the ideal. But does this equate to blind submission when authorities do not perform their instituted function? Verses 3–4 explain that rulers are supposed to discourage (be "a terror to") bad conduct and not good.

This focus, though, does not mean that Christians should not denounce evil. While philosophers such as the Stoics emphasized such submission to authorities like the government, this submission was not understood as unconditional or unqualified, meaning that one still should not obey commands to perform evil. An example would be that Christians still would not worship Caesar.[45] This call to accountability may also be found in passages such as the mini-apocalypse in 2 Thessalonians, and in the warning against the rich who take advantage of their workers in James 5:4–6:

> You have not paid any wages to those who work in your fields. Listen to their complaints! The cries of those who gather in your crops have reached the ears of God, the Lord Almighty. Your life here on earth has been full of luxury and pleasure. You have made yourselves fat for the day of slaughter. You have condemned and murdered innocent people, and they do not resist you. (GNT)

---

42. Jewett, *Romans*, 795.
43. Dunn, *Romans 9–16*, 764.
44. Keener, *Bible Background Commentary*, 450.
45. Keener, 450.

As God's servants, the ruling authorities are supposed to "promote good and restrain evil" and it is crucial to read both statements together.[46] Called deacons (*diakonos*, twice in v. 4) and servants (*leiturgoi*, v. 6), these rulers are under the oversight of God. While *leitourgos* referred to those in "cultic religious service," it pertains to public servants in this context.[47] Regardless of the claims of Roman authorities as to the source of their authority, their power essentially came from the Judeo-Christian God.[48] This notion is also present in the "OT (Jer 27:5–6; Dan 4:17, 25, 32; 5:21) and in Hellenistic Judaism."[49] Because authority is ultimately from God, the purpose of the delegation of such power should be kept in mind.[50]

Conscience and Paying What Is Due (vv. 5–7)

> [5] Therefore one must be subject, not only because of wrath but also because of conscience. [6] For the same reason you also pay taxes, for the authorities are God's servants, busy with this very thing. [7] Pay to all what is due them – taxes to whom taxes are due, revenue to whom revenue is due, respect to whom respect is due, honor to whom honor is due.

Conscience (v. 5)

Paul gives two reasons for submission: the wrath we discussed previously, and conscience. In verse 5, Paul concludes explaining the necessity (Greek *ananke*) of submission as not simply because one is afraid of punishment, but on account of one's conscience. Dunn explains that the use of the word "must" (*ananke*) here refers to "the way things are and have to be," or the "laws of nature and fate or destiny." There is an appeal to the "(divine) givenness of things."[51]

---

46. Isabelo F. Magalit, "Rightful Rule: Romans 13 for the Philippines Today," in *Doing Theology in the Philippines*, eds. E. Acoba, Asian Theological Seminary, et al. (Quezon City: Asian Theological Seminary, 2005), 139.

47. Magalit, "Rightful Rule," 139. These are ones "engaged in special service" in cultic or other spheres. Danker, *Greek-English Lexicon*, 214. See also HELPS Word-studies, "3011 leitorgós," Bible Hub, accessed 22 September 2021, https://biblehub.com/greek/3011.htm.

48. Jewett, *Romans*, 789.

49. Jewett, 789.

50. Magalit, "Rightful Rule," 139.

51. Dunn, *Romans 9–16*, 765.

This conscience, which sets apart right from wrong, should align with the purposes of government. Conscience balances the harshness of wrath – for Christians, fear alone should not be the sole motivator of political conduct.[52] Although the functioning of the conscience is not exclusive to Christians, what steers Christian behavior is love (13:8–10) and faith.[53] For Dunn, Paul merges responsibilities in the moral-spiritual realm and the political world and so the civic obligation to be subject to the authorities has the impact of moral responsibility.[54] Thus, when one supports the government's mandate, one is also "promoting good and restraining evil,"[55] so to speak. In this manner, one's submission to the government is in line with God's will, which the government is supposed to implement.

The discussion of the notion of one's conscience as the ultimate motivation behind our civic behavior segues into a summary of Paul's reinterpretation of the law throughout chapters 1–12: it is love that fulfills the law (13:8–10). Since Christ has fulfilled the requirements of the law and has given us freedom and new life, the expression of our transformed life is our love for our neighbors. For Paul, this love for the other also encompasses commitment to public welfare, shown in respecting governing authorities.

Paying Taxes (vv. 6–7)

As an example Paul then discusses paying one's due. In general, taxes were collected by both the empire and local provinces or kingdoms. These funded the government, roadbuilding, Roman armies, and the temples used for emperor worship. Months before Paul wrote his letter, certain taxes were disputed in Rome. Jews who were not Roman citizens and who returned from AD 54 onwards were also taxed.[56] Dunn views this discussion of the payment of taxes as the climax of the passage because such instructions are not found elsewhere in Paul's letters.[57]

In Rome, the matter was a delicate one.[58] By AD 58, there were growing complaints against indirect taxes levied by companies and the eagerness of tax collectors; there was likely a buildup of such complaints in the years prior,

---

52. Dunn, 765.
53. Dunn, 765.
54. Dunn, 765.
55. As Magalit phrases it. Magalit, "Rightful Rule," 139.
56. Keener, *Bible Background Commentary*, 450.
57. Dunn, *Romans 9–16*, 772.
58. Dunn, 766.

when the letter to the Romans was written.[59] Also, it was through taxation that individuals were forced to interact with government authorities. Jews also enjoyed certain benefits, such as special arrangements for the temple tax.[60] Thus, they, and the Christians associated with them, would have been in a vulnerable position.[61]

The matter that government officials diligently occupied themselves with was collecting taxes: "busy with this very thing" (v. 6c). Dunn cites the NEB: "thoroughly engaged in their task for this very purpose"; "to these duties they devote their energies."[62] The use of *proskartereo*, meaning to "occupy oneself diligently with, pay persistent attention to,"[63] implies that Paul may have viewed "dedicated public service" as the goal of service by the government. He may have had a high view of civil service, including tax collection.[64] On the one hand, ruling officials both demanded and received honor because of their station,[65] but on the other hand, Paul also recognizes that tax collectors might not be committed to the welfare of the public.[66] Paul's point is that the tribute taxes had to be paid despite pressure to do otherwise.[67] The implication of this is that the congregation accepted that those officials who collected taxes were *leitourgoi tou theo*, "ministers of God."[68] The churches within the Roman administration would also have welcomed such a view from Paul.[69]

So Paul reiterates that governments are God's servants and are thus occupied with administrating or governing on behalf of God. When the government does its job, it is only right that those under its authority (in Paul's time, both citizens and non-citizens) cooperate. Because the ruling authorities were serving them, there had to be a mutual exchange with those who received their service.[70] This submission included the payment of taxes.

---

59. Dunn, 766.
60. Dunn, 766.
61. Dunn, 766.
62. Dunn, 767.
63. *TDNT* 3.618, quoted in Dunn, 767. See also "4342. *proskartereó*," Bible Hub, accessed 1 June 2021, https://biblehub.com/greek/4342.htm.
64. Dunn, 767.
65. Keener, *Bible Background Commentary*, 450.
66. Dunn, *Romans 9–16*, 767.
67. Jewett, *Romans*, 798.
68. Jewett, 798.
69. Jewett, 799.
70. Jewett, 801.

Allusion to Mark 12:17

> Jesus said to them, "Give to the emperor the things that are the emperor's, and to God the things that are God's." And they were utterly amazed at him.

The theme of giving everyone their due is reminiscent of Jesus's attitude toward the Roman Empire and taxes in Mark 12:13–17. In the passage, Pharisees and Herodians attempted to pit Jesus against the Roman government. Taxation was a sensitive issue even in Jesus's time. Jesus's claims about God's kingdom were by their nature opposed to the emperor's claims to divinity and absolute authority at the time. If Jesus incited the people to not pay their taxes, he would be effectively opposing the empire (and possibly could even be killed before his time). And so, even if God's kingdom is above all, Jesus says that the emperor should be given what is due to him, and God given what is due to him.

Assuming that Paul was alluding to what had been passed down as the sayings of Jesus, Christians would have known that the first part of the Mark 12:17 principle ("Well, then, pay to the Emperor what belongs to the Emperor," GNT) entails the second part ("and pay to God what belongs to God," GNT). That is, love for neighbor hinges on the first duty to love God.[71]

Thus, if the call to love our neighbor – including submitting to the government – contradicts the prior call to love God, we as Christians should rethink our position. Does our submission to the government violate the command to love our neighbor, who is made in the image of God? More so, in our submission to the government, are we putting it above our love for God? Do we obey so much that we disobey God himself and place another in his place?

Consider also the title "Son of God." In the letter's opening, Paul introduces himself as the servant of Jesus and called to be an apostle to proclaim the gospel about Jesus Christ our Lord, who "was declared to be Son of God with power according to the spirit of holiness by resurrection from the dead" (Rom 1:4). Most scholars argue that Jesus's being "declared" Son of God does not mean that he was not God's Son beforehand; rather, this refers to his "heavenly installation as God's Son" because of his lineage through David.[72] And it means

---

71. Dunn, *Romans 9–16*, 767.

72. Thomas Schreiner, *Romans*, Baker Exegetical Commentary on the New Testament, 2nd ed (Baker Publishing Group, 2018), accessed February 17, 2022, https://www.perlego.com/book/2051130/romans-baker-exegetical-commentary-on-the-new-testament-pdf. Citing A. Nygren, F. F. Bruce explains that this designation as Son of God does not mean that Jesus *became* the Son of God. Rather, Jesus underwent a transformation from being "the Son of God

not only that Jesus was the Son of God "in the ordinary royal sense," but that God himself established the king and his kingdom, based on the promises of the Old Testament.[73] So for some of the unbelieving Roman population, this title could have pitted Jesus against the emperor.[74]

Julius Caesar was also portrayed as "the son of royalty and the gods" who had "'risen up' to enact justice and triumph over the nations."[75] After Julius Caesar had been assassinated, he was deified and named "god of the Roman state."[76] His adopted son Octavian (also known as Caesar Augustus) was the first Roman emperor after the destruction of the Roman republic. Because Caesar was God, Octavian was thus "Son of God."[77] Thus one's loyalty was tested as two figures laid claim to the same title: Jesus as the Son of God against the Roman "Son of God," and the gospel of Jesus Christ as opposed to the "good news" enforced by Rome. Paul declared the triumph of "the son of Israel's God," who was descended from royalty and through his resurrection was "designated son of God in power."[78] What Paul proclaimed was "the gospel of God, not Caesar" – and unlike other cruel leaders, this Son attains victory through servanthood and being given up to death.[79] As opposed to Caesar, the only one who could be the Pax Romana of the Roman Empire, Paul declares the peace that is "from a new Lord, the Lord Jesus Christ."[80] Thus, Paul possibly made a dangerous claim by ascribing the title "Son of God" to Jesus in Romans 1:4.

Prayer Passages in the Pastoral and Petrine Epistles

Two of these letters are attributed to Paul (Titus is likely written by the apostle while 1 Timothy follows the Pauline tradition[81]), while the other one

---

in weakness and lowliness" during his ministry on earth to being "the Son of God in power" at his resurrection. In F. F. Bruce, *Romans*, Tyndale New Testament Commentary (Leicester: Inter-Varsity Press, 2008), accessed February 17, 2022, https://www.perlego.com/book/1470521/romans-pdf.

73. Craig S. Keener, *Romans*, A New Covenant Commentary (Cambridge: Lutterworth, 2009), 20.
74. Keener, *Bible Background Commentary*, 786.
75. Keesmat, "Reading Romans," 52.
76. Britannica, "Augustus," accessed 5 November 2020, https://www.britannica.com/biography/Augustus-Roman-emperor.
77. Britannica, "Augustus."
78. Keesmat, "Reading Romans," 52.
79. Keesmat, 52.
80. Keesmat, 53.
81. Keener, *Bible Background Commentary*, 600.

(1 Peter) follows the Petrine tradition and is likely pseudonymous.[82] We have already discussed that writings such as these were common both among secular philosophers and moralists as well as within first-century Christian communities. Admonishments with the themes of state loyalty and obedience to leaders were of the same kind as household codes; the latter were possibly even more important in thwarting talk about rebellion as the Romans in particular despised religious groups that seemed to incite rebellion.[83]

1 Timothy 2:1–4

> [2] First of all, then, I urge that petitions, prayers, requests, and thanksgivings be offered to God for all people; [2] for kings and all others who are in authority, that we may live a quiet and peaceful life with all reverence toward God and with proper conduct. [3] This is good and it pleases God our Savior, [4] who wants everyone to be saved and to come to know the truth. (GNT)

The call to pray for government authorities in 1 Timothy 2:1–4 occurs in the context of public worship and prayer. These prayers are to be offered for everyone, including "kings and all who are in high positions" (NRSV). That is, the subjects of these prayers would be "the emperor, provincial officials, local magistrates."[84] This attitude of inclusive prayer is top priority, according to Guthrie, and these prayers should be offered whether the government rulers are "perverted or not." In this way, Christians would be able to affect civic affairs.[85] These public prayers for different levels of civic rulers showed that Christians were "good citizens of the society in which they lived."[86]

The purpose (rather than the content) of the prayers is for "peace and security" to prevail,[87] translated in the NRSV as leading "a quiet and peaceable life in all godliness and dignity." Those under said authorities would be able to lead their own lives, although under some governments, such a quiet and

---

82. Paul J. Achtemeier, *1 Peter*, Hermeneia: A Critical and Historical Commentary on the Bible (Minneapolis: Augsburg Fortress, 1996), 43.

83. Keener, *Bible Background Commentary*, 630.

84. Gordon D. Fee, *1 and 2 Timothy, Titus*, New International Biblical Commentary (Peabody, MA: Hendrickson, 1988), 63.

85. Donald Guthrie, *The Pastoral Epistles*, Tyndale New Testament Commentary (Nottingham: Inter-Varsity Press, 2009), accessed February 17, 2022, https://www.perlego.com/book/1470519/pastoral-epistles-pdf.

86. Keener, *Bible Background Commentary*, 604.

87. Guthrie, *Pastoral Epistles*. See also Fee, *1 and 2 Timothy, Titus*, 63.

peaceful life is not certain.[88] This does not mean, however, that Christians would have lives without any difficulties, but rather that their lives would not be a cause for anyone to "'speak evil of the name of God and of our teaching' (6:1)."[89] Thus, Paul's intention was not only to maintain peace, but also to proclaim the gospel.[90]

Titus 3:1–2

> [3] Remind your people to submit to rulers and authorities, to obey them, and to be ready to do good in every way. [2] Tell them not to speak evil of anyone, but to be peaceful and friendly, and always to show a gentle attitude toward everyone. (GNT)

Both 1 Timothy and Titus served as letters that strengthened the authority of Timothy and Titus in their congregations, Ephesus and Crete respectively.[91] These letters mainly addressed the problems caused by false teachers who promoted asceticism according to the law, which subverted the work of Paul and his ministry companions.[92] Rather than being "directly theological," the letters are more "personal and institutional."[93]

Paul wrote Titus not only as a personal letter but also as a letter that gave authorization to Titus.[94] After reminding Titus, in chapter 2, of the "sound doctrine" he needed to teach the congregation, Paul moves in chapter 3 to the focus of the letter – "good works" as a testimony for outsiders, as a contrast with the false teachers in 3:9–11.[95] The congregation in Crete needed to be reminded of the importance to submit, which was their civil obligation.[96] Paul here may have been concerned that Cretans could have easily incriminated the church in political disturbances and thus put the gospel in a bad light.[97] The situation in Romans 13 may have been similar. For the communities of Timothy and

---

88. Guthrie, *Pastoral Epistles*.
89. Fee, *1 and 2 Timothy, Titus*, 63.
90. Keener, *Bible Background Commentary*, 604.
91. Keener, 601, 625.
92. Keener, 601.
93. Keener, 601.
94. Keener, 625.
95. Fee, *1 and 2 Timothy, Titus*, 200.
96. Guthrie, *Pastoral Epistles*.
97. Guthrie.

1 Peter 2:13–17

> ¹³ For the sake of the Lord submit yourselves to every human authority: to the Emperor, who is the supreme authority, ¹⁴ and to the governors, who have been appointed by him to punish the evildoers and to praise those who do good. ¹⁵ For God wants you to silence the ignorant talk of foolish people by the good things you do. ¹⁶ Live as free people; do not, however, use your freedom to cover up any evil, but live as God's slaves. ¹⁷ Respect everyone, love other believers, honor God, and respect the Emperor. (GNT)

The immediate context of 1 Peter 2 is right living in the midst of Gentiles (2:11 – 3:7), and it gives more specific instruction after the more general call to holy living (1:13 – 2:10). Submission here is required both to the highest authority, the emperor, and to those under him, the governors. Peter explains the function of governors: "to punish the evildoers and to praise those who do good" (v. 14 GNT). This "good" involves submitting to civic authorities. This concept is reminiscent of Romans 13:3–4.

Based on the values of the aristocracy of that time, the household reflected the city-state government, which is why civic duties are often addressed alongside the household.[98] Such codes were adopted by Jews and other religions that were maligned to show that they upheld the values of Roman society; by doing so, they would minimize persecution.[99] Thus, the behavior of the believing community had to be such that there would be no grounds for outsiders to accuse them of any offense.[100]

For both Paul and Peter, one's allegiance to God is the main reason behind acquiescence to human rule.[101] They both focus on what should be the ultimate function of government, namely to maintain "order in society," and so do not tackle situations when governments act wrongly.[102] Peter's generally positive view here fits best with the first decades of the church, near the end of Claudius's

---

98. Keener, *Bible Background Commentary*, 690.
99. Keener, 690.
100. Dennis Edwards, *1 Peter*, The Story of God Bible Commentary (Grand Rapids, MI: Zondervan, 2017), 106.
101. Edwards, *1 Peter*, 105.
102. Edwards, 105.

rule (AD 41–54) or at the start of Nero's (AD 54–68).[103] Some scholars point to a much later date, between AD 80 and 100, as there is no explicit mention of martyrdom, although the letter could have reflected persecution that may have led to the condemnation of Christians later on.[104] Because of the more peaceful tone of 1 Peter, it is likely that it was not written during Nero's terrible persecution of the church in Rome or after the martyrdom of Christians as ordered by the government.[105] While the Christians were being shunned in social or possibly professional circles, they were not yet experiencing "state-sponsored persecution as a matter of policy."[106] And so Peter seems optimistic that the church could continue some degree of positive rapport with the government because of its connection with Judaism.[107] Peter seems to estimate that as long as believers live as good citizens, government authorities will not disturb them at the very least, and possibly even favor them at best.[108]

Peter explains that God's desire is that they would "silence the ignorant talk of foolish people" (GNT). The ignorance being discussed here has to do with the wrong notion of Christianity that was circulating among those not part of the Christian community.[109] When smaller religious groups did not easily adapt to Roman ideals, the Roman nobility swiftly slandered them.[110]

Here, Peter does not challenge the emperor's status as the "supreme authority on earth" and stays clear of anything seditious by supporting human rulers.[111] Thus, whatever suffering the church experienced the public would perceive as unjust; and since Peter has only advocated proper behavior as citizens, his teachings could actually embarrass officials when they abused others.[112]

The three letters discussed (1 Timothy, Titus, and 1 Peter) have similar contents and contexts: (1) their placement within the household codes since civic

---

103. Karen Jobes, *Baker Exegetical Commentary on the New Testament* (Baker Publishing Group, 2005), accessed February 17, 2022. https://www.perlego.com/book/2051296/1-peter-baker-exegetical-commentary-on-the-new-testament-pdf. Dates of emperors' reigns in Achtemeier, *1 Peter*, 49–50.
104. Achtemeier, 49–50.
105. Jobes, *1 Peter*.
106. Jobes.
107. Jobes.
108. Jobes.
109. Keener, *Bible Background Commentary*, 691.
110. Keener, 691.
111. Edwards, *1 Peter*, 106.
112. Edwards, 106.

obligations were often lumped with household instructions; (2) the need to combat persecution and literally survive as a religious minority; and (3) the need to display integrity and good works as a testimony to the gospel (in contrast to false teachers and the Roman aristocracy who slandered Christianity and its teachings). In such a context, it was imperative for Christians to live peaceably within a broader gentile community and thus submit to the government.

I agree with all of these letters in their call to prayer for and compliance with civic leaders – in that we seek to live peaceably with others, contribute to the broader society by submitting to the structure of government, and pray for those in authority. There is an organized way for things to be and government service can be an honorable vocation. What is crucial, though, is that we gain a proper understanding of the cultural context that merited these directives and the differences between the political structures then and now. Following these passages does not mean that we should not correct what is wrong in our context.

What, then, reduces a Christian's relationship to government to merely that of a subject and not an active participant, as in a democracy? Are we disempowered to call out evil because we have to "submit"? When should we submit to government – when it does evil or good, or all the time, regardless of what it does? What if the government itself does evil: should we hold it to account?

We have had our own version of these evils in Philippine history. We could ask questions like the following: Was the revolt against Spain merited, given that it was an oppressive colonial power? Or among fellow Filipinos, was it right to overthrow the dictatorship under Marcos, when his theft, corruption, and murders had been proven multiple times in court?

Even during the Marcos era, evangelicals involved in protests struggled with Romans 13 – having understood that "evangelism and socio-political involvement" were both part of Christian obligation under the Lausanne Covenant.[113] There was indeed more to Christian obligation than "prayer and obedience" and so they needed to understand Romans 13 in its own context and also interpret it for their time. Bringing the conversation into the present, we need to reflect on what is the proper Christian response to the string of extrajudicial killings targeting suspected drug addicts or dealers, red-tagged community leaders, lawyers defending human rights, and even unarmed citizens at the receiving end of unreasonable police wrath.

---

113. Magalit, "Rightful Rule," 143.

One new feature that we need to consider in contemporary times is "participatory democracy."[114] The preamble of the Philippine Constitution describes the Filipino people as sovereign. One of the aims in establishing government is to "secure to ourselves and our posterity the blessings of independence and democracy under the rule of law and a regime of truth, justice, freedom, love, equality, and peace."[115]

One advantage of participatory democracy is that every person is regarded as having the same "dignity and worth before the Creator," removing any space to dictate to or enslave another.[116] So our duty as believers does not merely rest in submission, including following laws and paying taxes; it also involves enabling rulers to perform their mandate from God to "promote good and restrain evil."[117]

Article XI of the 1987 Constitution ensures the accountability of government officials. Section 1 declares that "public office is a public trust" and so officers and employees in public service "must at all times be accountable to the people, serve them with utmost responsibility, integrity, loyalty, and efficiency, act with patriotism and justice, and lead modest lives." Sections 2–4 indicate which public officials may be impeached and removed from their positions, and provide the process for doing so.[118]

The government has also formed bodies that are venues for graft and corruption complaints against public servants. Created in 1978 under Presidential Decree 1486, the Sandiganbayan is the government's anti-graft court which handles criminal and civil cases against public officials and employees.[119] Its function is upheld by the 1987 Constitution (Article XI, Section 4). Meanwhile, the Office of the Ombudsman was created under the 1987 Constitution and investigates graft and corruption covered by the Sandiganbayan.[120]

---

114. Magalit, 143.

115. The Constitution of the Republic of the Philippines, 2 February 1987, accessed 10 November 2021, https://www.officialgazette.gov.ph/constitutions/1987-constitution/.

116. Magalit, "Rightful Rule," 143.

117. Magalit, 146.

118. Constitution of the Republic of the Philippines.

119. Presidential Decree No. 1486, 11 June 1978, accessed 10 November 2021, https://mirror.officialgazette.gov.ph/1978/06/11/presidential-decree-no-1486-s-1978/.

120. Its structure as well as "functions, powers, and duties" are detailed in Article XI, Sections 5–14, Constitution of the Republic of the Philippines.

Since we are "not subjects but citizens; participants, not spectators" in a democracy, much is also required from leaders.[121] But was this always the case? Are good works always rewarded and bad always punished? What if the reverse is the case – good works are thwarted while evil is enabled? Ironically, the president who signed the decree creating the Sandiganbayan later himself became embroiled in massive corruption and human rights violations. A brief look at another passage, Revelation 13, shows us the potential of evil that governments can unleash and what the Christian response should be.

Revelation 13 as a Critique of the Empire

In this section, I will focus on the historical background of Revelation and the initial referents of the symbolism for John, the writer of Revelation, and the recipients of the book. I will not go into the details of interpreting apocalyptic literature and the subsequent (post-first-century, current, or future) equivalents of its symbols. While still dealing with political and religious issues relevant to the congregations who received the letter, the referents remain enigmatic because of the nature of the visions and the delicate political overtones.[122]

In Revelation 13:1–18, the struggle moves from the cosmic scene in chapter 12 to a setting that the initial audience would have been familiar with.[123] In 12:1–17, Satan the dragon has been hurled to the earth, where he instigates violence against believers.[124] In chapter 13, Satan employs two agents: the beast from the sea (13:1–10) and the beast from the land (13:11–18).[125]

The first beast arose from the sea and was given his own power, throne, and great authority by the dragon. This beast seemed undefeatable and blasphemed God, from the names on its horns to the proud claims it made that insulted God. The number of the first beast was 666, which served as a clue to the beast's name. This first scene in chapter 13 emphasizes the tight association between the dragon and the beast, both being monsters from the sea with "ten horns

---

121. Magalit, "Rightful Rule," 146.

122. Catherine Gunsalus Gonzales and Justo L. Gonzales, *Revelation*, Westminster Bible Companion (Louisville, KY: Westminster John Knox, 1997), 85.

123. Gonzales and Gonzales, *Revelation*, 85.

124. Craig R. Koester, *Revelation: A New Translation with Introduction and Commentary*, Anchor Yale Bible (New Haven: Yale University Press, 2014), 576.

125. Koester, *Revelation*, 576.

and seven heads."[126] This is the "first parody or great imitation," as the dragon assumes the position of God the Father, the first beast takes on God the Son, and the second beast completes the "counterfeit trinity."[127]

The beast from the sea depicts the Roman Empire as from Asia Minor, the Romans would arrive from the west or the sea.[128] This evokes the beasts in Daniel's vision, which portrayed political forces that aimed to annihilate God's people at that time.[129] John combined imagery from Daniel with the contemporary realities of the Roman Empire.[130] For the original recipients of John's book, this beast represented the Roman Empire, personified by the emperor who was "the god of this world."[131]

The beast's "blasphemous name" on each of its heads portrayed its "claim to deity and desire to supplant God as an object of worship."[132] Among these divine titles that the emperor used were "lord," "savior," "son of god," and "our lord and god."[133] Before the first century, Roman emperors were considered deities after their death. This practice, however, later changed as these emperors began to use "divine titles," as in the case of Domitian, who wanted to be referred to as "lord" and "god" from AD 81 to 96.[134] Domitian himself was given sacrifices and considered to be "the person who united the human and the divine," which clearly imitated Jesus.[135] The blasphemy was not in the emperors slandering the Christian God but in their taking the names ascribed to the true God alone and usurping God's place and authority.[136]

The second beast came from the earth, and he used the power of the first beast and directed worship to it. This beast probably represents the imperial cult's outworking in the religion and politics of that time.[137] It was in the province of Asia, where the seven churches of Revelation 2–3 were located,

---

126. Grant Osborne, *Revelation Verse by Verse*, Osborne New Testament Commentaries (Lexham Press, 2016), accessed February 17, 2022. https://www.perlego.com/book/2055089/revelation-verse-by-verse-pdf.
127. Osborne, *Revelation Verse by Verse*.
128. Gonzales and Gonzales, *Revelation*, 85.
129. Gonzales and Gonzales, 85.
130. Gonzales and Gonzales, 85.
131. Osborne, *Revelation Verse by Verse*.
132. Osborne.
133. Osborne.
134. Gonzales and Gonzales, *Revelation*, 87.
135. Osborne, *Revelation Verse by Verse*.
136. Gonzales and Gonzales, *Revelation*, 87, 89.
137. Gonzales and Gonzales, 89.

that the imperial cult particularly flourished.[138] It is possible that the beast from the earth represented the "traditional local institutions in Asia Minor" that were congruent with and used to serve the imperial cult.[139]

Another serious threat from the beast from the earth was that it blended the religious and economic sectors such that one had to participate in emperor worship in order to engage in economic life.[140] This could pertain to the image of the emperor on coins or to religious rituals associated with different trade groups.[141] The manner by which the worshippers of the beast are marked is similar to the marking of Christians in baptism; both are marked by a seal.[142]

The circumstances behind the writing of Romans and Revelation are totally different. We discussed earlier that Romans was written during the early years of Nero's reign, when he had helpful mentors, and prior to the persecutions. Paul's view of the government in Romans 13 stands in opposition to John's perspective in Revelation, where he paints the Roman Empire as demonic. Although the worship of the emperor was not yet compulsory when Revelation was written, it did eventually happen.[143]

By the end of the first century, there was a huge increase in emperor worship, as seen in Domitian's status in Ephesus as well as the various temples dedicated to emperor worship in Asia Minor.[144] This new occurrence was a menace to John and could have been a threat to Christians once it was noticed that they were not willing to renounce their faith and worship the emperor to show state allegiance.[145]

In Romans 13:4, Paul implies that it is only those who violate the law who will be subject to punishment by the government.[146] But a few years after the letter was written, in AD 64, the recipients of Paul's letter were blamed for a fire in Rome; according to a report by Tacitus, they were "torn to death by dogs," hung on crosses, or their bodies burned as lamps at night.[147] Paul here

---

138. Osborne, *Revelation Verse by Verse*.
139. Gonzales and Gonzales, *Revelation*, 89.
140. Gonzales and Gonzales, 90.
141. Gonzales and Gonzales, 90.
142. Gonzales and Gonzales, 90.
143. Gonzales and Gonzales, 87.
144. Gonzales and Gonzales, 89.
145. Gonzales and Gonzales, 89.
146. Jewett, *Romans*, 796.
147. Jewett, 796.

had not yet assessed the "evil potential of totalitarian regimes, including the Neronian government then in power."[148]

It is worth noting that Christians had different attitudes toward the Roman government and that John's negative portrayal of the Roman Empire might have been shared by some of his readers but not by those who benefited from such rule.[149] Paul indeed validated government authority to curtail evil (Rom 13) and other early Christians prayed for the emperor and acknowledged his authority (1 Tim 2 and 1 Pet).[150] Revelation, however, had to change the perception of imperial rule and in the vision of the beast, it exposed the empire's proud claims through parody.[151] John ridicules imperial rule by depicting it as a vicious beast.[152] He rejected the Roman Empire's claim that its power to dominate was the reason for its "legitimacy and invincibility," and portrayed it instead as a vehicle of oppression.[153]

Conclusion

We see from the New Testament that the Bible does not have a singular voice as to how Christians should relate to government. Historical contexts matter – the circumstances, the political systems, and even the mindsets of their age. Reading the text closely gives glimpses of Paul's understanding of the function of the governing authorities and, as such, qualifies his statement on submission to governing authorities.

First, placing Romans 13 in its literary and historical contexts shows a more nuanced approach. It needs to be understood according to the realities that the Jewish and Christian faith communities faced in their day. Moreover, we need to see the external social tensions that led Paul to give such practical advice that upheld the social order of that time.

Romans 13 is just a small portion of a broader section calling Christians to a transformed life. This is placed in the wider framework of unity and reconciliation within the church in light of the internal tensions between Jewish and gentile members of the faith community. The letter seeks to redefine the relationship between Jews and Gentiles. It seems that Paul was calling

---

148. Jewett, 796.
149. Koester, *Revelation*, 578.
150. Koester, 578.
151. Koester, 578.
152. Koester, 578.
153. Koester, 579.

for external order or submission just as he was asking Roman Christians to consider one another. The whole passage may be part of Christian testimony to live harmoniously – within the community and also outside in an external submission to power, given the tension between the Roman Empire and Jews. Their community needed to survive while providing faithful testimony to the gospel. The letter was also written during the earlier part of Nero's reign, when the empire was still benign towards Christians. Reading the text closely gives glimpses of Paul's understanding of the function of government. The reason for the existence of human authorities qualifies such voluntary subjection. Paul also possibly alluded to Mark 12:7 with regards to payment of taxes and in Romans 1:4, likely contented against the imperial claim of divine sonship. Thus, Paul's appeal to humility amid diversity does not mean stifling dissent against structural injustice.

Also, the Christian obligation and stance toward the ruling authorities or government is often limited to prayer. Paul's other passages on prayer for the authorities also indicate the need for order according to the standards of Roman society, survival by avoiding persecution, and the preservation of Christian witness for the sake of the gospel. This does not mean blind submission. What needs to be taken into account are the centuries of massive change in terms of citizen participation in government alongside prayer. Most countries today have democratic forms of government where the rule of law prevails. The Philippines is among them. Are we in the same vulnerable, powerless position as the Christians in imperial Rome, such that we need to live harmoniously both as a testimony and as a means to survive?

What would be required today as a better testimony of being in Christ – obedience regardless of evil, or the exercise of the powers of a citizen in a democracy that holds our rulers accountable? May this lead us to contemplate these questions for our times today: What is our condition as a people, what are the contours of our government, and what is the best response as followers of Jesus?

Bibliography

"436. *anthistémi*." Bible Hub. Accessed 5 November 2020. https://biblehub.com/greek/436.htm.

"498. *antitassó*." Bible Hub. Accessed 5 November 2020. https://biblehub.com/greek/498.htm.

"3011. *leitorgos*." Bible Hub. Accessed 22 September 2021. https://biblehub.com/greek/3011.htm.

"3162. *machaira.*" Bible Hub. Accessed 5 November 2020. https://biblehub.com/greek/3162.htm.

"4342. *proskartereó.*" Bible Hub. Accessed 1 June 2021. https://biblehub.com/greek/4342.htm.

Achtemeier, Paul J. *1 Peter.* Hermeneia: A Critical and Historical Commentary on the Bible. Minneapolis: Augsburg Fortress, 1996.

Britannica. "Augustus." Accessed 5 November 2020. https://www.britannica.com/biography/Augustus-Roman-emperor.

Bruce, F. F. *Romans.* Tyndale New Testament Commentary. Nottingham: Inter-Varsity Press, 2008. https://www.perlego.com/book/1470521/romans-pdf.

The Constitution of the Republic of the Philippines. 2 February 1987. Accessed 10 November 2021. https://www.officialgazette.gov.ph/constitutions/1987-constitution/.

Danker, Frederick William. *The Concise Greek-English Lexicon of the New Testament.* Chicago: University of Chicago Press, 2009.

Dunn, James D. G. *Romans 1–8.* Word Biblical Commentary 38A. Dallas: Word, 1988.

———. *Romans 9–16.* Word Biblical Commentary 38B. Dallas: Word, 1988.

Edwards, Dennis. *1 Peter.* The Story of God Bible Commentary. Grand Rapids, MI: Zondervan, 2017.

Fee, Gordon D. *1 and 2 Timothy, Titus.* New International Biblical Commentary. Peabody, MA: Hendrickson, 1988.

Gonzales, Catherine Gunsalus, and Justo L. Gonzales. *Revelation.* Westminster Bible Companion. Louisville, KY: Westminster John Knox, 1997.

Guthrie, Donald. *The Pastoral Epistles.* Tyndale New Testament Commentary 14. Nottingham: Inter-Varsity Press, 1990. https://www.perlego.com/book/1470519/pastoral-epistles-pdf.

Jewett, Robert. *Romans: A Commentary.* Hermeneia: A Critical and Historical Commentary on the Bible. Minneapolis: Fortress, 2006.

Jobes, Karen. *1 Peter.* Baker Exegetical Commentary. Grand Rapids, MI: Baker Academic, 2005. https://www.perlego.com/book/2051296/1-peter-baker-exegetical-commentary-on-the-new-testament-pdf.

Keener, Craig S. *The IVP Bible Background Commentary: New Testament.* 2nd ed. Downers Grove, IL: InterVarsity Press, 2014.

———. *Romans.* A New Covenant Commentary. Cambridge: Lutterworth, 2009.

Keesmat, Sylvia C. "Reading Romans in the Capital of the Empire." In *Reading Paul's Letter to the Romans,* edited by Jerry Sumney, 47–64. Atlanta: SBL, 2012.

Koester, Craig R. *Revelation: A New Translation with Introduction and Commentary.* Anchor Yale Bible. New Haven: Yale University Press, 2014.

Magalit, Isabelo F. "Rightful Rule: Romans 13 for the Philippines Today." In *Doing Theology in the Philippines,* edited by E. Acoba, Asian Theological Seminary, et al., 131–49. Quezon City: Asian Theological Seminary, 2005.

Moo, Douglas. *The Epistle to the Romans.* New International Commentary on the New Testament. Grand Rapids, MI: Eerdmans, 1996.

Osborne, Grant. *Revelation Verse by Verse.* Osborne New Testament Commentaries. Bellingham, WA: Lexham Press, 2016. https://www.perlego.com/book/2055089/revelation-verse-by-verse-pdf.

Presidential Decree No. 1486. 11 June 1978. Accessed 10 November 2021. https://mirror.officialgazette.gov.ph/1978/06/11/presidential-decree-no-1486-s-1978/.

Schreiner, Thomas. *Romans.* Baker Exegetical Commentary. Grand Rapids, MI: Baker Academic, 1998. https://www.perlego.com/book/2051130/romans-baker-exegetical-commentary-on-the-new-testament-pdf.

Wigram, George V. *The Englishman's Greek Concordance of the New Testament.* 9th ed. Grand Rapids, MI: Zondervan, 1970.

Wright, N. T., and Michael Bird. *The New Testament in Its World.* London: SPCK, 2019.

4

Why the Church Needs to Learn How to Complain and Not Just "Trust and Obey"

Federico G. Villanueva

I hear a lot of complaining these days. There are those who are complaining about what they perceive to be failures of the government. Then there are those who are arguing that we should not complain ("Huwag nang pumuna"). Actually, the latter is also a form of complaining – complaining about those who are complaining.

But when you go to church, you rarely, if at all, hear anything about complaining. I have been attending church worship for almost five decades now, but I have not heard a single sermon on the importance of complaining. If there is anything on complaining, the emphasis is on its prohibition, using as an example the murmuring and complaining of the Israelites in the desert and how they were punished by God as a warning. The New Testament text that says, "Do everything without grumbling or arguing" (Phil 2:14) is always cited.[1] One hymn famous among evangelicals that encapsulates the Christian response is "Trust and Obey." This is the only acceptable Christian response to everything – "unquestioning trust and obedience."

But is all complaining wrong? When a Christian complains, does that mean he or she no longer trusts in God?

---

1. All Scripture quotations in this chapter are from the NIV unless specified otherwise.

This chapter focuses on the topic of complaining. And it is not just about complaining, but complaining against God. While it is true that some forms of complaining are wrong and unacceptable to God (for example, the murmuring of the Israelites in the desert), not all complaints were rejected by God. As will be demonstrated below, God allowed his people to complain against him, and he listened to them. The complaints against God are important for three reasons. First, they constitute one of the responses to God in the Bible. The response of God in the Bible is not limited to "trust and obey." God's people did trust in God, but they also complained. Second, the complaints reveal to us who God is. And third, they provide inspiration and guidance for the church's engagement with society. Part of the reason for the failure of the church to engage with society may be traced to the loss of the important tradition of the complaint against God.

Complaints against God in the Bible

There are many complaints against God in the Bible. In addition to those in the books of Job, Lamentations, and Psalms, we find many scattered throughout the Bible. In his article "The Complaint against God," Westermann cites the following texts in addition to the books mentioned above: Genesis 25:22; 27:46; Exodus 5:22; Numbers 11:11; Judges 15:18; 6:13; 21:3; Jeremiah 4:10; 15:10–20; 20:7–11; 20:14; 20:18; 1 Maccabees 2:7; 2 Baruch (Syriac Apoc.) 11:4; 2 Esdras 3:8; 5:28. Westermann argues that the complaints against God can be found from the earliest to the later period of Israel's history.[2] As will be shown below, the complaint against God is not limited to the Old Testament. Even Jesus himself complained to God. The New Testament ends with a book that contains a complaint against God. In the first part of this chapter, we look

---

2. Claus Westermann, "The Complaint against God," in *God in the Fray: A Tribute to Walter Brueggemann*, eds. Tod Linafelt and Timothy K. Beal (Minneapolis: Fortress, 1998), 233–40. Westermann's list is not comprehensive. He notes that the complaint against God is "more frequent" in the communal laments in the Psalms, though it is also present in the individual laments. He cites Pss 13 and 22 as examples. For the prophets, he does not mention Isa 63:7 – 64:12 which contains some of the most impassioned complaints (see, for example, Isa 63:17 – "Why, LORD, do you make us wander from your ways and harden our hearts so we do not revere you?"). See also Samuel E. Balentine, *Prayer in the Hebrew Bible: The Drama of Divine-Human Dialogue* (Minneapolis: Fortress, 1997), 146–98, for what Balentine calls the "Lament tradition: Holding to God against God" in Jeremiah, Job, and Habakkuk.

at some of these complaints. We begin with Moses and Abraham – two of the great servants of God.[3]

We may think that complaining and being a servant of God are a contradiction in terms. We do not normally associate complaining with being a servant of God. In Filipino, a person who complains is called *maangal*. This word has a negative connotation. It's not good to be branded as *maangal*. To be *maangal* is to be *mayabang* (boastful). Interestingly, Moses was described as a "very humble man." According to Numbers 12:3, "Moses was a very humble man, more humble than anyone else on the face of the earth." And yet, according to Exodus 32, Moses complained to God ("umangal siya sa Diyos").

Moses Asked God "Why?"

Moses asked God "why?" twice:

1. "*Why* should your anger burn against your people, whom you brought out of Egypt with great power and a mighty hand?" Exod 32:11).

2. "*Why* should the Egyptians say, 'It was with evil intent that he brought them out, to kill them in the mountains and to wipe them off the face of the earth'?" (32:12).

This was after God had told him that he was going to destroy the Israelites because they had made the golden calf and worshipped it. God told Moses to step aside so he could destroy the people (v. 10). But instead of saying, "Yes, Lord, let it be done according to your will," Moses asked God "why?" He reasoned with God. Why deliver the people out of Egypt only to destroy them in the desert (v. 11)? In verse 12, Moses said to God, "What will the other people say?" ("Ano na lang ang sasabihin ng iba?"). What other people say is of utmost value in shame cultures like Israel as well as in most Majority World cultures. Moses used this argument to argue with God.

Rather than calling Moses *mayabang* (boastful), God allowed Moses to argue with him. Not only that – God even allowed Moses to "win" the argument! In response to Moses's questioning and arguing, the Bible says: "The LORD relented and did not bring on his people the disaster he had threatened"

---

3. For a discussion of Abraham and Moses's complaints against God, see Reuven Kimelman, "Prophecy as Arguing with God and the Ideal of Justice," *Interpretation* 68, no. 1 (Jan. 2014): 17–27. He sees a "similarity of structure between Moses' argument with God in Sinai and Abraham at Sodom" and compares the two (p. 25).

(Exod 32:14). The word "relented" comes from a Hebrew word which could also mean to "change one's mind." So not all *maangal* (complainers) are *mayabang* (boastful). And not all who complain lack faith.

Abraham Challenged God

If there is one person who trusted and obeyed God, it's Abraham. He is the embodiment of the song "Trust and Obey." Abraham is known as a man of faith (Heb 11:8–12). He trusted God even though he did not understand God's command. When God asked him to offer his son Isaac as a sacrifice, he obeyed (Gen 22). But though Abraham submitted to God and obeyed him, he also complained to God. Westermann did not include Genesis 15:2 as one of the complaints against God, but in this text we see Abraham complaining. He had been waiting for some time for the fulfillment of God's promise of a son. God assured him that he should not be afraid, for "I am your shield, your very great reward" (Gen 15:1). But notice how Abraham responded: "Sovereign LORD, what can you give me since I remain childless?" (v. 2). We have a softer analogy of Abraham's response – "Credit is good, but we need cash." Your promise is good, but what I need is a son!

Later, in Genesis 18, after Abraham learned about God's plan for Sodom and Gomorrah, he asked God: "Will you sweep away the righteous with the wicked?" (v. 23). This is not just a simple questioning. Notice the direct and bold address – "Will *you* . . . ?" Though he viewed himself as "nothing but dust and ashes" (v. 27), Abraham did not shrink from standing up to God. As Salkin comments, "One of the most notable aspects of Abraham's character" is that "he had the courage to challenge God."[4] Abraham did not remain silent and simply submit. He also protested against the "potential taking of innocent lives"[5] when he said to God, "Will not the Judge of all the earth do right?" (v. 25).

Abraham's approach to God in Genesis 18 is one example of what is called *chutzpah* (or *hutzpah*) in Jewish tradition.[6] *Chutzpah* is "boldness with regard

---

4. Jeffrey K. Salkin, *Va-Yera' (Genesis 18:1 – 22:24) and Haftarah (2 Kings 4:1–37): The JPS B'nai Mitzvah Torah Commentary* (Philadelphia: Jewish Publication Society, 2018), 5.

5. Darrell J. Fasching, "Faith and Ethics after the Holocaust: What Christians Can Learn from the Jewish Narrative Tradition of Hutzpah," *Journal of Ecumenical Studies* 27, no. 3 (1990): 455.

6. Adele Reinhartz, "The Hermeneutics of Chutzpah: A Disquisition on the Value/s of 'Critical Investigation of the Bible,'" *Journal of Biblical Literature* 140, no. 1 (Mar. 2021): 15.

to heaven."⁷ It is the audacity to challenge God instead of simply bowing down in utter submission. It is the courage to protest against God. We also see this way of responding to God in the prophets as well as in the book of Psalms.

Jeremiah Questioned the Justice of God

Like Abraham, Jeremiah questioned God too:

> You are always righteous, LORD,
>   when I bring a case before you.
> Yet I would speak with you about your justice:
>   Why does the way of the wicked prosper?
>   Why do all the faithless live at ease? (Jer 12:1)

Like Moses, he asked God "why?" twice.[8]

A fundamental belief in the Bible is that if you are righteous, you will be blessed, but if you are wicked, you will be punished. God makes the righteous successful but judges the wicked. For example, in Psalm 1, the righteous who meditate on God's word are called "blessed." They are always successful: "whatever they do prospers [$ṣlḥ$]" (v. 3).

But this is not what Jeremiah saw. It is not the righteous who prosper ($ṣlḥ$) but the wicked (Jer 12:1). In the Hebrew, the same word for "prosper" is used in Psalm 1:3 and Jeremiah 12:1. The wicked are described in the last line of verse 1 as "treacherous" (ESV); in Tagalog, "mandaraya" (MBB).[9] Jeremiah complains that not only are "all who are treacherous" prospering, but they also "live at ease" (Jer 12:1). In Tagalog, the Hebrew word translated "live at ease" is captured by the expression "ansarap ng buhay."[10] Jeremiah is complaining: "Why is it that those who are wicked are the ones living at ease?" Or in Filipino, "Bakit kung sino pa ang masama, sila pa ang masarap ang buhay?"

---

7. Belden C. Lane, "Hutzpa K'Lapei Shamaya: A Christian Response to the Jewish Tradition of Arguing with God," *Journal of Ecumenical Studies* 23, no. 4 (Sep. 1986): 567.

8. Though the interrogative "why?" (*maddûaʿ*) occurs only once in the Hebrew, this is because of the use of ellipsis, a poetic feature employed to create or free up space in the next colon for the purpose of emphasis. Thus, in verse 1, there is a foregrounding of the "faithless" who "live at ease."

9. José M. de Mesa, *A Theological Reader* (Manila: De La Salle University Publishing House, 2016), 354–62, argues that in Filipino culture and language, sin is best understood and its meaning becomes more effective through the word *pandaraya*. Pandaraya is "corruption within and without" (p. 356). When someone calls you *madaya*, it sinks in better than the word "sinner."

10. The Hebrew word is *tsalakh*, meaning "be at ease"; Hausmann, "צָלַח," TDOT, 12:382.

Habakkuk Asked God, "How Long?" and "Why?"

Some Christians remain silent even when the poor are oppressed while the wicked prosper and live at ease. But the prophets were not silent. They were greatly disturbed. When Habakkuk saw the injustices around him, he complained to God:

> How long, LORD, must I call for help,
>   but you do not listen?
> Or cry out to you, "Violence!"
>   but you do not save?
> Why do you make me look at injustice?
>   Why do you tolerate wrongdoing? (Hab 1:2–3)

The question "how long, LORD?" also occurs in the lament in Psalm 13. But the lament in Psalm 13 is directed more toward personal struggles, whereas the complaint in Habakkuk is specifically directed to the issue of justice in society. Habakkuk's complaint is similar to Jeremiah's complaint discussed above. Both complain about injustice. The difference in Habakkuk is the emphasis on the fact that the situation has been going on for a long time, as reflected in the question "how long?" It is urgent and serious, as signaled by the word "violence." And yet God seems to be doing nothing. Thus, the cry "how long?" and the complaint "why?"

The complaint in Psalm 10 reflects a similar situation.

The Psalmist Complained against God (Pss 9–10)

In Psalm 10, those who are weak are being hunted down by the wicked man (v. 2). The "helpless" are being dragged into his net (v. 9). And yet God is doing nothing. God has become like many Filipinos who don't seem to care even if poor people are killed.[11] The psalmist complains to God:

> Why, LORD, do you stand far off?
>   Why do you hide yourself in times of trouble? (Ps 10:1)

---

11. According to one survey, "88% of Filipinos are supportive of the War on Drugs." This is despite the fact that, according to the same survey, "73% believe that 'extrajudicial killings (EJK)' are also happening." See Bea Cupin, "Most Filipinos Believe EJKs Happen in War on Drugs – Poll," Rappler, 16 October 2017, https://www.rappler.com/nation/185424-pulse-asia-september-2017-war-on-drugs-survey.

This is contrary to what the psalmist knows of God. The psalmist proclaims that the LORD "has established his throne for justice" (Ps 9:7 ESV).[12] The Lord reigns (9:7a) and "he rules the world in righteousness and judges the peoples with equity" (v. 8). God is a God of justice. The psalmist believes that the Lord is "a refuge for the oppressed, a stronghold in times of trouble" (v. 9). So why is God hiding "in times of trouble" (10:1)? The phrase "in times of trouble" is repeated, creating a tension in the two psalms between his earlier declaration and what he sees around him.

In Psalms 9–10, there is an emphasis on the poor and helpless. Six out of the ten words used for poverty/the poor in the psalms are used:

1. *'ani* (poor) (9:12; 10:2, 9)
2. *'anaw* (poor) (9:18)
3. *'ebyon* (needy) (9:18)
4. *dak* (oppressed) (9:9; 10:18)
5. *helkha* (helpless) (10:8, 10, 14)
6. *yatom* (fatherless) (10:14, 18)

This is because it is usually these people who are deprived of justice. They do not know anyone at the higher levels of society. They do not have anyone else to go to. And so they come to God. Psalm 10:14a literally says, "To you the helpless abandons himself" (my own translation).[13] Westermann notes that "the individual may call out in despair, 'God, why have you forsaken me?' but not once does the caller say, 'so I shall forsake you too, I shall also turn away from you.'"[14]

---

12. The lament in Ps 10:1 is connected to the thanksgiving in Ps 9 such that the two psalms are actually one. The two are composed using a Hebrew acrostic, whereby Ps 9 begins with the first letter in the Hebrew alphabet and the acrostic continues to Ps 10.

13. The word "abandon" in Hebrew is the same word used in Ps 22 – "My God, my God, why have you abandoned [or 'forsaken'] me?" For God to abandon the weak and the powerless is the most tragic thing of all. That was how the psalmist felt, and he did not shrink from telling God honestly what he felt and saw as the right thing to do. God is a God of justice and so he should defend the cause of the oppressed.

14. Westermann, "Complaint against God," 239.

The Community Complained to God Despite Awareness of Their Sins (Lamentations)

The above discussion demonstrates that even God's servants complained to God. But some may argue that we should not complain to God because we are sinners. What right have we, sinful human beings, to complain to God? And yet the people in the Bible complained to God even though they too were aware that they had sinned. Their knowledge of their sin did not prevent them from questioning the justice of God's actions. We see this in the book of Lamentations.[15]

Lamentations was written in response to the destruction of Jerusalem by the Babylonians. Based on their history, it is clear that the destruction was a consequence of their failure to be faithful to the covenant. It was because of their sins, their disobedience, that their city was destroyed. The people do not deny this. They admit their sin (see Lam 1:8). But they also complain about the severity and, thus, the justice of their punishment. They could not accept that even little children had to die. According to Lamentations 2:11, "children and infants faint in the streets of the city."

One of the most harrowing sights is that of children dying of hunger. So horrible was the situation that even mothers lost their humanity:

> Look, LORD, and consider:
> > Whom have you ever treated like this?
> Should women eat their offspring,
> > the children they have cared for?
> Should priest and prophet be killed
> > in the sanctuary of the Lord? (Lam 2:20)

This is a question of fairness, of justice, of what's right. The people feel that though they have sinned, what they are experiencing is way beyond what they deserve. Three times in Lamentations 2 they speak of God as one "without pity":

1. "*Without pity* the Lord has swallowed up all the dwellings of Jacob; in his wrath he has torn down" (v. 2).

2. "He has overthrown you *without pity*" (v. 17).

3. "You have slain them in the day of your anger; you have slaughtered them *without pity*" (v. 21).

"Walang awa" (without pity). That's how they describe God. Some Christians would consider that to be blasphemy. Try to post that on social media

---

15. We also see this in the book of Psalms (see Pss 74; 79).

and you will be bashed. Yet what is remarkable about Lamentations is that the words were not deleted. Even when God is presented as the "perpetrator" of the actions "without pity," he did not remove their words. Perpetrators do everything to silence complaints. But in Lamentations 2, God did not silence the people. Neither did he become angry with them for daring to question his justice even though they had sinned. In Lamentations, everyone speaks except God. God simply allowed his people to pour out their complaints, as an expression of his mercy.[16]

Thus, we see that even sinners can and did complain against God. The verses cited above on God as one "without pity," as well as the complaints of God's people mentioned earlier, were allowed to be preserved in the Old Testament. The Old Testament was the Scriptures of the New Testament church (2 Tim 3:16–17). It was the Bible that Jesus read. It is important to highlight this because some Christians may say that the complaints against God are an "Old Testament thing," no longer applicable to Christians today. But even Jesus complained to God and allowed complaining to him.

Jesus Complained to God and Allowed Others to Complain to Him

To many Christians, Jesus is the ultimate picture of submission. The image of Jesus is often used to counter complaining.[17] It is true that Jesus knew how to submit. In the garden of Gethsemane, Jesus said to his Father, "Not as I will, but as you will" (Matt 26:39). Three times he uttered this prayer, which indicates that his submission was not without struggle. But in spite of the struggle, he obeyed the Father. On the cross, he also said, "Father, into your hands I commit my spirit" (Luke 23:46), which was a prayer of surrender and trust. This prayer was quoted from Psalm 31:5.

But Jesus's response was not limited to submission. Jesus also complained to God. Quoting the famous lament from Psalm 22, he cried on the cross, "My God, my God, why have you forsaken me?" This prayer is recorded in Matthew and Mark, and in both it represents the final words of Jesus on the cross (Matt 27:46; Mark 15:34).[18] The final word of Jesus while on earth was

---

16. Federico G. Villanueva, "Is There Mercy in the Book of Lamentations?," *Journal of Asian Evangelical Theology* 21, no. 1–2 (2017): 39–51.

17. Our colonizers used the image of Jesus as gentle and meek to maintain their control over us (Jose Mario C. Francisco, "Panitikan at Kristiyanismong Pilipino: Ang Nagbabagong Larawan Ni Kristo," *Philippine Studies* 25 [1977]: 186–214).

18. Matthew S. Rindge, "Reconfiguring the Akedah and Recasting God: Lament and Divine Abandonment in Mark," *Journal of Biblical Literature* 131, no. 4 (2012): 757.

a word of complaint against God. In Jesus the two traditions of *chutzpah* and trust meet and merge like two streams forming one river.

Not only did Jesus complain to God, but he also allowed others to complain to God. In one of the most intriguing stories in the New Testament, we find a woman arguing with Jesus.[19] Her approach to Jesus also includes *chutzpah*.[20] First, she comes to Jesus pleading, "Lord, Son of David, have mercy on me! My daughter is demon-possessed and suffering terribly" (Matt 15:21). To be demon-possessed is like having critical COVID-19. The woman is desperate. But Jesus did not at first even respond to the woman's pleading (v. 22). It was only after his disciples asked him to send her away that Jesus responded.

Curiously, Jesus did not allow his disciples to send the woman away. He could have done that. Why did he not? Why did he keep responding to the woman? I think it was because Jesus wants to allow the woman to engage with him. He wants to give her the opportunity to reason with him. He senses strong determination in her. So Jesus said, "I was sent only to the lost sheep of Israel" (v. 24). This is a discouraging statement. But the woman does not give up, but instead cries out, "Lord, help me!" (v. 25). Seeing that she is undeterred by his discouraging remark, Jesus brings the conversation to a new low – in fact the lowest: "It is not right to take the children's bread and toss it to the dogs" (v. 26). Jesus throws the woman into the lowest pit. But it is from there that we hear one of the most moving *chutzpah*s ever uttered in the Bible: "Yes it is, Lord . . . Even the dogs eat the crumbs that fall from their master's table" (v. 27).

The statement sounds compliant, beginning with the word "yes." The Greek word for "yes" here is *nai*, which expresses "strong affirmation, *yea, verily*."[21] But the woman is far from being a "yes-woman," even in front of the Master. Her statement is a strong protest: You say you are a compassionate Messiah, whose heart was filled with compassion when you saw the crowds who "were harassed and helpless" (Matt 9:36); who cares even for the little children, bringing them into the midst of your disciples (Matt 18:2–5); who taught your disciples to care for the least among their brothers and sisters (Matt 25:40). So why can't you even care for my daughter who is demon possessed!

Jesus could have gotten angry with the woman's audacity in confronting him. He could have rebuked her, "How dare you lecture the rabbi!" But Jesus

---

19. The story is found in two places in the gospels: Mark 7:24–30 and Matt 15:21–28.

20. Reinhartz, "Hermeneutics of Chutzpah," 15. Gail R. O'Day, "Surprised by Faith: Jesus and the Canaanite Woman," *Listening* 24 (1989): 294, argues that the story in Matt 15:21–28 is a *"narrative embodiment of a lament psalm."*

21. George Liddell and Robert Scott, *A Greek-English Lexicon*, 9th ed. (Oxford: Oxford University Press, 1940), 1159.

admired her. He not only listened to her, but praised her for her faith: "You have great faith! Your request is granted" (v. 28). Some scholars paint Jesus in the most ugly colors in this story. Smith compares the woman to Bland, an African-American who was murdered by the police for simply answering back or doing sass talk.[22] Though she does not explicitly compare Jesus to the police, her silence and the rhetoric of her writing points to the comparison. But she fails to mention that, unlike the police, Jesus does not punish the woman for her sass talk. On the contrary, he opened himself to the woman, listened to her, and allowed himself to be "changed" in the encounter. This is like the God Moses encountered on Mount Sinai – the God who allows humans not only to reason with him but also to "win" the argument!

Theology of the Complaints against God

In the above discussion I have demonstrated that complaining is one of the responses of God's people in the Bible, including Jesus himself. And the fact that the complaints to God were allowed to be written down and preserved in the Bible means that they have become part of God's word. They have a message for us. Specifically, they reveal to us who God is. As Zimmerli points out, "God himself can be recognized as in a mirror" in the responses of his people.[23] Through the complaints against God in the Bible we come to know more of our God.

What do the complaints teach us about God?

An Empowering God

The complaints against God mirror to us an empowering God. As we have seen above, he allows his people to ask him questions. Unlike some human leaders

---

22. Mitzi J. Smith, "Race, Gender, and the Politics of 'Sass': Reading Mark 7:24–30 through a Womanist Lens of Intersectionality and Inter(Con)Textuality," in *Womanist Interpretations of the Bible: Expanding the Discourse*, ed. Gay L. Byron and Vanessa Lovelace, Semeia Studies (Atlanta: SBL Press, 2016), 95–112.

23. Walther Zimmerli, *Old Testament Theology in Outline* (Edinburgh: T&T Clark, 1978), 141. Zimmerli does not specifically discuss the complaints against God. For Zimmerli the responses come in the form of actions of obedience, thanksgiving, or petition (pp. 141–55). This is true in our human relationships as well. For example, if children are always afraid whenever their father arrives home, that tells us about the kind of father he is. Or if a leader gets mad every time he hears complaints, this betrays his character as a dictator.

whom you cannot even ask where they are,[24] the God of the Bible allows his people to complain against him and to ask, "Where is he?":

- "*Where* is he who brought them through the sea, with the shepherd of his flock? *Where* is he who set his Holy Spirit among them . . . ?" (Isa 63:11).
- "*Where* are all his wonders that our ancestors told us about when they said, 'Did not the LORD bring us up out of Egypt?'" (Judg 6:13).

And it is not just the question "where?" Almost all of the interrogatives have been applied to God.[25] In addition to "where?," we have "what?," "how long?" (the equivalent of "when?"), and "why?":

- "*What* can you give me since I remain childless . . . ?" (Gen 15:2). This is another of Abraham's complaints against God when God's promise kept being delayed.
- "*How long*, LORD? Will you forget me forever? How long will you hide your face from me?" (Ps 13:1).
- "*How long*, LORD, must I call for help, but you do not listen? Or cry out to you, "Violence!" but you do not save?" (Hab 1:2).
- "*How long*, Sovereign Lord, holy and true, until you judge the inhabitants of the earth and avenge our blood?" (Rev 6:10).

Of all the interrogatives, it is the question "why?" which occurs most frequently. According to Westermann, the "why?" question "is at the core of the complaint against God throughout the entire Old Testament."[26]

- "*Why* should your anger burn against your people, whom you brought out of Egypt with great power and a mighty hand?" (Exod 32:11).
- "*Why* have you dealt ill with your servant? And *why* have I not found favor in your sight, that you lay the burden of all this people on me?" (Num 11:11 ESV).
- "*Why* does the way of the wicked prosper? Why do all the faithless live at ease?" (Jer 12:1).

---

24. For example, when Filipinos asked, "Nasaan ang pangulo?" ("Where is the president?"), the president got angry. GMA News Online, "Angry over 'Nasaan ang Pangulo'?," updated 18 November 2020, accessed 6 May 2021, https://www.gmanetwork.com/news/news/nation/764537/angry-over-nasaan-ang-pangulo-duterte-calls-leni-a-liar/story/.

25. For a more comprehensive list of interrogatives used to address God, see Samuel E. Balentine, *The Hidden God: The Hiding of the Face of God in the Old Testament* (Oxford: Oxford University Press, 1983), 118–19.

26. Westermann, "Complaint against God," 238.

- "*Why* do you make me look at injustice? Why do you tolerate wrongdoing?" (Hab 1:3).
- "*Why*, Lord, do you stand far off? Why do you hide yourself in times of trouble?" (Ps 10:1).
- "My God, my God, *why* have you forsaken me?" (Matt 27:46; Ps 22:1).

Unlike some human leaders who shame and threaten anyone who complains to them, God is not insecure. When his people complained against him, he did not respond like a Philippine president by saying, "Kayo na kaya maging Diyos!" ("Why not be God yourself!"). God is an empowering God; he is not a dictator. Before a dictator, you are nothing ("Siya lang ang magaling"). But in the presence of the Lord, you have a voice. God allows his people to speak their minds. Their ideas, what they feel, are matters of great importance to him. As Jacob wrestled with God, so God allows his people to wrestle with him and even win.[27] God does not view his people as slaves, but as covenant partners. Jesus calls his disciples "friends."

A God Who Allows His People to Pour out Their "Sama Ng Loob" (Feelings of Hurt)

The complaints against God are the outpouring of grievances or feelings of hurt, what we call in Filipino "pagbubuhos ng sama ng loob." This is related to the Filipino concept of *tampo*.[28] Tampo is a feeling of hurt which results from a failure on the part of those we love to do what is expected of them. Tampo occurs only in intimate relationships. We experience tampo only with our close friend or loved one. We do not have tampo with a mayor, for example, unless we feel close to him or her. The feeling of hurt is therefore also an indication of intimacy. When Abraham, Moses, the prophets, and the people of God we mentioned above complained against God, they did so because they were close to God. We expect our loved ones to be there for us in our difficult times and

---

27. He allowed Moses, Jacob, and Job to "win" against him. Fasching, "Faith and Ethics," 456, writes concerning Job: "Job has the hutzpah to reverse the roles, put God on trial, and win (Job 42:7–9)."

28. For further discussion of the concept of tampo and lament, see Federico G. Villanueva, "'My God, My God, Why Have You Forsaken Me?' Christology amid Disasters," in *Christologies, Cultures, and Religions: Portraits of Christ in the Philippines*, eds. Pascal D. Bazzell and Aldrin Peñamora (Mandaluyong City: OMF Literature, 2016), 83–86; Federico G. Villanueva, "My God, Why?: Natural Disasters and Lament in the Philippine Context," in *Why, O God?: Disaster, Resiliency, and the People of God*, ed. Athena E. Gorospe, Charles Ringma, and Karen Hollenbeck-Wuest (Manila, Philippines: OMF Literature and Asian Theological Seminary, 2017), 94–97.

we feel hurt when they are not. Likewise, God's people in the Bible feel hurt when God seems to be inactive or hiding.

The difference between the Filipino concept of tampo and the complaint against God is that the former is indirect while the latter is direct. Filipinos express their tampo indirectly.[29] The complaints against God challenge us to bring our hurt directly to God, to be honest to God about what we really feel. Westermann explains that in the complaints against God, the people "do not try to analyze the discrepancy; rather, they say how it affects them."[30] There is a directness in the complaints against God as reflected in our own saying, "Ang nagsasabi ng tapat nagsasama nang maluwat" (Honesty brings the relationship to greater intimacy). Could it be that one of the reasons why we do not become more intimate with God is because we are not that honest to God about what we really feel?

A God of Justice

But the complaints against God are not only a matter of feelings or emotions. The feelings of hurt are connected to the people's convictions and beliefs. Central to the complaints is the people's belief in the justice of God. This is the basis of the complaints of Abraham, Jeremiah, Habakkuk, the psalmist, and the people in Lamentations. They complain to God because they believe in the God of justice. They know that the foundation of God's reign is righteousness and justice (Ps 97:2). Their complaints reflect their knowledge of God as one "who exercises kindness, justice and righteousness on earth" (Jer 9:24). As in a mirror, the complaints against God reveal to us a God who values justice highly. In his sovereignty God has placed himself, as it were, "under the law" when it comes to matters of justice.

This has strong political implications. For issues of justice involve questions of power and authority. If God can be questioned and complained against when it comes to issues of justice, why shouldn't the same be true of human leaders? Are human leaders higher than God?

---

29. Melba Padilla Maggay, *Pahiwatig: Kagawiang Pangkomunikasyon ng Filipino* (Quezon City: Ateneo de Manila University Press, 2002), 138.

30. Westermann, "Complaint against God," 239. Though Westermann does not know about tampo, what he says here reflects the same idea.

The Politics of the Complaints against God

The complaints against God are not only theological; they are also political. According to Wilce, "laments in nearly all of the world's traditions have a political edge to them."[31] This is true in the case of the laments in the Bible. The laments in the Psalms are not private prayers, but public. As Lakkis points out, the "psalms of lament . . . represent prayer formulas which were constantly reused. Their poetic force and condensed language alone rules out the possibility that they were written by individuals in their time of need. In the rituals of that environment, the texts were maintained by cultic officials."[32] Sheppard argues that "these prayers were traditionally spoken out loud and intended to be overheard by friends and enemies alike."[33] Since they are public and are meant to be heard, "those who pray take a political risk of response from the 'enemies' who overhear, or hear about, these prayers."[34]

The complaints against God are related to the imprecatory prayers. One of the characteristics of these prayers is that they are "from below." Those who pray them do so from the perspective of the weak and vulnerable. For example, when the psalmist prays "May burning coals fall on them; may they be thrown into the fire" (141:10), it is because he believes that "the LORD secures justice for the poor and upholds the cause of the needy" (v. 12). Earlier, we mentioned the complaint in Psalm 10:1. Later in that psalm, the psalmist asks God to "break the arm of the wicked" (v. 15). The imprecatory prayers can be dangerous in the hands of powerful people. But these prayers are not for them. Those who pray them do so because they no longer have anyone or anywhere to go to. The fact that they come to God with their complaints manifests that they have reached a point where all the systems of check and balances have broken down. Humanly speaking, there is no more hope for them. So they go to God where "the one praying is challenged to become fairly articulate to God about the injustice in order to name it and to instruct those who stand nearby, even when the enemy may be included in that group."[35]

---

31. James MacLynn Wilce, *Crying Shame: Metaculture, Modernity, and the Exaggerated Death of Lament* (Malden, MA: Wiley-Blackwell, 2009), 49.

32. Stephen Lakkis, "'Have You Any Right to Be Angry?' Lament as a Metric of Socio-Political and Theological Context," in *Evoking Lament: A Theological Discussion*, eds. Eva Harasta and Brian Brock (London: T&T Clark, 2009), 173.

33. Gerald T. Sheppard, "'Enemies' and the Politics of Prayer in the Book of Psalms," in *The Bible and the Politics of Exegesis: Essays in Honor of Norman K. Gottwald on His Sixty-Fifth Birthday*, eds. David Jobling, Peggy L. Day, and Gerald T. Sheppard (Cleveland, OH: Pilgrim, 1991), 69.

34. Sheppard, "Politics of Prayer," 69.

35. Sheppard, 80.

Westermann sees a connection between the complaint and the prophetic call for justice. He writes:

> That the lament is heard implies that God has accepted their protest. Hence, we can see a connection between the lament of the oppressed which God hears, and the prophetic accusation against society. For in their accusations against society, the prophets in a sense became the articulators of the lament of the oppressed and the defenseless.[36]

Because they had learned how to complain in the presence of God, the prophets were able to complain against injustice in their society. Protest against injustice and oppression is learned in prayer. As O'Connor puts it: "If we cannot challenge the governance of this world, then we cannot challenge the governors of the world. The churches' unwillingness or incapacity to bring radical discontent, protest, and anger before God silences and denies reality. It teaches sheepishness, lying and cowardice."[37]

The Tragic Loss of the Complaint Tradition

Tragically, the tradition of the complaint against God has become lost to many Christians. There are several factors that have led to this. According to Fasching, "when Christianity broke off from Judaism . . . [the] complex dialectic of faith as trust and questioning came to be reduced in Christianity to a very different understanding of faith as unquestioning trust and obedience."[38] The acceptable Christian response is "trust and obey."

Complaints against God arise out of extremely difficult situations. As Lane puts it: "One can never speak forcefully to God from a position of security. Some levels of spirituality are grasped only when balancing on the edge of the abyss."[39] The complaints are a matter of life and death. The contexts of Abraham's and Moses's complaints concern the destructions of entire peoples, those in Sodom and Gomorrah and the Israelites, respectively. The complaints are prayers "from below." The sociological context of such prayer is "generally

---

36. Claus Westermann, "Role of the Lament in the Theology of the Old Testament," *Interpretation* 28, no. 1 (1 Jan. 1974): 30.

37. Kathleen O'Connor, "The Book of Lamentations," in *The New Interpreter's Bible*, vol. 6 (Nashville: Abingdon, 2001), 1044.

38. Fasching, "Faith and Ethics," 454.

39. Lane, "Hutzpa K'Lapei Shamaya," 579.

characterized . . . by poverty and need."[40] We see this in the complaints of Jeremiah, Habakkuk, and the psalmist (see above).

But while their extreme sufferings and issues of injustice led the people of God in the Bible to complain against God, such is not the case for many Christians today. Even when Christians are suffering severely, they generally do not complain to God. For instance, when Super Typhoon Yolanda (international name: Haiyan) devastated Tacloban, destroying houses and lives, one of the observations of a group of seminary students visited the place was that the people did not complain to God.[41] Even in the midst of the COVID-19 pandemic, when social media has become like an obituary because of so many deaths, Christians do not complain. One of the most common verses cited is Job 1:21 – "Naked I came . . . may the name of the LORD be praised." Recently, I even saw on social media a pastor leading a group in singing, "God is good, all the time." This was while the worst situation in the pandemic was transpiring in India.

Even when there are injustices happening right before our very eyes comparable to those which Habakkuk saw, many Christians remain silent. How deeply seated is the doctrine of "unquestioning trust" dawned on me when one Christian leader simply said, "Trust in God," after all the preaching and teaching I had done on the injustices of the so-called "war on drugs."

The loss of the complaint against God is tragic. Fasching argues that one of the reasons why Hitler succeeded was because Christians had lost the tradition of the complaint against God. "Even if the Nazis had invented Antisemitism instead of simply adapting the church's traditions of anti-Judaism, the church would probably still have gone along with the Nazis, based on its teaching of faith as unquestioning obedience."[42] The Christian response in terms of "unquestioning obedience" was applied even to the state, using Romans 13 as a key scriptural text. Fasching writes, "It is this statement to which Luther appealed in formulating his extreme position in response to the peasant revolts of his time."[43] The Christian teaching in terms of trusting and obeying resulted

---

40. Lane, 579.

41. Karl M. Gaspar, *Desperately Seeking God's Saving Action: Yolanda Survivors' Hope beyond Heartbreaking Lamentations* (Quezon City: Institute of Spirituality in Asia, 2014), 109–10. For an alternative narrative, see Annabel Manzanilla-Manalo, "Strengthening Resilience of Disaster Survivors: Integrating Psychospiritual Support in Mental Health and Psychosocial Support Response," in *Why, O God? Disaster, Resiliency, and the People of God*, eds. Athena E. Gorospe, Charles Ringma, Karen Hollenbeck-Wuest, and Terence E. Fretheim (Manila: OMF Literature and Asian Theological Seminary, 2017), 159–60.

42. Fasching, "Faith and Ethics," 464.

43. Fasching, 465.

in the "lack of counterauthorities resisting."[44] Very few among the church leaders preached against Hitler.[45] We cannot help but wonder if, had there been more church protests, could the ensuing genocide have been prevented, or at least hindered?[46]

Fasching asks a very important question: "What needs to be changed in Christianity so as to prevent that kind of complicity with evil from occurring again?"[47] He proposes that we "reexamine" and "reformulate" the "understanding of Christian faith and ethics grounded in *unquestioning obedience*" "in light of the lessons of history."[48]

Unfortunately, the fact that Christians have allowed another such leader to arise, who at the very beginning of his term compared himself to Hitler, demonstrates the sobering reality that we have not yet learned from history. And we have yet to learn from our very own sacred Scriptures. The need to "reexamine" and "reformulate" our Christian responses is urgent.

Conclusion

Complaint against God, along with trust and obedience, form the two responses of God's people in the Bible. In Jesus, these two streams meet together, forming one complex response to God. In Gethsemane, Jesus said, "Your will be done." But on the cross, he cried, "My God, my God, why have you forsaken me?" Like the prophets and people of old, Jesus did not limit himself to one response. The fact that we find this in the Bible and in the life of Jesus himself indicates that the complaint against God is important for the life of faith.

The complaints reveal to us God himself. The complaints against God mirror the God who is empowering, compassionate, and just. An encounter with this God strengthens human agency – something which has been severely weakened due to a one-sided focus on "unquestioning trust." The complaints against God are not only theological; they are also political. God's justice is meant to be lived out not only inside the church but "on earth" (Jer 9:24; Matt 6:9–10). If the church is to learn how to engage with its world, it has to learn how to engage with its God. Protest against injustice is learned in the prayers of lament.

---

44. Fasching, 462.
45. Fasching, 463.
46. Cf. Fasching, 462–63.
47. Fasching, 468–69.
48. Fasching, 469.

One of the striking characteristics of the prayers we have looked at in this chapter is that they are prayers not for the person praying, but for others. Moses intercedes on behalf of the Israelites who are on the brink of annihilation. Abraham questions God for the sake of Lot and his family and the people in Sodom and Gomorrah. Jeremiah, Habakkuk, and the psalmist cry out for justice on behalf of the oppressed. The people in Lamentations cry out for the lives of their children. The Syrophoenician woman confronts Jesus for the sake of her sick child. And Jesus's complaint, though it was a direct result of his suffering on the cross, is also a way of being one with those who suffer. Theologically, Jesus's prayer of abandonment is an affirmation of the laments of the people in the Old Testament. The prayer is quoted from one of the lament psalms (Ps 22). Jesus's cry also reveals to us the Son of God who is one with us in our suffering (Heb 4:14–16).

From the biblical point of view, it is not true that complaining is a sign of a lack of faith. On the contrary, it is the absence of complaining in the midst of injustice that is a sign of a lack of faith. We complain because we believe in God and trust his word. We complain because we care. We care about what is just and fair. It is not fair that if you are poor, you get imprisoned right away if you get caught violating lockdown rules, but if you are a high-ranking officer, you are not penalized, but even get promoted.[49] It is not just to spend money on non-urgent projects while many are dying of hunger. It is not wrong to complain. For complaining can and does initiate the necessary corrective actions. What is wrong is when you never complain, even when injustices are being committed right before your very eyes.

> Why then do you tolerate the treacherous?
> Why are you silent while the wicked
> swallow up those more righteous than themselves?
> (Hab 1:13)

Bibliography

Balentine, Samuel E. *The Hidden God: The Hiding of the Face of God in the Old Testament.* Oxford: Oxford University Press, 1983.

———. *Prayer in the Hebrew Bible: The Drama of Divine-Human Dialogue.* Minneapolis: Fortress, 1997.

---

49. Sofia Virtudes, "Mañanita Cop Promoted? Sinas Slammed Anew over PNP Chief Appointment," Rappler, 9 November 2020, accessed 13 September 2021, https://www.rappler.com/nation/netizens-reaction-debold-sinas-new-pnp-chief.

Cupin, Bea. "Most Filipinos Believe EJKs Happen in War on Drugs – Poll." Rappler, 16 October 2017. https://www.rappler.com/nation/185424-pulse-asia-september-2017-war-on-drugs-survey.

Fasching, Darrell J. "Faith and Ethics after the Holocaust: What Christians Can Learn from the Jewish Narrative Tradition of Hutzpah." *Journal of Ecumenical Studies* 27, no. 3 (1990): 453–79.

Francisco, Jose Mario C. "Panitikan at Kristiyanismong Pilipino: Ang Nagbabagong Larawan Ni Kristo." *Philippine Studies* 25 (1977): 186–214.

Gaspar, Karl M. *Desperately Seeking God's Saving Action: Yolanda Survivors' Hope beyond Heartbreaking Lamentations.* Quezon City: Institute of Spirituality in Asia, 2014.

GMA News Online. "Angry over 'Nasaan ang Pangulo'?" Updated 18 November 2020. Accessed 6 May 2021. https://www.gmanetwork.com/news/news/nation/764537/angry-over-nasaan-ang-pangulo-duterte-calls-leni-a-liar/story/.

Hausmann. "צָלַח," *TDOT*, 12:382–385.

Kimelman, Reuven. "Prophecy as Arguing with God and the Ideal of Justice." *Interpretation* 68, no. 1 (Jan. 2014): 17–27.

Lakkis, Stephen. "'Have You Any Right to Be Angry?' Lament as a Metric of Socio-Political and Theological Context." In *Evoking Lament: A Theological Discussion*, edited by Eva Harasta and Brian Brock, 168–82. London: T&T Clark, 2009.

Lane, Belden C. "Hutzpa K'Lapei Shamaya: A Christian Response to the Jewish Tradition of Arguing with God." *Journal of Ecumenical Studies* 23, no. 4 (Sep. 1986): 567–87.

Liddell, George, and Robert Scott. *A Greek-English Lexicon.* 9th ed. Oxford: Oxford University Press, 1940.

Maggay, Melba Padilla. *Pahiwatig: Kagawiang Pangkomunikasyon ng Filipino.* Quezon City: Ateneo de Manila University Press, 2002.

Manzanilla-Manalo, Annabel. "Strengthening Resilience of Disaster Survivors: Integrating Psychospiritual Support in Mental Health and Psychosocial Support Response." In *Why, O God? Disaster, Resiliency, and the People of God*, edited by Athena E. Gorospe, Charles Ringma, Karen Hollenbeck-Wuest, and Terence E. Fretheim, 158–77. Manila: OMF Literature and Asian Theological Seminary, 2017.

de Mesa, José M. *A Theological Reader.* Manila: De La Salle University Publishing House, 2016.

O'Connor, Kathleen. "The Book of Lamentations." In *The New Interpreter's Bible*, vol. 6, 1013–72. Nashville: Abingdon, 2001.

O'Day, Gail R. "Surprised by Faith: Jesus and the Canaanite Woman." *Listening* 24 (1989): 290–301.

Reinhartz, Adele. "The Hermeneutics of Chutzpah: A Disquisition on the Value/s of 'Critical Investigation of the Bible.'" *Journal of Biblical Literature* 140, no. 1 (Mar. 2021): 8–30.

Rindge, Matthew S. "Reconfiguring the Akedah and Recasting God: Lament and Divine Abandonment in Mark." *Journal of Biblical Literature* 131, no. 4 (2012): 755–74.

Salkin, Jeffrey K. *Va-Yera' (Genesis 18:1 – 22:24) and Haftarah (2 Kings 4:1–37): The JPS B'nai Mitzvah Torah Commentary*. Philadelphia: Jewish Publication Society, 2018.

Sheppard, Gerald T. "'Enemies' and the Politics of Prayer in the Book of Psalms." In *The Bible and the Politics of Exegesis: Essays in Honor of Norman K. Gottwald on His Sixty-Fifth Birthday*, edited by David Jobling, Peggy L. Day, and Gerald T. Sheppard, 61–82. Cleveland, OH: Pilgrim, 1991.

Smith, Mitzi J. "Race, Gender, and the Politics of 'Sass': Reading Mark 7:24–30 through a Womanist Lens of Intersectionality and Inter(Con)Textuality." In *Womanist Interpretations of the Bible: Expanding the Discourse*, edited by Gay L. Byron and Vanessa Lovelace, 95–112. Semeia Studies. Atlanta: SBL Press, 2016.

Villanueva, Federico G. "Is There Mercy in the Book of Lamentations?" *Journal of Asian Evangelical Theology* 21, no. 1–2 (2017): 39–51.

———. "'My God, My God, Why Have You Forsaken Me?' Christology amid Disasters." In *Christologies, Cultures, and Religions: Portraits of Christ in the Philippines*, edited by Pascal D. Bazzell and Aldrin Peñamora, 78–86. Mandaluyong City: OMF Literature, 2016.

———. "My God, Why?: Natural Disasters and Lament in the Philippine Context." In *Why, O God?: Disaster, Resiliency, and the People of God*, edited by Athena E. Gorospe, Charles Ringma, and Karen Hollenbeck-Wuest, 87–99. Manila, Philippines: OMF Literature and Asian Theological Seminary, 2017.

Virtudes, Sofia. "Mañanita Cop Promoted? Sinas Slammed anew over PNP Chief Appointment." Rappler, 9 November 2020. Accessed 13 September 2021. https://www.rappler.com/nation/netizens-reaction-debold-sinas-new-pnp-chief.

Westermann, Claus. "The Complaint against God." In *God in the Fray: A Tribute to Walter Brueggemann*, edited by Tod Linafelt and Timothy K. Beal, 233–41. Minneapolis: Fortress, 1998.

———. "Role of the Lament in the Theology of the Old Testament." *Interpretation* 28, no. 1 (1 Jan. 1974): 20–38.

Wilce, James MacLynn. *Crying Shame: Metaculture, Modernity, and the Exaggerated Death of Lament*. Malden, MA: Wiley-Blackwell, 2009.

Zimmerli, Walther. *Old Testament Theology in Outline*. Edinburgh: T&T Clark, 1978.

5

Duterte, Democracy, and Dissent

Roberto G. Barredo

Duterte and the State of Democracy in the Philippines

The Philippines is a constitutional democracy, yet we are forced to ask the question: What is the state of our democratic institutions and practices today? Loyal supporters of President Duterte may insist on the narrative that democracy remains robust in this nation. To the contrary, I will argue that our democracy is currently confronted by a very serious problem, namely, that under Duterte's administration one can easily discern a deliberate attempt to constrain the space for political dissent and contestation. To sharpen my argument, I will focus my discussion for the moment on Duterte's crucial political move: the "centralization of powers."

But first, briefly, let me define democracy as a distinct political conception. Democracy is the ideal government of the people – the *demos*. Simply put, the obligation to arrange a just social order ultimately rests on the people as the prime political subject, and this necessarily entails disruption and dissent. But democracy is also a political conception of power. That is to say, power tends toward corruption and injustice – hence there is a tacit suspicion of power. For modern democracy "has not come into being beneath the banner of license. At the source of democratic claims, we find a rejection of arbitrary power."[1] This is exactly the reason why modern democratic regimes set institutional rules and mechanisms that allow for dissent and contestation.

To actualize this suspicion, democratic societies divide governmental powers into three major branches, namely, the judiciary, the legislature,

---

1. Claude Lefort, "Modern Democracy and Political Philosophy," in *Writing the Politics of Difference*, ed. Hugh Silverman (New York: SUNY Press, 1991), 245.

and the executive. The purpose of this is to ensure the mechanism of checks and balances. We refer to this as the principle of the "separation of powers." Montesquieu understood this well, writing:

> [Political liberty] is there only when there is no abuse of power. But constant experience shows us that every man invested with power is apt to abuse it, and to carry his authority as far as it will go.... To prevent this abuse, it is necessary from the very nature of things that power should be a check to power.[2]

This conception suggests that power need not be concentrated in one locus; that in fact power is divisible. Yet we are not so quick to appreciate this democratic insight. It is necessary thus to revisit Montesquieu's fundamental argument:

> When the legislative and the executive powers are united in the same person, or in the same body of magistrates, there can be no liberty; because apprehension may arise, lest the same monarch or senate should enact tyrannical laws, to execute them in a tyrannical manner. Again, there is no liberty, if the judiciary power be not separated from the legislative and executive. Where it joined with the legislative, the life and liberty of the subject would be exposed to arbitrary control; for the judge would be then the legislator. Were it joined to the executive power, the judge might behave with violence and oppression. There would be an end of everything, were the same man or the same body, whether of the nobles or of the people, to exercise those three powers, that of enacting laws, that of executing the public resolutions, and of trying the causes of individuals.[3]

The separation of powers is therefore designed to check and impose limits on the exercise of political powers.[4] For to ensure the basic rights of the people, power must be legitimate and not merely arbitrary.[5]

---

2. Baron de Montesquieu, *The Spirit of the Laws*, ed. Robert Maynard Hutchins (Chicago: William Benton, 1952), 69.

3. Montesquieu, *Spirit of the Laws*, Book XI, Section 6.

4. In Christian tradition, the prime theological reason for imposing limits and the mechanism of checks and balances in the exercise of political power is the doctrine of sin or "radical evil." On this, see the discussion in Glenn Timber, *Liberty: Rethinking the Imperiled Ideal* (Grand Rapids, MI: Eerdmans, 2007), 29–60. A modern classic appropriation of the doctrine of sin in relation to political philosophy is that of Reinhold Niebuhr, *The Nature and Destiny of Man* (New York, NY: Charles Scribner's Sons, 1964). The philosophical account of "radical evil" inherent in the human condition is offered by Kant in his *Religion within the Bounds of Reason*, trans. Theodore M. Greene and Hoyt H. Hudson (New York: Harper & Brothers, 1960).

5. On the principles of legitimacy, see the discussion in Michael Curtis, ed., *The Nature of Politics* (New York: Avon, 1962), 202–39.

But what of the case of the present regime? Keen and sympathetic observers of our political situation lament the fact that, under Duterte, the democratic principle of separation of powers has been deliberately undermined. And many believe that the president is now too powerful, having consolidated all political powers necessary for him to do whatever he wants. But how has he been able to accomplish this?

In the legislature, Duterte secured majority support in both chambers. In the lower house it is a super majority, which on several occasions has showed unwavering support for the president's legislative agenda. In the upper house, Duterte has been able to build strategic alliances. Recent developments demonstrate this hold of Duterte over the legislative body – for example, the closure of the media corporation ABS-CBN and the passing of the Anti-Terror Law.[6] In the case of the former, it was public knowledge that Duterte had expressed bitter resentment against the network and thus vowed to reject its franchise renewal which, as he himself admitted, basically rests on the decision of the legislature.[7] It was a bitter drama that resulted first in an investigation conducted by Congress. But eventually the lawmakers through a special committee decided to reject the network's application for franchise renewal.

The Anti-Terror Bill also demonstrates Duterte's irresistible influence in the legislative house. Against the mounting resistance of many, the legislature still approved and passed the bill in a speedy manner, only because it was deemed a priority bill by the Duterte administration. This despite complaints, on procedural grounds, that there was not sufficient deliberation in the house. Nor there was proper public consultation to get the feedback and support of the people. For its part the Senate, Duterte's loyal supporters, continues to defend the validity of the bill, even in the face of strong resistance coming from various sectors of Philippine society.

In the case of the judicial branch, Duterte similarly wanted it to be subservient to his wishes. That is why, when the former Chief Justice Maria Lourdes Sereno vocally expressed her dissent against Duterte's controversial policies, it was a signal for the president that he had to do something. Thus, in

---

6. See Eimor Santos, "Here Are the Major Issues Raised against the Anti-Terrorism Act," CNN Philippines, 30 January 2021, https://cnnphilippines.com/news/2021/1/30/Anti-Terrorism-Act-oral-arguments-Supreme-Court.html; Senator Leila De Lima, "Anti-Terror Law? Or Anti-Filipino Law," Rappler, 17 June 2020, https://r3.rappler.com/thought-leaders/263715-anti-terror-law-or-anti-filipino-law; accessed February 9, 2022. ABS-CBN stands for Alto Broadcasting System and Chronicle Broadcasting Network.

7. See Michelle Abad, "Timeline: Duterte against ABS-CBN's Franchise Renewal," Rappler, 17 January 2020, https://www.rappler.com/newsbreak/iq/249550-timeline-duterte-against-abs-cbn-franchise-renewal/.

a manner that surprised many, Solicitor General Calida filed a quo warranto petition aimed at nullifying Sereno's high position in the Supreme Court.[8] From a political standpoint, the move was cunningly brilliant and strategic. Clearly it was not a simple issue of procedural legality that Sereno allegedly violated. In other words, the legal dispute raised by the Solicitor General arose only because of a political reason: if Sereno only remained silent, that is, supportive of Duterte's policies, she would stay as the Chief Justice. But the former Chief Justice could not be silenced. Hence Duterte, through the brilliant effort of his Solicitor General, removed Sereno from office.[9]

In various other ways, Duterte has further consolidated his power by silencing dissent and opposition. Senator Leila De Lima, one of Duterte's most vocal critics, has remained in prison for years now, despite pressure from the international community to release her. A similar political persecution happened to Senator Sonny Trillanes. Rappler and ABS-CBN, both influential media companies, suffered a similar fate. Many also believe that the recently passed Anti-Terror Bill aims to threaten political activism and to silence dissent. Moreover, Duterte has projected power and strength by making the police and the military institutions subservient to his wants and wishes. Thus, we have in Duterte's imagined democracy a political arrangement without dissent, conflict, and contestation.

On Modern Democracy (Lefort's Account)

Despite its unparalleled popularity today the idea of democracy has become increasingly problematic.[10] One of the recurring complaints is that democracy is messy, noisy, immensely pluralized, and marked by perennial conflict and contestation. This observation is of course warranted. In fact, early on, French political writer Alexis de Tocqueville already noted that a major feature of democracy is agitation. But why is that the case?

To appreciate this agitated feature of democracy, I propose exploring a philosophical and historical account of modern democracy from Claude

---

8. See Regine Cabato, "Former Chief Justice: Granting Quo Warranto Marks 'Doomsday for the Judiciary,'" CNN Philippines, 11 May 2018, https://cnnphilippines.com/news/2018/05/11/former-chief-justice-hilario-davide-quo-warranto-sereno-doomsday-judiciary.html.

9. On this issue, see chapter 8 of this book.

10. See Giorgio Agamben et al., *Democracy in What State?*, trans. William McCuaig (New York: Columbia University Press, 2011). Also see Rancière's "Does Democracy Mean Something?," in Jacques Rancière, *Dissensus: On Aesthetics and Politics*, trans. Steven Corcoran (New York: Bloomsbury, 2015), 53–69.

Lefort, a French political theorist. What makes this account attractive is that it provides an explanation of why democracy appears so messy, that is, divided, radically pluralized, disruptive, and conflictual. In particular, it explains well why dissent and contestation appear so central and constitutive to modern democratic practices.

In Lefort's account, modern democracy emerged in the late eighteenth century with the beheading of the French king. Within that historical milieu, the king served for the society as the central locus of symbolic order.[11] In his person, the spheres of *power*, *knowledge*, and *law* were condensed and concentrated. This symbolic order provided the society with a "body" – a sense of organic unity. However, the French democratic revolution in the eighteenth century disrupted this social arrangement, resulting in a tremendous mutation in the symbolic order: "The locus power becomes *an empty place* ... it cannot be occupied – it is such that no individual and no group can be consubstantial with it."[12] This revolutionary event engendered a radical problem for political representation. That power had become "an empty place" meant that power could no longer be embodied and represented. It now belonged to no one except the people, albeit in the abstract. For even the concept of "the people" remains bound with democratic indeterminacy. In other words, the practice of democracy was now defined by the legitimacy of division and conflict.

This implies that no one now has the basis to claim power unconditionally, and thus everyone has a right to contest the exercise of power, which transforms it into an object of struggle. This then entails the opening of the public space for the perennial contest of power. But this only demonstrates the deep fissures within democratic societies: the lost unity of the body politic. Lefort explains:

> If we bear in mind the monarchical model of the Ancient Regime [in France], the meaning of the transformation can be summarized as follows: democratic society is instituted as a society without a body, a society which undermines the representation of an organic totality. Neither the state, the people nor the nation represent substantial entities. Their representation is itself, in its

---

11. Lefort's analysis has been influenced by the now classic work of Ernst Kantorowicz, *The King's Two Bodies: A Study in Medieval Political Theology* (Princeton, NJ: Princeton University Press, 1957).

12. Claude Lefort, *Democracy and Political Theory*, trans. David Macey (Cambridge: Polity Press, 1988), 17.

dependence upon a political discourse ... always bound up with ideological debate.¹³

And one that is further sustained by the dissolution of the markers of certainty; a society in which the foundation of the social and political order has now vanished, and hence is marked by radical indeterminacy. "It inaugurates a history in which people experience fundamental indeterminacy as to the basis of power, law, and knowledge." And thus consequently "a process of questioning is implicit in social practice, that no one has the answer to the questions that arise, and the work of ideology, which is always dedicated to the task of restoring certainty, cannot put an end to this practice."¹⁴

Lefort insisted that we can appreciate the revolutionary import of modern democracy only against the background of modern totalitarianism¹⁵ which "proceeds from the furious negation of the democratic spirit." What then explains the rise of modern totalitarianism? For Lefort, modern totalitarianism arises

> from the mutation of a symbolic order, and the change in the status of power is its clearest expression. . . . What in fact happens is that a party arises claiming to be by its very nature different from traditional parties, to represent the aspirations of the whole people, and to possess a legitimacy which places it above the law. It takes power by destroying all opposition; the new power is accountable to no one and is beyond all legal control.¹⁶

This brief but succinct description needs to be unpacked. Note first that the formation of modern totalitarianism arises from the claim "to represent the aspirations of the whole people." This, however, is a complete contrast to the democratic conception, according to which the power to govern ultimately resides with the people. Totalitarian regimes assert the exact opposite by claiming that they themselves incarnate or embody power. Clearly the logic of identification is operative here.

> Totalitarianism is governed by the representation of power as embodiment. The proletariat and the people are one; the party and

---

13. Lefort, "Question of Democracy," in Claude Lefort, *Democracy and Political Theory*, trans. David Macey (Cambridge: Polity Press, 1998), 18.

14. Lefort, "Question of Democracy," 19.

15. See also Karl Jaspers, "Totalitarianism and Freedom," in Curtis, *Nature of Politics*, 343–47.

16. Lefort, *Democracy and Political Theory*, 18.

proletariat are one.... Whilst there develops a representation of a homogeneous and self-transparent society, of a People-as-One, social division in all its modes, is denied, and at the same time all signs of differences of opinion, belief or mores are condemned.[17]

Totalitarian regimes claim also "to possess a legitimacy which places [them] above the law" and hence have a conception of power "beyond all legal control." This again constitutes a stark contrast with the democratic experiment which now insists that "that which has been established never bears the seal of full legitimacy." In the democratic order, the exercise of political power is submitted to the perennial contest for legitimation, the result of what Lefort describes as the disentangling of the sphere of power, the sphere of law, and the sphere of knowledge.

Moreover, totalitarianism "takes power by destroying all opposition" and thus makes it accountable to no one.[18] Because it confidently claims to embody and represent the locus of power, it makes no room for political conflict and contestation. Such a regime is a closed society. It cannot sympathize with the cries and sufferings of the people. All the talk about representing the aspirations of the people is but an empty rhetorical gesture that hides its intent for total domination.[19]

This again sharply opposes the basic intentions of the modern democratic spirit. A totalitarian regime "takes power by destroying all oppositions because it [has] understood itself as accountable to no one." In the democratic social arrangement, by contrast, "*the exercise of power depends on conflict.*"[20] That is, power allows itself to be challenged and contested by other competing parties and groups. The practice of periodic elections, for instance, implies institutionalization of conflict. This constitutes the political originality of democracy which signals what Lefort calls a "double phenomenon": first, a conception of power which is involved in a constant search for its basis because law and knowledge are now no longer embodied in the person or persons who

---

17. Lefort, 13.

18. The fundamental belief of totalitarianism, according to Arendt, is that "everything is possible." Such a regime is capable of the worst evil and horror imaginable. It can destroy the humanity of others, deny their spontaneity, and reduce them to "uncomplaining animals." See Hannah Arendt, *The Portable Hannah Arendt*, ed. Peter Baehr (New York: Penguin, 2000), 120–40.

19. For Arendt, totalitarianism "strives to organize the infinite plurality and differentiation of human beings as if all of humanity were just one individual." Arendt, *Portable Hannah Arendt*, 119.

20. Arendt, 19. Emphasis mine.

exercise it; and second, a type of society "which accepts conflicting opinions and debate over rights because the markers which once allowed people to situate themselves in relation to one another in a determinate manner have disappeared."[21] This double phenomenon, according to Lefort, is a sign of single mutation, namely, that power must now win its legitimacy without becoming divorced from conflict between competing parties. For this reason, in the dissolution of the markers of certainty, the modern democratic arrangement invites us to replace the notion of a legitimate power by "the notion of a regime *founded upon the legitimacy of a debate* as to what is legitimate and what is illegitimate – a debate which is necessarily without any guarantor and without any end."[22]

Power and Dissent in the Old Testament[23]

What biblical-theological warrants are there for democracy's practice of imposing checks and for its suspicion of power? By framing such a question, there is no claim to necessarily equate ancient Israel's biblical politics with modern democracy. Rather, it is only to argue that already present in the political arrangement of ancient Israel was a sort of "institutionalization of conflict" that anticipated the practice of dissent and contestation constitutive of modern democratic politics. I would like to pursue this question, albeit briefly, by examining the relations between three major institutions in Israel, namely, the Torah, the kings, and the prophets.

Let us first consider the Torah, or the law. It should be obvious that the Torah plays a pivotal role in the life and self-understanding of ancient Israel. It defines and sets the terms of Yahweh's unique relationship to Israel, by means of which Yahweh asserts his exclusive claim to Israel as *his* people. In turn, by orienting their lives and practices in accordance with the claims of the Torah, Israel demonstrate their unique identity as the people of God. As Brueggemann

---

21. Claude Lefort, *Democracy and Political Theory*, 34.

22. Claude Lefort, *Democracy and Political Theory*, 39 (italics mine). Today advocates of deliberative democracy put at the center the idea of public reason as integral to the pursuit of social and political justice. See John Rawls, "The Idea of Public Reason Revisited," *The University of Chicago Law Review* 64, no. 3 (Summer 1997). Jürgen Habermas, "Reconciliation through the Public Use of Reason," *The Journal of Philosophy* 92, no. 3 (March 1995). Amartya Sen, *The Idea of Justice* (Cambridge, MA: Belknap Press, 2009), 321–37.

23. The deployment of biblical-theological materials here is tentative given the limited space. Hence there may be other practices and institutions such as the sage, the temple, and the priesthood, among others, that might elucidate further the complexity of the play in the relations of power in ancient Israel.

reminds us: "This establishment of Yahweh's new rule of law is the beginning point for Israel's utterance about Yahweh as king."[24] Indeed, one of the oldest and most central confessions of Israel is expressed in the assertion that Yahweh is King – over all creation and over all nations.[25]

The rhetorical import of this assertion is to relativize all temporal powers as merely derived.[26] Informed thus by this theological horizon, the institution of kingship in ancient Israel was not simply taken as something unproblematic.[27] Hence a major strand in the tradition even disputes the legitimacy of monarchy as potentially abusive and thus in conflict with the just rule of Yahweh (see 1 Sam 8:1–21). As Brueggemann notes, "This interpretive tradition, suspicious of concentration of power, anticipates that the centralized government is in principle exploitative, usurpatious, and self-serving . . . [and] this recognition is fundamental to a biblical critique of power."[28]

What then were the institutional mechanisms deployed by Israel to check and delimit the political powers of the king? A crucial institutional move in this direction was to subsume royal powers under the claims of the Torah, as explicitly stated in Deuteronomy 17:14–20. There are two things we must notice here. First, against the potential abuses of royal power (1 Sam 8:11–18), severe limits were imposed. The king must not put his confidence in the strength of his army by acquiring "great numbers of horses for himself" (Deut 17:16).[29] Nor must he rely on political alliances by taking many wives (v. 17a). He was also commanded not to acquire for himself great quantities of silver and gold (v. 17b). Second, against the royal tendency to amass military might, wealth, and political alliances, the king was commanded instead to define and orientate his rule in relation to the Torah. Thus upon his assumption of the royal throne, he must secure a copy of the Torah for himself (v. 18). "It is to be with him, and he is to read it all the days of his life." That is to say, the central duty of the king was to study and immerse himself in the Torah, so that "he may learn to fear the LORD his God, diligently observing all the words of this law and these statutes" (v. 19 NRSV). Moreover, it was underscored that the king

---

24. Walter Brueggemann, *Theology of the Old Testament* (Minneapolis: Fortress, 1997), 579.

25. See, for instance, the group of psalms classified by scholars as "Enthronement Psalms," which includes Pss 47; 93; 97; 98; 99.

26. On the nature, purpose, and limits of the state, see the discussion in Ronald J. Sider, *The Scandal of Evangelical Politics* (Grand Rapids, MI: Baker, 2008), 79–100.

27. See Walter Eichrodt's lengthy but insightful discussion of this problematic in his *Theology of the Old Testament*, vol. 1 (London: SCM, 1961), 436–56.

28. Eichrodt, *Theology of the Old Testament*, 603.

29. All Scripture quotations in this chapter are from the NIV unless specified otherwise.

must not claim a privileged status in relation to the Torah, that is, "neither exalting himself above other members of the community nor turning aside from the commandment, either to the right or to the left" (v. 20 NRSV). In short, the exercise of royal power must be legitimate, not arbitrary, but rather in accordance with the "rule of law."

To illustrate, consider King David when he acted as if he was above the law (see 2 Sam 11). Through sheer manipulation, he took Bathsheba as his wife and murdered her husband. Nathan the prophet announced the consequences and accused the king of despising "the word of the LORD" (2 Sam 12:9–10). Similarly, the promise to Solomon of royal success was conditioned on Torah obedience (1 Kgs 9:4–8). His royal records, however, end on a tragic note. He was judged for a major departure from the limits of the Torah (1 Kgs 11:9–11).

Perhaps a more striking example is the story about Ahab's attempt to possess Naboth's vineyard, narrated in 1 Kings 21. There we are told that Ahab proposes that Naboth give him his vineyard, and in exchange Ahab either will give him a better one or pay him for it. The proposition seems good and fair. But here is the complication: Naboth cannot accept what the king proposes because the property is an inheritance that belonged to his fathers, the sale of which outside the family is forbidden (see Lev 25:23; Num 27:1–11; 36:7). In short, Naboth cannot accede to the wishes of the king which clearly go against the prohibitions of the Torah. This angers the king: "So Ahab went home, sullen and angry because Naboth the Jezreelite had said, 'I will not give you the inheritance of my ancestors.' He lay on his bed sulking and refused to eat" (1 Kgs 21:4). That Ahab reacts in this way clearly indicates his strong desire to acquire the vineyard. But since Naboth refused the offer, the king could not do anything else, thus he went home very disappointed. Jezebel, the foreign wife of King Ahab, learns about what has happened (vv. 5–6). But what surprises her is Ahab's apparent helplessness in the face of Naboth's refusal. This, for Jezebel, is not the way kings should behave. Her assumption is that there are no limits to what the king may do. On this assumption, Jezebel then acts on her own. She devises a manipulative scheme which leads to Naboth's judicial murder (see vv. 8–14). Naboth's fate was tragic, yet the narrator reports that what happened did not fail to gain the notice of the prophet. This effort to subsume the royal power under the Torah insisted that kingship in Israel must be in accordance with the kingship of Yahweh, whose manner of ruling is marked by a commitment to justice (see Ps 72:1–4, 12–14).

As seen from the above, the royal claims in Israel were never granted absolute or unqualified power. The political arrangement instead already reflected (to borrow from Lefort) an "institutionalization of conflict." Hence one observes a dispute over the legitimacy of monarchy and the effort to subsume royal power under the Torah. This also reflects an early conception of legitimate power, not arbitrary nor tyrannical but rather based on the "rule of law." This delimiting and de-absolutizing function of the Torah further implies a legitimate space for dissent. And indeed, in the institutional arrangement of Israel, the voice of dissent is represented by the prophets.[30] It belongs to their dangerous vocation to rebuke the abuses of the kings and the ruling powers.[31]

The prophets generally are "uncredentialed" and "[live] at the margin of Israel's life."[32] They remain in this marginal social location because they speak against the dominant powers. Yet as John Barton notes, the prophets are "non-establishment figures who will not be silenced."[33] In fact, as Brueggemann observes, they are mainly "utterers" who "speak in outrageous and extreme figures because they intend to disrupt the 'safe' construals of reality, which are sponsored and advocated by dominant opinion makers."[34]

But what sustains their immense courage to speak against the dominant powers? It is the belief that they speak on behalf of Yahweh whose rule is marked by a commitment to justice, which should be manifested in the polity of his people. Thus we see in the biblical narratives this frequent confrontation between the prophet and the king. Recall the famous parable of Nathan, intended to expose David's adultery and murder, reminding the king that he was not above the law. We see this also in the story of Elijah, who relentlessly articulated dissent and resistance to the despotic rule of King Ahab. In the famous confrontation between the prophet and the royal apparatus on Mount Carmel, we are told by the narrator that when King Ahab saw Elijah, he referred to the prophet as the "troubler of Israel" (1 Kgs 18:17). But Elijah argues that the accusation applies to the king, on the grounds that the king and his family have failed to rule in accordance with the laws of Yahweh (1 Kgs 18:18).

Amos's impartiality confronts the nations and Israel in the name of Yahweh, whose wrath rages like a lion hunting its prey. But on what grounds? Because like Judah, "they have rejected the law of the LORD and have not kept

---

30. On the importance of "prophetic spirituality" in politics, see Jim Wallis, *The Soul of Politics* (New York: New Press, 1994), 31–47.

31. In a small but important book, Walter Brueggemann argues that prophetic imagination was engaged in the "formation of the consciousness that is a genuine alternative to royal consciousness." See his *Prophetic Imagination*, 2nd ed. (Minneapolis: Fortress, 2001), 39.

32. Brueggemann, *Theology of the Old Testament*, 628.

33. John Barton, *Oracles of God: Perception of Ancient Prophecy in Israel after the Exile* (London: Darton, Longman, and Todd, 1986), 112.

34. Brueggemann, *Theology of the Old Testament*, 625.

his decrees" (Amos 2:4). In other words, amid the affluence (3:10, 15; 6:4, 11) the land was filled with lawlessness, injustice, and lack of compassion for the poor (2:6–7; 8:4). It was an oppressive social arrangement that hid behind the mask of religion. Hence Amos had to pronounce the destruction of Bethel, the royal sanctuary, and tell them that Yahweh in fact hated and despised their religious rituals and sacrifices, and demanded instead that "justice roll on like a river, righteousness like a never-failing stream" (5:24). This angered the establishment, who accused Amos of conspiracy, of being a prophet for hire (7:10–15). But for Amos, at the root of the social injustice in the land was the deadly alliance between the religious elite and the royal power – an alliance that refused to be disturbed.

Similarly, the prophet Hosea accused the house of Israel of a major departure from the ideals of the Torah (4:6):

> There is no faithfulness, no love,
>   no acknowledgment of God in the land.
> There is only cursing, lying, and murder,
>   stealing and adultery;
> they break all bounds,
>   and bloodshed follows bloodshed. (4:1–2)

The people and the rulers were regarded as prostitutes who "dearly love shameful ways" (4:18; 5:1–4). Hosea did not spare the royal house in his relentless critique (5:1). Instead of implementing the claims of the Torah, Israel broke the covenant and relied too much on the institution of monarchy for their political survival.

> They set up kings without my consent;
>   they choose princes without my approval. (8:4)

Thus Hosea "rejected the institution as such and regarded the passage to monarchy as the "'original sin' of Israel"[35] (13:9–11). Yet the people and rulers remained undisturbed, calling Hosea "a fool" and "a maniac" (9:7).

Micah's passionate demand for justice "takes aim at officialdom in the service of monarchy."[36] These ruling elites of Israel "despise justice and distort all that is right" (3:1–2a, 9). Thus in a shocking metaphorical image, Micah accuses them of cannibalism:

---

35. Joseph Blenkinsopp, *Sage, Priest, Prophet: Religious and Intellectual Leadership in Ancient Israel* (Louisville, KY: Westminster John Knox, 1995), 150.

36. Blenkinsopp, *Sage, Priest, Prophet*, 151.

> [You] who tear the skin from my people
> and the flesh from their bones;
> who eat my people's flesh,
> strip off their skin
> and break their bones in pieces;
> who chop them up like meat for the pan,
> like flesh for the pot. (3:2–3)

Isaiah had a similar concern for the law or Torah of Yahweh, and thus he cries: "Obedience, not sacrifice" (see Isa 1:10–17). However, for Isaiah, the real significance of the law does not lie in the law as such. As von Rad observes:

> [The law] only becomes significant in the wider, i.e. political, contexts. Quite a number of Isaiah's utterances reveal a remarkable concentration of thought about questions concerning the national life, that is to say, a concern for the forms of government appropriate to a society whose founder is Jahweh, and also for the necessary offices.... First and foremost, he thinks of the chosen people as a *polis*. At the *eschaton* Jerusalem is to be restored as a *polis*, complete with all its officials (Is. 1:26), and in the *polis* the delivered are to find refuge (Is. 14:32).... All that Isaiah has to say about Israel's deliverance and renewal rests on this *polis* concept.[37]

Thus Isaiah finds it necessary to issue dissent on the specific policies pursued by King Ahaz (Isa 7:1–17). He condemns the royal counselors and the corrupt judicial system that takes advantage of the poor (Isa 3:1–3; 5:18–23; 29:14).[38]

In the above discussion, two things come to the fore. First, between the "rule of men" and the "rule of law," biblical politics insists on the rule of law.[39] Thus we see the effort to submit royal power to the Torah. This accords well

---

37. Gerhard von Rad, *Old Testament Theology*, vol. 2, trans. D. M. G. Stalker (New York: Harper & Row, 1965), 150.

38. Blenkinsopp, *Sage, Priest, Prophet*, 151.

39. The apparent opposition between the "rule of law" and the "rule of men" may not be as simple as that. For in practice, we need good laws to be implemented by wise rulers. However, Bobio notes that in the history of political philosophy, the primacy of the "rule of law" prevails – perhaps on the premise that we cannot always rely on the "goodness" of the ruling class, who tend to use their political powers to serve their own interests. Hence the sovereignty of the law is a necessary remedy to protect the political community from the potential tyranny of the ruler. The principle of the "rule of men" is of course favored during exceptional circumstances. See further, Norberto Bobio, *The Future of Democracy: A Defense of the Rules of the Game* (Minneapolis: University of Minnesota Press, 1987), 138–56.

with the history of political thought in which the law is seen as a "a hedge or wall surrounding powerful men who without this limitation might abuse their strength."[40] Such a conception played a major role in the definition of tyranny as the worst form of political ruling, and that conversely good governance is founded on the rule of law. This biblical insistence on the rule of law accords and somehow anticipates the modern democratic constitutionalism whose guiding principle is the subordination of all power to legal constraints. Second, the institution of the prophetic office in Israel is designed to allow for the full articulation of dissent and contestation, which are only possible because of the rigors and impartiality of the Torah. Consequently, the prophets' passion for justice brings them into serious collision with the abuses of the kings and the ruling class.

Conclusion

Can there be a democracy without dissent, as the current regime in the Philippines forces us to imagine? If one should insist on it, then such is no longer a democracy. For as seen from the above discussion, the modern democratic revolution inaugurates a society without a body, a society where the locus of power has become empty. Consequently, it has disrupted the markers of certainty and thus marks the "institutionalization of conflict" or the practice of dissent constitutive of the democratic arrangement. Totalitarian regimes, by contrast, claim to represent and embody power, and thus promise a society without division, dissent, and contestation.

The democratic arrangement is of course noisy, messy, and precarious; yet we cannot trade it for what totalitarian regimes may offer. Moreover, as shown from the above discussion, the democratic style of polity is something that we may also appreciate. There are biblical-theological warrants that already anticipate its constitutive practice of dissent and contestation. The kings and rulers in ancient Israel were not simply granted absolute and unqualified political power. Instead, efforts were made to subsume royal powers under the claims of the law or the Torah. This indicates that even in this primitive society, the kings were not assumed to be above the law. Hence, this already anticipates the modern conception of legitimate political power, that is, of power that is not simply arbitrary but rather based on the "rule of law." That

---

40. Hannah Arendt, *Thinking without a Banister*, ed. J. Kohn (New York: Penguin, 2018), 44, 47.

royal power was not above the law is what ultimately granted authority to the prophets to contest and speak against the injustices and abuses of the kings.

Against a democracy without dissent, we must therefore insist on democratic practices and institutions that are designed to check and delimit political power. We must protect the constitutional rule of the separation of powers. We must insist on the rule of law and the protection of our basic political rights. Against rampant extra-judicial killings, we must insist on the basic right to life and the due process of law. And against the attempt to silence the voice of dissent, we must insist on the basic political right to contest and question government policies, especially those that aim to negate the life and dignity of individuals. Democracy presupposes the capacity of the people as political subjects – it is a conception of a citizenship that is not merely docile and passive but rather critical, participatory, and vigilant.

Bibliography

Abad, Michelle. "Timeline: Duterte against ABS-CBN's Franchise Renewal." Rappler, 17 January 2020. https://www.rappler.com/newsbreak/iq/249550-timeline-duterte-against-abs-cbn-franchise-renewal/.

Agamben, Giorgio. *State of Exception*. Translated by Kevin Attel. Chicago: University of Chicago Press, 2005.

Agamben, Giorgio, et al. *Democracy in What State?* Translated by William McCuaig. New York: Columbia University Press, 2011.

Arendt, Hannah. *The Origins of Totalitarianism*. New York: Harvest, 1968.

———. *The Portable Hannah Arendt*. Edited by Peter Baehr. New York: Penguin, 2000.

———. *Thinking without a Banister*. Edited by J. Kohn. New York: Penguin, 2018.

Baehr, Peter, ed. *Hannah Arendt Reader*. New York: Penguin, 2000.

Barton, John. *Oracles of God: Perception of Ancient Prophecy in Israel after the Exile*. London: Darton, Longman, and Todd, 1986.

Blenkinsopp, Joseph. *A History of Prophecy in Israel*. Louisville, KY: Westminster John Knox, 1996.

———. *Sage, Priest, Prophet: Religious and Intellectual Leadership in Ancient Israel*. Louisville, KY: Westminster John Knox, 1995.

Bobio, Norberto. *The Future of Democracy: A Defense of the Rules of the Game*. Minneapolis: University of Minnesota Press, 1987.

Brueggemann, Walter. *The Prophetic Imagination*. 2nd ed. Minneapolis: Fortress, 2001.

———. *Theology of the Old Testament*. Minneapolis: Fortress, 1997.

Cabato, Regine. "Former Chief Justice: Granting Quo Warranto Marks 'Doomsday for the Judiciary.'" CNN Philippines, 11 May 2018. https://cnnphilippines.com/

news/2018/05/11/former-chief-justice-hilario-davide-quo-warranto-sereno-doomsday-judiciary.html.

Child, Brevard. *Biblical Theology of the Old and New Testaments*. Minneapolis: Fortress, 1992.

Curtis, Michael, ed. *The Nature of Politics*. New York: Avon, 1962.

De Lima, Senator Leila. "Anti-Terror Law? Or Anti-Filipino Law." Rappler, 17 June 2020. https://r3.rappler.com/thought-leaders/263715-anti-terror-law-or-anti-filipino-law; accessed February 9, 2022.

Eichrodt, Walter. *Theology of the Old Testament*, vol. 1. London: SCM, 1961.

Foucault, Michel. *"Society Must Be Defended": Lectures at The Collège de France*. Translated by David Macey. New York: Picador, 2003.

Habermas, Jürgen. "Reconciliation through the Public Use of Reason." *The Journal of Philosophy* 92, no. 3 (March 1995): 109–131.

Heschel, Abraham. *The Prophets*. 2 vols. New York: Harper & Row, 1962.

Kant, Immanuel. *Religion within the Bounds of Reason*. Translated by Theodore M. Greene and Hoyt H. Hudson. New York: Harper & Brothers, 1960.

Kantorowicz, Ernst. *The King's Two Bodies: A Study in Medieval Political Theology*. Princeton, NJ: Princeton University Press, 1957.

Lefort, Claude. *Democracy and Political Theory*. Translated by David Macey. Cambridge: Polity Press, 1998.

Montesquieu, Baron de. *The Spirit of the Laws*, ed. Robert Maynard Hutchins. Chicago: William Benton, 1952.

Podhoretz, Norman. *The Prophets*. New York: Free Press, 2002.

Rancière, Jacques. *Dissensus: On Aesthetics and Politics*. Translated by Steven Corcoran. New York: Bloomsbury, 2015.

Rawls, John. "The Idea of Public Reason Revisited." *The University of Chicago Law Review* 64, no. 3 (Summer 1997): 765–807.

———. *Lectures on the History of Political Philosophy*. Edited by Samuel Freeman. Cambridge, MA: Belknap Press, 2007.

Santos, Eimor. "Here Are the Major Issues Raised against the Anti-Terrorism Act." CNN Philippines, 30 January 2021. https://cnnphilippines.com/news/2021/1/30/Anti-Terrorism-Act-oral-arguments-Supreme-Court.html.

Sen, Amartya. *The Idea of Justice*. Cambridge, MA: Belknap Press, 2009.

Sider, Ronald J. *The Scandal of Evangelical Politics*. Grand Rapids, MI: Baker, 2008.

Silverman, Hugh, ed. *Writing the Politics of Difference*. New York: SUNY Press, 1991.

Timber, Glenn. *Liberty: Rethinking the Imperiled Ideal*. Grand Rapids, MI: Eerdmans, 2007.

Tocqueville, Alexis de. *Democracy in America*. Edited by J. P. Mayer. New York: Anchor, 1966.

Von Rad, Gerhard. *Old Testament Theology*, vol. 2. Translated by D. M. G. Stalker. New York: Harper & Row, 1965.

Wallis, Jim. *The Soul of Politics*. New York: New Press, 1994.

6

Their Blood Cries Out from the Ground

An Ethic of *Malasakit* and the War on Drugs

Aldrin M. Peñamora

Introduction

"Salot sa lipunan" (plague on society). "Sayad na ang utak" (crazy). "Walang halaga ang buhay" (worthless life). These are but some of the ways drug addicts have recently been depicted in our society. I was once among them before I accepted Christ as Lord and Savior back in 1998, which has led me to reflect more deeply in light of recent events. Does a person truly lose his or her dignity as a human being, and become a *salot* deserving to be killed, because of drug use? I am indeed thankful that I know Jesus Christ, without whom I could not have gotten out of that phase of my life, a life beset with problems with family and school, and battles with loneliness, insecurities, and anxieties. I am grateful to God that he did not consider my life back then to be worthless because of my drug addiction, and who mystifyingly even called me to serve him in the ministry.

There is no denying the seriousness of illegal drugs as a social problem, one which affects not only the person using them but also his or her family members and the wider community. In order to address this, the Philippine Government launched its flagship program in 2016: the "war on drugs." The program, a cornerstone of President Rodrigo Duterte's presidential campaign during that same year, seeks to put to an end the nation's problem with drug dealing and drug addiction through large-scale crackdowns on drug syndicates, dealers, and users.[1] In his inaugural address on 30 June, the president made the ominous remark that he would "have to slaughter these idiots for destroying my country." He has kept his promise, as he has led, and continues to lead, with the support of the majority of the Filipino people, one of the world's most blood-drenched antidrug campaigns in recent memory.[2] For this reason, on 15 September 2021, the International Criminal Court (ICC) formally opened an investigation upon allegations that President Duterte had committed crimes against humanity.[3]

In view of this, I believe we Filipinos need to deeply examine our personal and national moral compass, for whether we like it or not, we all partake in one way or another in this gruesome bloodbath. As Christians whose ultimate loyalty is supposedly to Christ, we need to examine in light of Scripture the claim of our nation's leaders who are spearheading this war, especially our President Rodrigo Roa Duterte, that moral obligation applies only to law-abiding citizens, and therefore that persons using illegal drugs deserve to be killed. "Nararapat pa nga ba na pagmalasakitan ang mga tinaguriang salot dahil sa kanilang pagkakalulon sa droga?" (Should people have concern for drug addicts, who are considered to be a plague on society?) In this chapter, I aim to articulate an *ethic of* malasakit (deep concern and compassion) that reflects an evangelical Christian view of responsibility toward those involved in illegal drugs.

Cain's Ethic of Violence and Non-Responsibility

In one of his writings the Jewish intellectual figure Rabbi Jonathan Sacks insightfully remarked that the distinctive contribution of Judaism is its *ethics of responsibility*, the idea that "life is God's call to responsibility," that the purpose of one's life is to enhance the lives of others living in community where goods

---

1. John Gershman, "Human Rights and Duterte's War on Drugs," interview by Michelle Xu, Council on Foreign Relations, 16 December 2016, https://www.cfr.org/interview/human-rights-and-dutertes-war-drugs.

2. Robert Muggah, "Duterte's Drug War in the Philippines Is Out of Control, He Needs to Be Stopped," *The Guardian*, 5 January 2017, https://www.theguardian.com/global-development-professionals-network/2017/jan/05/rodrigo-dutertes-drug-war-in-the-philippines-is-out-of-control-he-needs-to-be-stopped.

3. Carlos H. Conde, "Duterte Is Worried about the ICC. He Should Be," *Washington Post*, 4 October 2021, https://www.washingtonpost.com/opinions/2021/10/04/rodrigo-duterte-philippines-icc-opinion/.

are shared – goods that exist in virtue of being shared.⁴ Said another way, we exist for each other, we were created to be responsible for each other, and goods are only goods when they are shared. The significance of humanity's calling to be responsible for each other is indeed a key moral of the prediluvian story of Cain and Abel in Genesis 4. It is a calling that Cain violated by murdering his brother.

Like Cain, who sought to bring about a perverse sense of order, what undergirds the "war on drugs" is the idea that killing people involved in illegal drugs will bring about peace and social order; that blood needs to be shed to subdue the chaos brought about by criminality. Such a perspective can be found on a grand mythological scale, as pointed out by Paul Ricœur regarding the "essential" nature of violence that is embedded in the very order of creation as depicted in the creation myth of the Babylonian epic *Enuma Elish*.⁵ The *Enuma Elish* portrays how the body of the vanquished goddess Tiamat was mutilated by the victorious god Marduk in order to create the universe and humankind. Violence is thus embedded in the very fabric of the cosmos. It runs in the very veins of human beings. As Ricœur incisively remarks, "Man himself is born from a new crime . . . from the blood of an assassinated god, that is to say, from the life of a god, but from his life ravished by a murder."⁶ In other words, the image of God (*imago Dei*) in human beings is the image of a violent and murderous god, which according to the Babylonian myth is fully manifested in the person of the king. Bearing this divine image means that the king, as Marduk's representative, can create order in society only by destroying enemies. Violence is therefore extolled for its necessary and redemptive qualities.⁷

The biblical account of creation rejects utterly such a myth of "redemptive violence" which emerges from divine wars and deicide. In contrast, Genesis 1, says Gerhard von Rad, does not know of any struggle between personified primordial beings. It does not have even the smallest trace of opposition to God, and chaos can be spoken of only in reference to the superior creative will of God.⁸ There is no theomachy or enthronement motif in Genesis 1, for the simple reason that God has never been *not enthroned* – he has never been

---

4. Jonathan Sacks, *To Heal a Fractured World: The Ethics of Responsibility* (New York: Continuum, 2005), 3.

5. Paul Ricœur, *The Symbolism of Evil* (Boston: Beacon, 1967), 180, 182.

6. Ricœur, *Symbolism of Evil*, 180.

7. Walter Wink, *The Powers That Be* (New York: Doubleday, 1998), 46–48; Ricœur, *Symbolism of Evil*, 194–98.

8. Gerhard von Rad, *Genesis: A Commentary*, rev. ed. (Philadelphia: Westminster, 1972), 65.

less than sovereign.[9] The sanctification of the seventh day by God makes it even clearer that violence is not embedded in the cosmos, that violence can never be the origin and goal of creation. For just as the setting apart of the seventh day is solely determined by God's action, so the origin of creation lies exclusively in the sovereign God, who in sanctifying a day discloses the goal of *his* creation – "to give the holy a special place in the stream of events . . . a goal that corresponds to that which God set for himself."[10] The biblical creation account therefore tells us that, despite Cain's murder of Abel and the subsequent increase of violence on the earth, killing is not "in our blood." Nor is it in God's.

What caused Cain, then, to murder his brother? Let us retrace the steps that led to it. We are not told by the text exactly why God looked with disfavor upon Cain's offering (Gen 4:5), which was the immediate circumstance that prompted Cain to make a murderous decision. Was it because his offerings were taken from the ground that God had already cursed? Was he frugal in what he offered? Did he lack proper regard for the offering and therefore toward God, which seems to be what is implied in Hebrews 11:4 where Abel's faith is mentioned as the reason for God's acceptance of his offering?[11] We can only speculate. What Cain's experience of rejection shows, Claus Westermann remarks, are circumstances that seriously endanger life in community. That is, the narrative tells us how living in community will always carry the danger of inequality, and, indeed, murder.[12] God's warning in verses 6 and 7 shows, however, that if he so chose, Cain could do what was right and avoid the path of sinning (4:7), and thus lift up his countenance again. But he chose the way of murder instead of the way of being responsible as his "brother's keeper." Scripture thus ascribes to Cain full responsibility for what he did.[13] By concealing Abel's blood under the ground, he tried to entirely repudiate what in Emmanuel Levinas's view is an enduring or interminable ethical responsibility to be a brother to Abel, a relationship born beyond legality and contract.[14] That is to say, murder does not cut off completely one's responsibility to be a brother (or a sister) or neighbor to another, for this call to responsibility is not chosen by us – it is a gift which comes from God.

---

9. Bill T. Arnold, *Genesis* (Cambridge: Cambridge University Press, 2009), 32.

10. Claus Westermann, *Genesis 1–11: A Commentary* (Minneapolis: Augsburg, 1984), 172.

11. See Westermann, *Genesis 1–11*, 294–96; Arnold, *Genesis*, 78.

12. Westermann, 297.

13. Westermann, 300.

14. Emmanuel Levinas, *Of God Who Comes to Mind* (Stanford, CA: Stanford University Press, 1998), 71.

In responding to Cain's lie that he did not know the whereabouts of Abel, God uttered in Genesis 4:10 what is considered one of the most monumental sentences in the Bible:[15] "Your brother's blood cries out to me from the ground."[16] Reading it together with verse 11, we are led to envision the ground as a living being that gulps Abel's blood down its throat and responds by denying the soil its power to produce. Like his parents before him, Cain sought to hide his evil deed, but as the passage clearly enunciates, when blood cries out, God hears.[17] We can only imagine how deafening it must be for God to hear the cries of the thousands killed in this war on drugs. But why can we not hear it?

One may think, due to the portrayal of the ground as "opening its mouth" and the blood "crying out," that the term "blood" is merely symbolic, having no actual reality. In the Old Testament, however, blood is understood to have concrete, objective existence.[18] It is seen as containing the vitality of human and animal life (Deut 12:23), and is intrinsically connected to the *imago Dei* in human beings, so that shedding blood is considered a direct attack on God himself (Gen 9:6). Hence, God acted as "avenger" even against Jerusalem, whose people brazenly poured out the blood of their victims on a bare rock for all to see (Ezek 24:7–8). For shedding blood causes ethical, and not just ritual, pollution (Ezek 36:17–18), seriously endangering the well-being of the entire Israelite nation. As Joel 3:19 shows, the lands of nonbelievers were turned desolate because of their shedding of innocent blood.[19] Scripture tells us of God's anger and judgment whenever blood is shed, especially the blood of the innocent (Rev 6:10).

"Kung kaya't sa pagdanak ng dugo ng mga napaslang sa War on Drugs, hindi nga ba't tayong mga Pilipino ay humaharap rin ngayon sa paghatol ng ating Panginoon?" (Therefore, aren't we Filipinos also facing God's judgment because of the blood that is being shed in this war on drugs?)

Guilty or Not Guilty?

Can we Filipinos as a nation be guilty in the killings that are happening in the drug war? We can learn from the thoughts of the German philosopher and

---

15. Levinas, *Of God Who Comes to Mind*, 305.
16. All Scripture quotations in this chapter are from the NIV.
17. Levinas, 305–6.
18. Pamela Barmash, *Homicide in the Biblical World* (Cambridge: Cambridge University Press, 2005), 96.
19. Barmash, *Homicide in the Biblical World*, 96, 100–1.

psychiatrist Karl Jaspers, who lived as a political outcast in Hitler's Third Reich and addressed the question of collective guilt. That is, the question whether, and how, the German nation could be collectively guilty of the crimes of the Third Reich, especially against the Jewish people. According to Jaspers, there were four ways that the German *Volk* (people) could be guilty: (1) *criminally* – incurred by those who are shown to have committed violations of unequivocal laws; (2) *politically* – incurred by citizens through the leaders of their nations; (3) *morally* – the guilt of those who are capable of repentance, knowing that they walked in wrong ways for reasons such as passivity (blindness to the misfortunes of others, indifference toward the evil that was taking place), wrong submission to authorities (soldierly disposition), assimilation of the wrong idea/policy, self-deception, and outward compliance; and (4) *metaphysically* – incurred due to one's lack of solidarity with humanity.[20]

As members of the one family that is humanity, it is ideal that we all cultivate the capacity for what Jasper calls metaphysical guilt. For our purposes in regard to the war on drugs, however, it is with the *moral* aspect that we, the Filipino people, should be immediately concerned. As Jaspers remarks,

> Moral failings cause the conditions out of which both crime and political guilt arise. The commission of countless little acts of negligence; . . . the imperceptible promotion of wrong; the participation in the creation of a public atmosphere that spreads confusion and thus makes evil possible – all that has consequences that partly condition the political guilt involved in the situation and the events.[21]

In other words, guilt in the criminal and political spheres is in large part made possible by a people's moral failures. In the war on drugs, one of the ways this failure is expressed is through the lack of *pagmamalasakit* of the majority of our people for persons involved in illegal drugs, and the families left behind by those who have been killed. Such an outlook is often socially conditioned, especially in relation to the phenomenon of dehumanization.

---

20. Karl Jaspers, *The Guilt of the German People*, trans. E. B. Ashton (New York: Fordham, 2000), 25–26, 45–66.

21. Jaspers, *Guilt of the German People*, 28.

Dehumanization and the War on Drugs

In a supposedly secret speech given in 1943 by SS Chief Heinrich Himmler to his troops, he said that exterminating the Jews was the "unwritten and never-to-be-written page of glory" in their country's history. He further said:

> We had the moral right, we had the duty towards our people to destroy this people that wanted to destroy us. . . . We do not want . . . to be infected by this bacillus and to die. . . . We can say that we have carried out this most difficult of tasks in a spirit of love for our people. And we have suffered no harm to our inner being, our soul, our character.[22]

By the time World War II was over, Nazi Germany had murdered more than 6 million Jews, which Himmler said was a glorious page in his country's history.

The phenomenon of *dehumanization* can often be located in the center of such brutalities. Dehumanization occurs in the partial or total denial of a person's humanity, whether as an individual or as a collective, which justifies the exclusion of that person or group from one's moral community.[23] As a state of mind, this phenomenon is a way of seeing people as totally "Other," as *sub-* or *nonhumans*.[24] Two "metaphors of inhumanity" are useful for understanding the process of dehumanizing others, according to Nick Haslam. The first is *animalistic*, whereby people are perceived as lacking in human qualities, such as rationality and civility, and are viewed as more like animals, *Untermenschen*, vermin, dogs, rats, *mga salot* (a plague) that must be exterminated. The second metapohor is *mechanistic*, where the victims are seen as fungible or interchangeable, lacking agency; and being more like machines than humans, they can be utilized for slave labor, experimented upon, and disposed of when they reach the end of their usability.[25] It is not the mere *perception*, however, of rejected persons as animals or mere objects which characterizes dehumanization; as Avishai Margalit points out, it is *behaving as*

---

22. Yitzhak Arad et al., eds., *Documents on the Holocaust*, quoted in Israel W. Charny, ed., *Encyclopedia of Genocide* (Santa Barbara: ABC-CLIO, 1999), 241.

23. Sophie Oliver, "Dehumanization: Perceiving the Body as (In)Human," in *Humiliation, Degradation, Dehumanization: Human Dignity Violated*, eds. Paulus Kaufman et al. (New York: Springer, 2011), 86.

24. David Livingstone Smith, *On Inhumanity: Dehumanization and How to Resist It* (New York: Oxford University Press, 2020), 19.

25. Nick Haslam, "Dehumanization: An Integrative Review," *Personality and Social Psychology Review* 10, no. 3 (2006): 257–58.

if the rejected persons are indeed animals or mere objects, hence they deserve to be rejected from the human community.[26]

In an insightful essay on President Rodrigo Duterte's war on drugs, Danilo Andres Reyes discusses how drug addicts are dehumanized, "humiliated and killed in a spectacle of violence that politicises their lives, sending a message that intimidates others."[27] "Spectacle" refers to the way the bodies of the victims are dehumanized and humiliated in death. Often dumped in public places for all to see, the head or mouth and at times the entire body is found wrapped in packaging tape, with a placard attached to the body saying, "Pusher ako, wag tularan" (I am a drug pusher, don't imitate me), "Tulak" (drug pusher), or similar messages.[28] Such reduces the body of a person to a commodity, utilized to carry a political message and to frighten the populace through the inhumanity the victimizers are capable of against those considered subhumans. As the former Justice Secretary Vitaliano Aguirre once said in defending the war on drugs against charges of inhumanity, "How can that be when your war is only against drug lords, drug addicts, drug pushers? You consider them humanity? I do not."[29]

Such dehumanization not only affects the persons who are involved in illegal drugs, but also extends to the families of the victims, who aside from suffering the trauma of the killing also experience the stigma and humiliation of being closely related to the "subhumans."[30] As such, the response of nonparticipants in this gruesome narrative is vital, for it can determine whether or not this cycle of violence will endure. In other words, "bystanders" can help in countering dehumanization and restore the humanity of the victims, for as Sophie Oliver remarks, "The failure of the bystander . . . to acknowledge the victim's experience, to listen to her story, and to recognize as human the traumatized body of atrocity is itself a reiteration of the logic of dehumanization."[31] To put it differently, citizens of good standing are needed to stand in the gap, to have

---

26. Avishai Margalit, *The Decent Society* (Cambridge, MA: Harvard University Press, 1996), 112.

27. Danilo Andres Reyes, "The Spectacle of Violence in Duterte's 'War on Drugs,'" *Journal of Current Southeast Asian Affairs* 35, no. 3 (2016): 111.

28. Reyes, "Spectacle of Violence," 120.

29. Agence France-Presse, "Criminals Are Not Human – Aguirre," *Inquirer*, 1 February 2017, http://newsinfo.inquirer.net/867331/criminals-are-not-human-aguirre.

30. Gil Espenido, "Philippines' War on Drugs: Its Implications to Human Rights in Social Work Practice," *Journal of Human Rights and Social Work* 3 (Sep. 2018): 142.

31. Oliver, "Dehumanization," 93.

an ethic of *pagmamalasakit* for those considered nonhumans in this war on drugs in order to restore the humanity of our human society.

The social phenomenon of dehumanization, nonetheless, does not happen overnight. It is often the case that its "seed" is "planted" in a society where it is cultivated, fertilized, and allowed to grow.[32] Shedding light on this is an answer given by Matt Ford to a moral dilemma that the *New York Times Magazine* asked its readers in 2015: "If you could go back and kill Hitler as a baby, would you do it" – knowing what he would do later on, in order to prevent the Holocaust and save millions of people? Killing baby Hitler, Ford insightfully says, would not automatically prevent the Holocaust, since the relevant contributing factors, such as the anti-Semitism that impacted state policies and civic discourse in many Western countries during that period, did not depend entirely on Hitler.[33] Indeed, dehumanization draws on numerous factors, including well-established traditions, habits, images, and vocabularies.[34] Alexis de Tocqueville made a similar observation regarding the situation of African slaves in America in the early nineteenth century, during which time their legal standing was improving, saying, "The legal barrier between the two races is tending to decrease, but not the barriers of mores. Slavery is receding; the prejudice to which it gave rise remains unaltered."[35]

The construction of dehumanization thus consists of a social component, and one of the ways it is embedded socially is through myths where the victimizers are extolled and the victims denigrated.[36] Aristotle's "Great Chain of Being" (*Scala Naturae*), for instance, was originally conceived to situate all creatures – divine, semidivine, natural, inanimate, devilish – in a vast interconnected network. This was later appropriated and utilized as a scale of morality, with so-called "subhumans" placed at the bottom of the chain, and those who embodied "humanity" occupying a much higher or even divine place that allowed for the smooth functioning of the mechanisms of oppression

---

32. Oliver, 88.

33. Matt Ford, "The Ethics of Killing Baby Hitler," *The Atlantic*, 24 October 2015, https://www.theatlantic.com/international/archive/2015/10/killing-baby-hitler-ethics/412273.

34. Herbert C. Kelman, "Violence without Moral Restraint: Reflections on the Dehumanization of Victims and Victimizers," *Journal of Social Issues* 29, no. 4 (1973): 50.

35. Alexis de Tocqueville, *Democracy in America*, trans. Arthur Goldhammer (New York: Library Classics, 2004), 395.

36. David Livingstone Smith, *Less Than Human: Why We Demean, Enslave, and Exterminate Others* (New York: St. Martin's, 2011), chapter 4.

and extermination.[37] Tocqueville's remark on African slaves in America illustrates this point: "This man, who was born in degradation, this alien . . . we scarcely recognize him as possessing the common features of humanity. To us his visage is hideous, his intelligence limited . . . *we come close to regarding him as something intermediate between brute and man.*"[38] Thus we see Aristotle writing about "natural slavery" in his political and ethical treatises; the Nazis manufacturing the myth of Aryan superiority and Jewish subhumanity; the slaveowners of America tracing the biblical origins of African slaves to the curse of Ham in Genesis 9; and our Spanish and American forebears spinning tales of Moro vileness that justified wars and oppressive policies toward them.

Similarly, the war on drugs has an underlying narrative in *apocalyptic* form. In this narrative, writes Dan Barrera, the administration plays the protagonist who is saving the law-abiding Filipinos from drug lords and drug users, who are portrayed as destroying the country and innocent children. The motivation for this is projected as springing primarily from love and pure *pagmamalasakit sa bayan* (deep concern for the nation) and for the Filipino people. What is involved in the struggle is the very destiny of our nation, hence sacrifices must be made in areas such as human rights and human lives; collateral damage needs to be accepted. Barrera observes that the widespread success and support of the Filipino people for the war on drugs can be traced to the successful use of this genre, which was able to voice many of our fellow citizens' anxieties over the danger posed by illegal drugs.[39]

Sadly, for the thousands who have been killed and for the families they have left behind, this is a tragic story of injustice. Equally tragic, if not more so, is the way many Filipinos, including evangelical Christians, continue to be supportive of the killings. For "malasakit sa bayan" has excluded "malasakit sa kapwa-tao, at higit sa lahat, malasakit sa Diyos" (concern for one's country has excluded concern for people, and above all, concern for God).

Renouncing Cain

"Am I my brother's keeper?" These lethal words that renounce all fraternal responsibility reverberate to this very day, existing, as Jesus said, in every act

---

37. Mark J. Brandt and Christine Reyna, "The Chain of Being: A Hierarchy of Morality," *Perspectives on Psychological Science* 6, no. 5 (2011): 428–30.

38. Tocqueville, *Democracy in America*, 394. Emphasis mine.

39. Dan Jerome Barrera, "Drug War Stories and the Philippine President," *Asian Journal of Criminology* 12, no. 4 (2017): 350–52.

and attitude of hatred and contempt toward our neighbors (Matt 5:21–22). Andre LaCocque insightfully says that in uttering these words Cain also transgresses the sacred by placing a limit on what God can require of him. He can choose to not be his brother's keeper; it was God's duty to do so – to be a keeper and protector of Abel, in which duty God utterly failed.[40] Cain thus shows humanity's ability to "de-create" God's creation and defy his sacred mandate. By murdering Abel and rejecting responsibility, Cain, says LaCocque, "euthanizes all morality."[41]

Clearly, Cain misunderstood what being his brother's keeper meant, for God did not sanctify the human being as an isolated individual, but in relationship with fellow human beings. To keep or care for one's fellow human being relates not just to the person-as-an-individual, but also to the person-in-relationship-with-others, that is, to the human being in the collective and relational sense, for human community and kinship relations themselves belong to the sacred.[42] This undergirds the insight of the rabbinic sages, who say it is not coincidental that the Hebrew term for "blood" is in plural form in Genesis 4:10 – "Your brother's *damim* cries out to me from the ground" – for it indicates the unity of all humanity. Therefore, the killing of another person is likened to causing the whole world to perish.[43] Thus, by killing Abel, Cain also murdered someone of which he himself was a part.

Sadly, the way the war on drugs (mis)treats persons involved in illegal drugs as subhumans or nonhumans contrasts with the utmost regard that God has for human life. Not even Cain was treated by God as less than human, despite his murderous act. That Cain did not lose his dignity as a human being was clearly disclosed when God called and punished Cain *as a human being*. That is to say, because he was human, and despite his crime, *Cain remains human* – for which reason he deserves forgiveness and expiation.[44] Cain, however, did not seek God's forgiveness, nor did he acknowledge any responsibility for the murder; he only lamented that his punishment was more than he could bear (Gen 4:13). By killing his brother without showing a shred of remorse, Cain exemplified Friedrich Nietzsche's conception of the "noble human being," who is characterized by power and pride, and who stands against values Nietzsche

---

40. Andre LaCocque, *Onslaught against Innocence: Cain, Abel and the Yahwist* (Cambridge: James Clarke & Co., 2010), 69–70.

41. LaCocque, *Onslaught against Innocence*, 69.

42. LaCocque, 67, 69.

43. Shimon Bakon, "Thoughts on the Death Penalty: From the Written Law to the Oral Law," *Jewish Bible Quarterly* 42, no. 3 (2014): 175.

44. Westermann, *Genesis 1–11*, 303.

saw as fit only for slaves, such as forgiveness, pity, compassion, and acting for others.[45]

Cain thus stands for all who murder and defiantly renounce responsibility for their *kapwa* or fellow humans. It is precisely such renunciation that must itself be renounced if we Filipinos are to recover our own humanity and that of our blood-drenched society. With the apparent lack of concern in our society for alleged drug addicts who are being mowed down and brutally killed, it is vital for "Asia's only Christian nation" to embrace responsibility for others by perceiving the nature and character of God as someone who in Christ, as Bonhoeffer says, is *"for others,"*[46] or as the prophet Isaiah says, is Immanuel, "God with us." Indeed, God, especially as demonstrated in and through Jesus Christ, is intensely and personally concerned with the good of others, especially the poor and oppressed – yes, including drug addicts – for he is a God of *malasakit*.

An Ethic of *Malasakit*

The Filipino virtue of *malasakit*, says the Filipino anthropologist F. Landa Jocano, refers to one's sincere concern and selfless service toward others. It is derived from the combined words *malasin* (to look intently at) and *sakit* (physical, emotional, or mental pain), pointing to looking intently at another person's pain.[47] Foundational to malasakit is the core concept of *kapwa*, which generally refers to a sense of equality, unity, "shared identity," or togetherness between two persons.[48] For Katrin De Guia, kapwa as "'shared Self' extends the I to include the Other. It bridges the deepest individual recesses of a person with anyone outside him or herself, even total strangers."[49]

---

45. Friedrich Nietzsche, *Beyond Good and Evil: Prelude to a Philosophy of the Future*, trans. Walter Kaufmann (New York: Vintage, 1966), 204–10.

46. Dietrich Bonhoeffer, *Letters and Papers from Prison*, ed. Eberhard Bethge (New York: Collier, 1972), 381. Emphasis mine.

47. F. Landa Jocano, *Filipino Worldview: Ethnography and Knowledge* (Quezon City: PUNLAD, 2001), 129.

48. Jeremiah Reyes, "*Loob* and *Kapwa*: An Introduction to a Filipino Virtue Ethics," *Asian Philosophy* 25, no. 2 (2015): 155–57. Reyes translates *kapwa* in terms of "togetherness with the person," which has as starting point the interconnection of the *loob* or relational will of persons. For Reyes, the idea of "shared identity" as popularized by Virgilio Enriquez, father of *Sikolohiyang Pilipino* (Filipino Psychology), which Katrin De Guia follows in conceiving *kapwa* as "shared Self," is deficient because it started from a Western concept wherein self and the other stand in opposition.

49. Katrin De Guia, *Kapwa: The Self in Other; Worldviews and Lifestyle of Filipino Culture-Bearers* (Pasig: Anvil, 2005), 28.

Certainly, there are various ways of being a kapwa to others. Malasakit focuses on the relational aspect of sharing in the suffering of those who suffer, as if the pain and suffering of others is one's own. For this reason, malasakit and *damay* (empathy) are interrelated. As Benigno Beltran remarks, "*Damay* is . . . partaking in the act of another. . . . Related to *damay* is the Filipino trait of *malasakit*. It is the concern for another that proves itself in action, no matter what price one has to pay or what pain one must suffer."[50] The opposite of this is *walang malasakit*, which means apathy toward the plight of others; it means to be shorn of the other-regarding feelings and concerns (*manhid*) that are vital in *pakikipagkapwa-tao*, or the continuing interaction to express and forge the sharedness between *mga tao* or persons.

Indeed, the virtue of malasakit is crucial for the humanization (*pagpapakatao*) of people and society, which can be viewed as the *telos* (goal) of ethical values.[51] It is not enough for people to be formal members of society; it is imperative that people be concerned with others so that society will truly be a human(ized) society. Put another way, through malasakit we become more human; in forgoing it we become more like beasts. This recalls the Filipino saying "Madaling maging tao ngunit mahirap magpakatao" (It is easy to become a human being, but being human is much more difficult).

If without malasakit humans cannot truly be human beings, might we not also say that without malasakit God could not be God? In Book 12 of his *Metaphysics*, Aristotle did conceive of such a "stone-faced" God, an "Unmoved Mover" who was "eternally solitary, immovable, immutable, self-absorbed and apathetic."[52] It is a conception of a god who has no malasakit and *pagdamay*. When contrasted with the God presented in the Scriptures, such a divine being who is unmoved and cannot be moved by the suffering and pain of his creation can only be a dead god. For God overflows with malasakit for his people, as we see in Exodus 3:7–8, where Yahweh declares: "I have indeed seen the misery of my people. . . . I have heard them crying out because of their slave drivers, and I am concerned about their suffering. So I have come down to rescue them from the hand of the Egyptians." God's cry is indeed a cry of divine disgust

---

50. Benigno P. Beltran, *The Christology of the Inarticulate* (Manila: Divine Word, 1987), 179.

51. Dionisio M. Miranda, *Buting Pinoy: Probe Essays on Value as Filipino* (Manila: Logos, 2001), 76–77. That is, what makes values ethical is *pagpapakatao*, or "the process of becoming human." Without this ethical imperative to be human, says Miranda, we cannot truly be human beings.

52. Aldrin M. Peñamora, "The Christ of the Eucharist and Moro-Christian Relations," in *Christologies, Cultures, and Religion: Portraits of Christ in the Philippines*, eds. Pascal D. Bazzell and Aldrin Peñamora (Quezon City: Asia Theological Association, 2016), 171.

with the human exploitation of their fellow human beings and any form of dehumanization. It is also a declaration of divine intrusion into history for the cause of the oppressed.[53] Marites Redona incisively points out that malasakit is the heart of God for the miserable; it is the "Filipino face of God's mercy."[54] Indeed, malasakit is central to God's ethical dealings with human beings.

Nowhere is God's ethic of malasakit more evident and more powerfully manifested than in God's sending of his Son, Jesus Christ, to atone for humanity's sins by dying on the cross (John 3:16; Rom 5:8). Jesus exemplified this ethic of malasakit for others during his earthly ministry, entering the community of the weak and drawing to himself the sick, oppressed, and disadvantaged in order to bring them within the sphere of God's kingdom that through him had already dawned. God's ethic of malasakit is therefore inclusive and participatory in nature. "The *basileia* vision of Jesus," as aptly pointed out by Elisabeth Schüssler-Fiorenza, is the "praxis of inclusive wholeness."[55] This is especially evident in Jesus's table fellowship with sinners and outcasts, which was a key reason why he was called "a glutton and a drunkard, a friend of tax collectors and sinners" (Matt 11:19; Luke 7:34). Indeed, because of his malasakit, Jesus became sin for us (2 Cor 5:21); he was "numbered with the transgressors" (Isa 53:12) and "assigned a grave with the wicked" (Isa 53:9). In view of Jesus's ethic of malasakit, would he have approved – as many Filipino Christians do – of the brutal killings of drug addicts?

The war on drugs rejects such an ethic of malasakit that, as Jesus demonstrated, each and every person deserves. Moral responsibility, according to the proponents of this war, is limited only to the moral and upright members of our country. This war teaches that we must have malasakit only for people who are "good," that is, those who are not involved in drug-related activities. It thus conversely inculcates a disposition of *walang pagmamalasakit* or apathy, of fear and hatred toward people with drug addictions. This requires us – especially Christians – seriously to ask the question, *Whose ethic do we follow?* It is a question of knowing where, or from whom, we derive our notion of right

---

53. Levi Oracion, *God with Us: Reflections on the Theology of Struggle in the Philippines* (Dumaguete City: Silliman University, 2001), 61.

54. Marites Rano Redona, "Malasakit: The Filipino Face of God's Mercy," in *Fearful Futures: Cultural Studies and the Question of Agency in the Twenty-First Century: The Asian Conference on Cultural Studies 2018 Official Proceedings* (Kobe: IAFOR, 2018), 97; available from http://papers.iafor.org/wp-content/uploads/conference-proceedings/ACCS/ACCS2018_proceedings.pdf.

55. Elisabeth Schüssler-Fiorenza, *In Memory of Her: A Feminist Reconstruction of Christian Origins* (New York: Crossroad, 1994), 118.

and wrong, of what is good and what is evil. Simply put, it is a question about discipleship, requiring us to ask whether the ethic of *walang pagmamalasakit* toward people with drug addictions conforms to Jesus's ethic of malasakit – or whether such an ethic of indifference is a blatant disregard and denial of Jesus's way for sinful humanity, a way which was marked by compassion, solidarity, and suffering. In short, we are faced with answering the question of whether this war conforms to, or is a denial of, Jesus's way of the cross.

Conclusion

Thousands of people have already been killed and continue to be killed brutally in connection with the war on drugs, leaving many more thousands of grieving and traumatized families. Do we have any malasakit for them at all? Or have the tape-wrapped and mangled bodies of those killed completely hidden from our view the clear fact that these people also carry God's very image? In our attitude and actions toward the drug addicts who are being targeted for slaughter, are we moving toward being conformed to and transformed in the image of Christ, or are we being formed in the image of Cain, who in renouncing responsibility for his brother, and in justifying his slaying, became a restless wanderer on the earth? May we seek and follow the way of Jesus of being "for others," of having malasakit for the lives of those society has deemed worthless, knowing that we are all equally valuable in God's sight. Only then can we lift up our countenance and declare humbly before God that we are our brother's and sister's keepers.

Bibliography

Agence France-Presse. "Criminals Are Not Human – Aguirre." *Inquirer*, 1 February 2017. http://newsinfo.inquirer.net/867331/criminals-are-not-human-aguirre.
Arnold, Bill T. *Genesis*. Cambridge: Cambridge University Press, 2009.
Bakon, Shimon. "Thoughts on the Death Penalty: From the Written Law to the Oral Law." *Jewish Bible Quarterly* 42, no. 3 (2014): 173–77.
Barmash, Pamela. *Homicide in the Biblical World*. Cambridge: Cambridge University Press, 2005.
Barrera, Dan Jerome. "Drug War Stories and the Philippine President." *Asian Journal of Criminology* 12, no. 4 (2017): 341–59.
Beltran, Benigno P. *The Christology of the Inarticulate*. Manila: Divine Word, 1987.
Bonhoeffer, Dietrich. *Letters and Papers from Prison*. Edited by Eberhard Bethge. New York: Collier, 1972.
Brandt, Mark J., and Christine Reyna. "The Chain of Being: A Hierarchy of Morality." *Perspectives on Psychological Science* 6, no. 5 (2011): 428–46.

Charny, Israel W., ed. *Encyclopedia of Genocide*. Santa Barbara: ABC-CLIO, 1999.
Conde, Carlos H. "Duterte Is Worried about the ICC. He Should Be." *Washington Post*, 4 October 2021. https://www.washingtonpost.com/opinions/2021/10/04/rodrigo-duterte-philippines-icc-opinion/.
De Guia, Katrin. *Kapwa: The Self in Other: Worldviews and Lifestyle of Filipino Culture-Bearers*. Pasig: Anvil, 2005.
Espenido, Gil. "Philippines' War on Drugs: Its Implications to Human Rights in Social Work Practice." *Journal of Human Rights and Social Work* 3 (2018): 138–48.
Ford, Matt. "The Ethics of Killing Baby Hitler." *The Atlantic*, 24 October 2015. https://www.theatlantic.com/international/archive/2015/10/killing-baby-hitler-ethics/412273.
Gershman, John. "Human Rights and Duterte's War on Drugs." Interview by Michelle Xu. Council on Foreign Relations, 16 December 2016. https://www.cfr.org/interview/human-rights-and-dutertes-war-drugs.
Haslam, Nick. "Dehumanization: An Integrative Review." *Personality and Social Psychology Review* 10, no. 3 (2006): 252–64.
Jaspers, Karl. *The Guilt of the German People*. Translated by E. B. Ashton. New York: Fordham, 2000.
Jocano, F. Landa. *Filipino Worldview: Ethnography and Knowledge*. Quezon City: PUNLAD, 2001.
Kelman, Herbert C. "Violence without Moral Restraint: Reflections on the Dehumanization of Victims and Victimizers." *Journal of Social Issues* 29, no. 4 (1973): 25–61.
LaCocque, Andre. *Onslaught against Innocence: Cain, Abel and the Yahwist*. Cambridge: James Clarke & Co., 2010.
Levinas, Emmanuel. *Of God Who Comes to Mind*. Stanford, CA: Stanford University Press, 1998.
Margalit, Avishai. *The Decent Society*. Cambridge, MA: Harvard University Press, 1996.
Miranda, Dionisio M. *Buting Pinoy: Probe Essays on Value as Filipino*. Manila: Logos, 2001.
Muggah, Robert. "Duterte's Drug War in the Philippines Is Out of Control, He Needs to Be Stopped." *The Guardian*, 5 January 2017. https://www.theguardian.com/global-development-professionals-network/2017/jan/05/rodrigo-dutertes-drug-war-in-the-philippines-is-out-of-control-he-needs-to-be-stopped.
Nietzsche, Friedrich. *Beyond Good and Evil: Prelude to a Philosophy of the Future*. Translated by Walter Kaufmann. New York: Vintage, 1966.
Oliver, Sophie. "Dehumanization: Perceiving the Body as (In)Human." In *Humiliation, Degradation, Dehumanization: Human Dignity Violated*, edited by Paulus Kaufman et al., 85–97. New York: Springer, 2011.
Oracion, Levi. *God with Us: Reflections on the Theology of Struggle in the Philippines*. Dumaguete City: Silliman University, 2001.

Peñamora, Aldrin M. "The Christ of the Eucharist and Moro-Christian Relations." In *Christologies, Cultures, and Religions: Portraits of Christ in the Philippines*, edited by Pascal D. Bazzell and Aldrin Peñamora, 169–183. Quezon City: Asia Theological Association, 2016.

Redona, Marites Rano. "Malasakit: The Filipino Face of God's Mercy." In *Fearful Futures: Cultural Studies and the Question of Agency in the Twenty-First Century*: The Asian Conference on Cultural Studies, 2018 Official Proceedings. Kobe: IAFOR, 2018, 103–112. Available from http://papers.iafor.org/wp-content/uploads/conference-proceedings/ACCS/ACCS2018_proceedings.pdf.

Reyes, Danilo Andres. "The Spectacle of Violence in Duterte's 'War on Drugs.'" *Journal of Current Southeast Asian Affairs* 35, no. 3 (2016): 111–37.

Reyes, Jeremiah. "*Loob* and *Kapwa*: An Introduction to a Filipino Virtue Ethics." *Asian Philosophy* 25, no. 2 (2015): 148–71.

Ricœur, Paul. *The Symbolism of Evil*. Boston: Beacon, 1967.

Sacks, Jonathan. *To Heal a Fractured World: The Ethics of Responsibility*. New York: Continuum, 2005.

Schüssler-Fiorenza, Elisabeth. *In Memory of Her: A Feminist Reconstruction of Christian Origins*. New York: Crossroad, 1994.

Smith, David Livingstone. *Less Than Human: Why We Demean, Enslave, and Exterminate Others*. New York: St. Martin's, 2011.

———. *On Inhumanity: Dehumanization and How to Resist It*. New York: Oxford University Press, 2020.

Tocqueville, Alexis de. *Democracy in America*. Translated by Arthur Goldhammer. New York: Library Classics, 2004.

Von Rad, Gerhard. *Genesis: A Commentary*. Rev. ed. Philadelphia: Westminster, 1972.

Westermann, Claus. *Genesis 1–11: A Commentary*. Minneapolis: Augsburg, 1984.

Wink, Walter. *The Powers That Be*. New York: Doubleday, 1998.

7

"Your Kingdom Come, Your Will be Done"

Disclosing the Ethics of the New Testament's Parousia

Christopher D. Sabanal

In Martin Scorsese's film *Silence* (2016), the anxious Portuguese priest Rodrigues wondered why the Japanese Christian peasants were so calm when they were bound to suffer the fate of Ichizo and Mokichi, who were tortured to death. With confidence, Monica responded that if they died, they would go straight to Paraiso, where there is no work, no hunger, no illness, no taxes, and no suffering. This popular belief continues to this day. And for some, this view is the ultimate solution to evil and suffering.

Filipino evangelicals hold a version of this popular eschatology. For example, Felipe[1] believes there is an end to this world's seemingly endless pain and suffering: "But that will only happen when Christ returns to establish God's kingdom on earth. Working for peace and justice is, therefore, a waste of time. What is the point if people will only end up in hell when Christ suddenly returns?"

---

1. Felipe is an imaginary character whose views reflect those held by many Filipino evangelicals today.

Moreover, Felipe argues that the work of justice is not essential for Christians.

> Non-Christians can do the work of justice. These are all "filthy rags" in the sight of God. In the end, if I fail to lead people to Christ as their personal Lord and Savior, then the work of justice is pointless. If these people die without Christ, I doubt they would sit in hell fondly remembering how I fought injustice but never told them about the Gospel of Christ.

In short, Felipe believes that the world's conditions are declining, so he confidently offers belief in the gospel and the parousia as the only available solutions to the world's ills. In such a gloomy "premillennialist" view of history, only Christ's parousia will "stem the tide of degeneration and inaugurate the millennium."[2] To this, we must inquire: Can the New Testament's diverse emphases on the parousia be reduced to Felipe's neat and popular understanding without distorting the New Testament evidence? This first question concerns the field of *hermeneutics*, the critical discipline of making sense of (sacred) texts.

The second question for this chapter has to do with *ethics*. Does Felipe's notion of the parousia already succumb to a defeatist stance toward history, thus reinforcing a maladaptive reaction to society's problems? Is there a way to evaluate the ethical soundness of his notion of the parousia? While he may have recognized society's conditions as marred by evil and injustice, his eschatology's implied "ethics" is mainly concerned with expediting the parousia through efforts other than confronting society's unjust structures.

---

2. Barry Hankins identifies premillennialism as a popular view among evangelicals in the United States. The opposite of premillennialism is "postmillennialism." Like premillennialism, postmillennialism subscribes to Christ's second coming. However, postmillennialism contradicts the former by holding that Christians have *an active role* (unfortunately including the problematic American Manifest Destiny) in the presumed progress of history. In this equally questionable view, Christ will return after the ongoing millennium of progress. This is discussed in the chapter entitled "Millennialism: Folk Religion and the Career of End-Times Prophecy" in Barry Hankins, *American Evangelicals: A Contemporary History of a Mainstream Religious Movement* (Plymouth: Rowman & Littlefield, 2008), 83–103. Hankins (*American Evangelicals*, 85) describes the distinction more dramatically through the words of two well-known nineteenth-century American evangelicals: "The exchange between Henry Ward Beecher and Dwight Moody epitomizes the difference between post- and premillennialists. . . . Moody [the premillennialist] said, 'I look upon this world as a wrecked vessel. God has given me a lifeboat and said to me, "Moody, save all you can."' In reply, Beecher [the postmillennialist] said, 'Mr. Moody thinks this is a lost world, and is trying to save as many as possible from the wreck; I think Jesus Christ has come to save the world, and I am trying to help him save it.'"

The Emergence of the Parousia in the Bible

The imminence of the parousia seems to have undergone a gradual theological development. A comprehensive study, which is beyond the scope of this chapter, must go back as early as the catastrophe of the exile in 586 BC when "the older forms of the faith and tradition came into crisis."[3] Before the birth of the New Testament parousia, people hoped for a dramatic deliverance through a second Moses to end the problems of the exile (cf. Isa 40–55). However, postexilic conditions were far from ideal as the returnees remained subject to the violence of both foreign and domestic powers (cf. Isa 56–66; Neh 9:32–37). The vision of God's redemption through David's offspring gradually merged with Daniel's Son of Man, transforming into a full-blown expectation of an apocalyptic messianic deliverer. We can see this emerging in the apocalyptic language developed by the sectarian community at Qumran in the second century BC,[4] down to the uprising of Bar Kochba (AD 135), whom the esteemed Rabbi Akiba proclaimed to be the Messiah they were all waiting for. This messianic excitement, however, was utterly undermined when Bar Kochba's revolt failed.

Before the Bar Kochba revolt, the expectation of an imminent parousia and the inbreaking of God's kingdom was central to the teachings of Jesus and his early followers. Between Jesus's tragic death and the production of Mark's gospel,[5] the Jesus movement continued to reproduce the belief in the parousia. As we shall see shortly, the apostle Paul firmly believed that this end-time event would occur in his lifetime. We find a similar belief in Mark and Revelation. This chapter will also reexamine Matthew, Luke-Acts, and John's alternative approaches in dealing with the parousia question, especially after the destruction of the Jerusalem temple in AD 70.

The Imminent Parousia in Paul, Mark, and the Book of Revelation
The Apostle Paul's Teaching

Most discussions on the parousia tend to overlook that this belief led to a crisis of faith when a growing number of early Christians realized that this

---

3. Frank Moore Cross, "A Note on the Study of Apocalyptic Origins," in *Canaanite Myth and Hebrew Epic: Essays in the History of the Religion of Israel* (Cambridge, MA: Harvard University Press, [1973] 1997), 343–46.

4. Cf. Frank Moore Cross, "The Early History of the Apocalyptic Community at Qumran," in *Canaanite Myth*, 326–42.

5. Mark's shorter version, which probably is the earlier form of the gospel, ends at 16:8, and therefore does not have vv. 9–20.

anticipated end-time event had not happened.⁶ For example, in Paul's first letter to the Thessalonians (4:13–18), written just two decades after Jesus's death and resurrection, we find one of the most explicit statements about the parousia:

> But we do not want you to be uninformed, brothers and sisters, about those who have died, so that you may not grieve as others do who have no hope. For since we believe that Jesus died and rose again, even so, through Jesus, God will bring with him those who have died. For this we declare to you by the word of the Lord, that we who are alive, who are left until the coming of the Lord, will by no means precede those who have died. For the Lord himself, with a cry of command, with the archangel's call and with the sound of God's trumpet, will descend from heaven, and the dead in Christ will rise first. Then we who are alive, who are left, will be caught up in the clouds together with them to meet the Lord in the air; and so we will be with the Lord forever. Therefore encourage one another with these words.⁷

Here, the confidence of Paul is unmistakable even though it is clear that at least some of the Thessalonians who believed that they would see the "coming of the Lord" had already died. Reading between the lines, it seems likely that the believers were wondering why the parousia, expected to occur soon, had not yet happened. To anticipate this problem, Paul assures the Thessalonian believers that the "dead in Christ will rise first" (v. 16), suggesting that their deaths should not be a cause of anxiety and hopelessness. Interestingly, he adds that "we who are alive" (and here Paul includes himself) "will be caught up in the clouds . . . to meet the Lord in the air" (v. 17). We find a similar eager expectation in 1 Corinthians 7:29 where Paul suggests that "the appointed time has grown short," and in Romans 13:11–12 where he states that "salvation is nearer . . . now than when we became believers; the night is far gone, the day is near."

Moreover, Paul divulges a fantastic mystery. "We will not all die," Paul claims in 1 Corinthians 15:51–52, "but we will all be changed, in a moment,

---

6. There are exceptions to this general neglect. In his enduring study published over a century ago, Albert Schweitzer recognized the centrality of eschatology and argued that the history of Christianity "is based on the delay of the Parousia, the non-occurrence of the Parousia, the abandonment of eschatology, the progress and completion of the 'de-eschatologising' of religion which has been connected therewith." See Albert Schweitzer, *The Quest of the Historical Jesus: A Critical Study of Its Progress from Reimarus to Wrede* (Baltimore: Johns Hopkins University Press, 1998), 360.

7. All Scripture quotations in this chapter are from NRSV.

in the twinkling of an eye, at the last trumpet." Here, the apocalyptic sign of the "last trumpet" reminds us of the parousia in 1 Thessalonians, suggesting that Paul reasserts his hope to see Jesus's parousia. Though some believers had already died, it is not difficult to imagine that Paul's letter must have encouraged the Thessalonian church back in the 50s to reaffirm their hope in the Lord's coming. Unfortunately, however, before the mid 60s, Paul himself had died.

The expectation of the Lord's swift return and the reign of God did not begin or end with the apostle Paul. Before Paul, the two best-known prophets in the New Testament are John the Baptist and Jesus of Nazareth, both of whom thundered forth God's demand for *metanoia* while proclaiming the soon coming of the mysterious kingdom of God. Let us now discuss the imminent parousia in the Gospel of Mark followed by the book of Revelation.

Mark's Imminent Eschatology

Scholars generally agree that the Gospel of Mark is the earliest canonical gospel, estimated to have been produced around the time of the First Jewish War against Rome (AD 66–73) and possibly before the second temple's destruction in Jerusalem. Mark's gospel intriguingly records the message of Jesus as having a distinctly apocalyptic tone. We find a clear example of this in Mark 1:14–15: "Now after John was arrested, Jesus came to Galilee, proclaiming the good news of God, and saying, 'The time is fulfilled, and the kingdom of God has come near; repent, and believe in the good news.'"

God's kingdom is now about to break in. Jesus is the leading figure in announcing the *nearness* of God's reign, and like John the Baptist before him, Jesus proclaims it with a sense of urgency and assurance. It is noteworthy that this kingdom proclamation was not entirely new. In essence, Mark's gospel is about the long-standing belief that God will finally intervene. It is remarkable to recall that the Hebrew prophets had already anticipated the good news of God's presence and its implications for the people's lives. For example, we read in Micah 4:2–4 (cf. Isa 2:3–4):

> "Come, let us go up to the mountain of the LORD,
>   to the house of the God of Jacob;
>   that he may teach us his ways
>   and that we may walk in his paths." . . .
>   [The nations] shall beat their swords into plowshares,
>   and their spears into pruning hooks;
>   nation shall not lift up sword against nation,
>   neither shall they learn war any more;

> but they shall all sit under their own vines and under their own fig trees,
>
> and no one shall make them afraid;
>
> for the mouth of the LORD of hosts has spoken.

Furthermore, Isaiah 65:17–21 echoes and transforms Micah's text in the postexilic period. Like Micah, Third Isaiah (chs. 56–66) envisions the end of violence as well as sitting under one's own vine and trees. But, unlike Micah, Third Isaiah introduces God's creative reign through the image of *new heavens and a new earth*. This image of the new creation will later be borrowed and reinterpreted in the book of Revelation. The Gospel of Mark is not an exemption. Mark, too, reinterprets the prophetic vision of God's reign and links this proclamation to the coming of the Son of Man in the Olivet Discourse (Mark 13). In the end, God intervenes, God reigns, and God redeems his people from evil and injustice. No more war among the nations. All will now sit under their own trees and enjoy the fruit of their labor. We can imagine how this message would have sparked hope in the minds of ordinary folk, who were constantly on the underside of history, especially if Mark addresses a troubled audience during the First Jewish War against Rome. To have heard the good news of God's reign must have been the most captivating and engaging experience for Mark's audience. And as a sign that God would surely intervene to deliver them from evil, Mark reintroduces the apocalyptic belief in the coming of the Son of Man (Mark 13:26–27).

During these troubled times, a most relevant question must have emerged: *When will God intervene in this way to save his people?* And this is precisely the type of question we find in Mark 13:4: "Tell us, when will this be, and what will be the sign that all these things are about to be accomplished?"[8]

To the oppressed and disenfranchised, agitated by wars and rumors of wars, the promised end was something to be desired simply because God's reign meant the termination of demoralizing tribulations. There was always too much evil for people living under Roman occupation, too much suffering, and extraordinarily little justice. God's reign and the parousia must have evoked an end to the corrupt conditions that normalized oppression and alienation. The Gospel of Mark audaciously reveals concrete signs of the parousia, the major one being the Jerusalem temple's destruction. "When you see these things taking place, you know that he is near, at the very gates. Truly I tell you, this

---

8. The First Evangelist strikingly reworked this question in Matt 24:3. Matthew rewrites this as: "Tell us, when will this be, and what will be the sign of your coming and of the end of the age?"

generation will not pass away until all these things have taken place" (Mark 13:29–30; cf. Matt 24:33–34).

No doubt this passage intensified, more than it weakened, the excitement and expectation of the people. As in Paul's letters, the timetable of the apocalyptic parousia was noticeably "short and impatient."[9] Nevertheless, the subscribers to Mark's good news would live to see the fulfillment of these things. As to the question of timing, Mark's gospel had only one confident answer: "The time is up, God's reign is coming shortly; turn your lives around immediately for the end is near."

At last, the appointed time had arrived. Jerusalem's temple crumbled in AD 70, and the First Jewish War (AD 66–73) ended. It was terrifying to have witnessed the casualties of war and destruction on such a grand scale. But, for the subscribers to the good news, it was an exciting time too, as they waited eagerly to see the Son of Man and experience the reign of God. They must have thought: "Finally, this is the moment we've all been waiting for! Redemption is here. God is with us. Salvation at last!"[10]

The Book of Revelation

The story, however, does not end here. In Revelation, written around AD 95, we learn how the Christian communities in Asia Minor experienced, *not* God's reign, but the most intense persecution. While the overall apocalyptic imagery employed in Revelation is surreal, it does not sanitize the painful struggle experienced by the faithful. The saints can be conquered and brutally killed. There is too much violence. And we can still hear their cry reverberating through the words: "Sovereign Lord, holy and true, how long will it be before

---

9. I owe the phrase "short and impatient" apocalyptic timetable to the lectures of Professor Lorenzo C. Bautista who taught Christology and Eschatology at the Asian Theological Seminary from 1980 to 2020.

10. But N. T. Wright challenges the common reading that expects the coming of Jesus and the end of time. In reinterpreting Mark 13, Wright questions both the long tradition of mainline Christianity and the "short tradition within mainline New Testament scholarship" that goes back to Johannes Weiss and Albert Schweitzer. According to Wright, the long tradition "supposes that, in Mark 13, Jesus was predicting his own coming at the end of time, a prediction still to be fulfilled," while the short scholarly tradition – namely Weiss, Schweitzer, and their successors – "have thought that Jesus here predicted the imminent end of the world, and that he was proved wrong." Wright claims "that both traditions, the old pietist one and the more recent scholarly one, are simply mistaken." See N. T. Wright, *Jesus and the Victory of God*, vol. 2 of *Christian Origins and the Question of God* (Minneapolis: Fortress, 1996), 341. For a critique of Wright's view, and a defense of the view that the coming of the Son of Man in the Gospel of Mark refers to Jesus's parousia, see Edward Adams, "The Coming of the Son of Man in Mark's Gospel," *Tyndale Bulletin* 56, no. 1 (2005): 39–61.

you judge and avenge our blood on the inhabitants of the earth?" (Rev 6:10). From the apocalyptic perspective of Revelation, evil seems to intensify continuously from one nightmarish level to another. Rome had turned itself into a giant killing machine. This harrowing experience must only have deepened the longing for the promised parousia and the vision of God's final judgment and ultimate reign. "See, I am coming soon; my reward is with me, to repay according to everyone's work" (22:12).

Does this mean that the faithful were reduced to longing and waiting and escaping? A leading scholar on Revelation, Craig Koester, argues that the book's overall perspective is "both critical and world-engaging." He notes that the visionary of Revelation claims to be "a prophetic witness who engages issues that have political, social, economic, and religious dimensions."[11] From beginning to end, Revelation is a story of resistance depicted in the conflict between the agents of creation (God and the Lamb) and the agents of destruction represented by the image of the mighty beast. Despite the bewildering and conflicting interpretations in church history's reception of the book, Koester's helpful proposal is to read Revelation as a "forward-moving spiral" that unfolds in six cycles "in which scenes of conflict lead to celebration in heaven over and over again."[12] In the end, Revelation foresees that the justice of God shall prevail over the destroyers of the earth.

But this triumph of God's retributive justice is not as straightforward as the cyclic pattern of the book seems to suggest. This warning should guard against a simple triumphalistic reading of the book. For the careful reader of Revelation, as Stephen L. Harris suggests, evil does not stay defeated. It must be fought again and again, just as real life "is a continual battleground in which the contestants must struggle to defend previous victories and combat the same opponents in new guises."[13] Whether the earliest readers of Revelation would have immediately agreed with the modern interpretive points of Koester and Harris remains an open question. But, again, the magnitude of evil experienced by the saints demanded swift and decisive action from God. And that is precisely the promise of Revelation (22:20): "Surely I am coming soon." To which the saints would reply: "Amen. Come, Lord Jesus!" This plea for the righteous and loving God to act *soon* is essential to what we may term

---

11. Craig R. Koester, *Revelation: A New Translation with Introduction and Commentary*, Anchor Yale Bible (New Haven: Yale University Press, 2014), xv.

12. Koester, *Revelation*, xiv.

13. Stephen L. Harris, *The New Testament: A Student's Introduction*, 8th ed. (New York: McGraw-Hill Education, 2015), 447.

Maranatha eschatology. One may wonder how the author of Revelation could retain this *Maranatha* belief toward the end of the first century given the repeated nonoccurrence of the parousia in Paul and Mark. Perhaps this is a testament to the resilience of the apocalyptic mindset.

Nevertheless, hindsight tells us that all apocalyptic reckonings, from the letters of Paul to the Gospel of Mark and the book of Revelation, have one thing in common: *a sad ending*, at least for the implied reader, who notices the nonoccurrence of the expected parousia. Contrary to the sincere promises in Paul, Mark, and Revelation, Jesus did not appear as expected.[14] We can imagine how the "fortunate ones" who survived the devastating war must have awakened one morning only to discover to their horror that nothing remarkable had happened except for the fierce torture and unjust suffering they had gone through. For some of them, a rather penetrating question must have crossed their minds before they died: Are we still waiting for the Son of Man and the kingdom of God, or are we just victims of the "good news" that turns out to be "fake news"?

From *Maranatha* to *Poimaine*: Theological Readjustment in Matthew, Luke-Acts, and John

How did the post-Markan gospels handle the parousia's nonoccurrence? It is intriguing that before they died, the writers who produced Matthew, Luke-Acts, and John left us with a fascinating body of literature. These gospel accounts allow modern readers to reimagine how the ancient communities survived the parousia's nonoccurrence in the first century.

Matthew's Emerging Ethical Eschatology

A decade after the destruction of the temple in Jerusalem, we find the emergence of a new and significantly longer gospel account that drew from Mark and "Q" (sayings source) while incorporating or adding unique material of its own. The Gospel of Matthew (produced around AD 80)[15] followed the

---

14. Apart from N. T. Wright's dismissal of the parousia as referring to the return of Jesus, there are others who argue that the nonappearance of Jesus after the destruction of the temple had to do with the "conditional" nature of the promise/prophecy. See Christopher M. Hays, *When the Son of Man Didn't Come: A Constructive Proposal on the Delay of the Parousia* (Minneapolis: Fortress, 2016), 82–87. We will return to this claim below.

15. Ulrich Luz, *Matthew 1–7*, Hermeneia: A Critical and Historical Commentary on the Bible (Minneapolis: Fortress, 2007), 58–59.

Gospel of Mark closely but did not wholly repeat the details of the earliest canonical gospel. Like Mark, the Gospel of Matthew reproduced the Olivet Discourse but deliberately edited the disciples' private question to Jesus: "Tell us, when will that be and what is the sign of your parousia and of the end of the world?"[16] Ulrich Luz comments that in comparison to Mark's gospel, Matthew's gospel "has reformulated [the question] by introducing two of his favorite terms," namely the "parousia" and "end of the world."[17] This "editorial reworking"[18] seems to be Matthew's way of explicitly connecting the temple's destruction with the end-time parousia, evidence that the author retained a firm belief in the imminent coming of the heavenly Jesus. Luz reminds us that the word "parousia," in the religious language of Hellenism, meant "the presence or arrival of a god or an exalted person." Since the time of Paul, the Greek term had become a technical word "for the second arrival of Jesus as the heavenly judge of the world."[19] Unlike Mark's readers, however, Matthew's readers knew about the destruction of the temple. But they were most likely wondering about the promised parousia, which Matthew believed must occur "*immediately* after the suffering of those days" (Matt 24:29, emphasis added).

For the first time in the history of the Synoptic tradition, we find Matthew seriously addressing the problem of the "delay of the parousia," an issue which we find lurking, though in a less pronounced way, in Paul, in Mark, and even in the book of Revelation. Thus, the Gospel of Matthew contains the first recorded attempt to tackle more directly the question as to why the Son of Man and the heavenly kingdom of God did not appear *immediately*.

Apart from reproducing the Markan eschatological discourse, Matthew expands his version by adding some unique material that, in effect, qualifies the inherited apocalyptic account. In chapter 25, we read the story of the bridegroom and the ten maidens. Unlike Mark's account, Matthew practically admits that there is a "delay": "As the bridegroom was *delayed*, all of them became drowsy and slept" (25:5, emphasis added).

The second story not found in Mark is about a master who went on a journey. Matthew narrates that the master's return took a *long time*: "After a *long time* the master of those slaves came and settled accounts with them" (25:19, emphasis added).

---

16. Translated by Luz. See Ulrich Luz, *Matthew 21–28*, Hermeneia: A Critical and Historical Commentary on the Bible (Minneapolis: Augsburg Fortress, 2005), 180.

17. Luz, *Matthew 21–28*, 189.

18. The technical term here is "redaction."

19. Luz, *Matthew 21–28*, 190.

Thus, Matthew slightly departs from Mark concerning the command to be vigilant. While he maintains the need to be alert (therefore aligning with Mark), Matthew interestingly acknowledges the "delay." In this sense, Matthew reinterprets the nearness of the parousia in light of the "delay." For Matthew and his readers, the contradiction of *imminence* and *delay* surprisingly becomes all the more reason to prepare actively (vv. 1–13). The argument implied in Matthew's reworking of the discourse is that there is no room to slacken even if one admits the postponement of the apocalyptic end. The lag increases the uncertainty but does not in any way affect the imminence of the parousia. Thus, in Matthew's Olivet Discourse, the parousia and the end have become *an immediate daily possibility*.[20]

Furthermore, Matthew goes beyond Mark's emphasis on alertness by suggesting that legitimate preparation for the parousia involves the *wise investment of resources* entrusted to them by the master who left for a "long time" (vv. 14–30). What is surprising in Matthew's version is that, unlike in Mark, both actions of vigilant preparation and wise investment ought to manifest in a new way of life, one that is deeply concerned with the concrete conditions of the "least of these" (vv. 31–46). As in the Gospel of Mark, in Matthew the Son of Man comes in glory. However, unlike in Mark, Matthew's Son of Man comes as the world Judge, which involves a striking twist. In Matthew, the Son of Man comes in a way that surprises even the righteous. Before the Son of Man sits on the throne to judge the nations, he "comes" daily and quietly: that is, he comes unidentified in the form of the hungry, the thirsty, the stranger, the naked, the sick, and the prisoner. The final judgment depends on whether the nations have exercised the deeds of love to the "least of these." In the end, the Son of Man will announce his verdict as the world Judge with the following words:

> Come, you that are blessed by my Father, inherit the kingdom prepared for you from the foundation of the world; for I was hungry and you gave me food, I was thirsty and you gave me something to drink, I was a stranger and you welcomed me, I was naked and you gave me clothing, I was sick and you took care of me, I was in prison and you visited me. (Matt 25:34–36)

The final judgment scenario must have surprised the readers of Matthew, especially those who were not familiar with the "twist" that he had developed. Even in the text, the righteous could only utter the words: "When was it that

---

20. Luz, 209.

we saw you hungry . . . ?" Thus, Matthew suggests that the followers of Christ are unaware of the Son of Man's daily but quiet presence. This lack of awareness is what some scholars call the "ignorance motif" in Matthew. "Truly I tell you, just as you did it to one of the least of these who are members of my family, you did it to me" (v. 40).

For Matthew, the downtrodden Jesus, who identifies with the least, should restructure the life of the faithful disciple while awaiting the parousia. This restructured life is well prepared and wisely invested in doing the works of love. Whoever wrote this gospel must have been a genuinely innovative sage. He managed to "hide" Jesus in the often ignored and easily forgotten lives of the less fortunate; even the righteous cannot recognize him. What ultimately counts for Matthew are the deeds of love exercised by the faithful disciples, which is a Matthean way of redefining what it means to inherit the kingdom of God, measured by the earnest effort to pursue righteousness and justice (Matt 6:33). This reinterpretation is consistent with the "greatest commandment" – to love God and neighbor (Matt 22:34–40). Luz, who interestingly favors a "universal interpretation" of Matthew's text,[21] regards the "ignorance motif" as crucial in Matthew's reformulation of the apocalyptic discourse.[22] The "ignorance motif" effectively transforms the story of the parousia in such a way that it can swiftly transport the readers to the heart of the gospel. The hiddenness of Jesus need not cause panic because what counts in the final judgment are the deeds of love. Though uncertain about the parousia's timing, the faithful disciples, having oriented their lives rightly, have paradoxically encountered the exalted Lord – Luz adds, *God* – hidden "in Jesus's lowliest brothers [and sisters] – be they members of the church or not."[23]

We have seen that Matthew retains many of the apocalyptic elements of the imminent coming of the Son of Man (Matt 24:3–35). But Matthew reworked this inherited tradition by expanding the story (Matt 24:36 – 25:46), thus in effect developing what we might call an "ethical eschatology." This reworking of the inherited discourse, I propose, is an early attempt to reinterpret the *Maranatha eschatology* without abandoning the belief in the imminent parousia.

---

21. For a discussion of the "universal," as well as the "classic" and "exclusive" interpretations in the history of reading the text of Matt 25:31–46, see Luz, 267–74.

22. Luz, 267–71.

23. Luz, 284.

Luke-Acts's Spirit-Led Eschatology

Our second example of theological readjustment regarding the nonoccurrence of the parousia is in Luke-Acts (AD 90), a groundbreaking attempt to produce the first account of salvation history connecting the ministries of John the Baptist, Jesus Christ, and the apostle Paul. Daniel Marguerat describes this two-volume work as a "diptych" in the sense that "Acts succeeds the gospel as a continuing story, with its necessary shifts."[24] Like the mirroring setup of a diptych, the Lukan work provokes a new style of reading, encouraging a "back-and-forth movement from the gospel to Acts and from Acts to the gospel."[25] Luke offers an unprecedented opportunity to reread the story of Jesus with the book of Acts in mind. We can, thus, imagine the interpretive possibilities such an innovative work can do to the question of the parousia.

Like Mark and Matthew, the Third Evangelist retains the account of the eschatological discourse in Luke 21. Like Matthew, Luke incorporates materials from Mark and Q while virtually relying on other traditional oral and written sources not found in Mark and Matthew. However, Luke's version of the eschatological discourse is surprisingly shorter than the Olivet Discourse of the first two gospel accounts. He cuts significant portions of the material and relocates them elsewhere (e.g. Luke 17 and 19). Unlike Matthew, Luke-Acts does not describe the problem as a "delay," which is a striking innovation in itself. While inheriting the early tradition of the imminent parousia, Luke steps back to rethink the pre-Markan and Markan apocalyptic language, cautioning against the arguably embarrassing emphasis on the *nearness of time*. More than Matthew's eschatological readjustment, Luke explicitly warns against the teaching of the imminent parousia: "Beware that you are not led astray; for many will come in my name and say, 'I am he!' and, '*The time is near!*' Do not go after them" (Luke 21:8).

Herman Hendrickx comments that Luke's warning possibly alludes to Daniel 7:22.[26] We can imagine that Luke's more sensitive readers in the first century, who had some familiarity with the pre-Markan tradition of the imminent parousia, must have been quite surprised by this passage. The text inevitably raises serious questions. Did Luke intend to caution his readers against Paul's emphasis on the swift coming of the Lord? Did he warn his

---

24. A fuller account of the argument is developed in Marguerat's chapter "The Unity of Luke-Acts: The Task of Reading," in Daniel Marguerat, *The First Christian Historian: Writing the "Acts of the Apostles"* (Cambridge: Cambridge University Press, 2004), 43–64.

25. Marguerat, *First Christian Historian*, 63–64.

26. Herman Hendrickx, *The End Will Not Be At Once*, Studies in the Synoptic Gospels (Makati: St. Paul's Publications, 1992), 27.

readers of Mark 1:14–15, which emphasized *fulfilled time* and the *nearness* of God's kingdom? What is more, Luke's revised eschatological account contradicts – although probably unintentionally – the passage in Revelation 1:3 (cf. 22:10), which states: "Blessed is the one who reads aloud the words of the prophecy, and blessed are those who hear and who keep what is written in it; for the *time is near*" (emphasis added).

This web of apocalyptic texts, reproduced in various life settings in the first century, contains the *Maranatha eschatology* against which Luke issues a stern warning. Then, in a provocative literary move that could easily have upset not a few apocalypticists, Luke walks past Mark and Matthew, signaling firmly but with deliberate uncertainty that the readers of his gospel will not see the day of the Son of Man (Luke 17:22–24):

> The days are coming when you will long to see one of the days of the Son of Man, and you will not see it. They will say to you, "Look there!" or "Look here!" Do not go, do not set off in pursuit. For as the lightning flashes and lights up the sky from one side to the other, so will the Son of Man be in his day.

Moreover, Luke also differs from Mark concerning the coming kingdom of God. Let us consider, for instance, how Luke-Acts handles the usual imminent expectation of God's kingdom. Luke is more than aware that the people longed for God's intervention and salvation. They were looking for concrete signs as to when this kingdom would break in. But Luke intentionally counters this assumption in Luke 17:20–21:

> Once Jesus was asked by the Pharisees when the kingdom of God was coming, and he answered, "The kingdom of God is not coming with things that can be observed; nor will they say, 'Look, here it is!' or 'There it is!' For, in fact, the kingdom of God is [hidden?] among you."

This passage is somewhat enigmatic. Is this Luke's version of the Markan messianic secret? The Lukan Jesus confronts the usual apocalyptic obsession with concrete signs. This literary strategy seems to be Luke's way to arrest the growth of unhealthy preoccupations concerning visible signs. However, Luke replaces it with a virtually enigmatic statement. What exactly does it mean that the "kingdom of God is among you"?

The book of Acts offers another clue to figure out Luke's eschatology. First, the resurrected Christ appeared to the disciples preaching God's kingdom (Acts 1:1–3). Then, Jesus instructed the disciples to wait in Jerusalem for the Father's promise, referring to the baptism of the Holy Spirit (Acts 1:4–5). We should note that Luke puts together Jesus's kingdom proclamation and the baptism of the Holy Spirit. But why make such a connection? What has God's kingdom to do with the baptism of the Holy Spirit? This strategy must have been enigmatic, as evident in the followers' response in the next verse: "They asked him, 'Lord, is this the time when you will restore the kingdom to Israel?'" (1:6).

This question is significant since they were under Roman occupation. In this context, the expectation of God's mighty intervention to redeem the nation from oppression is reasonable. In Luke's gospel, we recall that the disciples, represented by the two men on the road to Emmaus, pinned their hopes on Jesus: "We had hoped that [Jesus] was the one to redeem Israel" (Luke 24:21). However, from Luke's perspective, the disciples had missed the point about Jesus. The "kingdom" proclaimed by Jesus had to do more immediately with the promise of the Holy Spirit and only remotely with the actual political restoration of Israel's kingdom. Jesus replied:

> It is not for you to know the times or periods that the Father has set by his own authority. But you will receive power when the Holy Spirit has come upon you; and you will be my witnesses in Jerusalem, in all Judea and Samaria, and to the ends of the earth. (vv. 7–8)

The Lukan perspective expressed in Jesus's reply is instructive. Jesus could have aligned with Mark's gospel and affirmed that the "kingdom" they were waiting for was *near*. But that is not the answer we find in Acts. Consistent with Luke's warning against being obsessed with signs, the Lukan Jesus discouraged the disciples from yielding to the temptation to speculate about things only "the Father has set by his own authority." As such, Luke's Jesus deliberately avoided the retrospectively awkward apocalyptic speculation, suggesting it was simply not possible to know for sure.

However, if the inbreaking of the kingdom of God is beyond human knowledge, then why did the resurrected Jesus continue to proclaim God's kingdom? This question helps to bring out the Lukan eschatological flavor. First, Jesus proclaims God's kingdom by emphasizing *the coming of the Spirit* at Pentecost. Then, in Acts 2:17–21, Peter, now filled with the Holy Spirit, picks this up by quoting Joel's prophecy of how in the "last days" the Spirit of God will fall upon all flesh, so that before the "coming of the Lord" they will prophesy, see visions, and dream dreams. Peter's testimony exemplifies the task of "witnessing" that the Lukan Jesus emphasized before his ascension

(Acts 1:8). Thus, this addition of Pentecost, not found in Mark and Matthew, is what makes Luke's version of eschatology innovative and unique.

Nevertheless, Luke reaffirms that Jesus will come again in the same way they saw him ascend (Acts 1:9–11). This passage is evidence that Luke may have expected the Lord's return in the lifetime of his readers. But that is not precisely what Luke says. Overall, the Lukan work avoids any prediction or expectation of the *nearness* of the parousia. "Doubtless," says Hendrickx, "one can no longer speak of an expectation of the *temporal* nearness of the end in Luke."[27] Luke does not subscribe to the Matthean "delay" to explain the nonoccurrence of the parousia. In Luke-Acts, the parousia looks more like an event that will occur indefinitely in the future, akin to a perpetual deferral.[28]

Luke's eschatology redirects the readers' attention away from an obsession focused on apocalyptic speculation about the future. Instead of pumping up the people's expectations to wait eagerly for God's mighty intervention, the parting words of Jesus focus explicitly on the *Spirit's coming*. In this way, Luke's "Spirit-led" eschatology qualifies the imminent parousia. Thus, like Matthew's gospel, Luke modified the *Maranatha eschatology*. But unlike Matthew, Luke did not see the need to explain the "delay of the parousia," for the simple reason that, from the perspective of the Lukan salvation history, "the end will not be at once."[29]

In Acts, the point of the Holy Spirit's coming had to do with "witnessing." The Holy Spirit transforms the disciples, and they become witnesses taking up the universal mission, from Jerusalem to the ends of the world. But there is a problem because, since the Age of Exploration and down to the modern period, Christian missions have often accompanied political expansions. Thus, this contemporary appropriation of Christian missions can obscure rather than clarify the Lukan meaning of the passage. We must recall Marguerat's proposal to regard Luke-Acts as a literary diptych to avoid this problem. Thus, I propose that the invitation to become *"Spirit-filled" witnesses* (Acts 1:8) must have reminded Luke's readers of an earlier story where they would find a man who was also a *Spirit-filled witness to God's reign*. That is the story of the Lukan Jesus, who, filled with the power of the Spirit, began his teaching ministry (Luke 4:14–21). But there is more to this Lukan technique. Luke 4:14–21 is precisely

---

27. Hendrickx, *The End Will Not Be At Once*, 122.

28. The term "perpetual deferral" is also used in Christopher M. Hays et al. to refer to the delay of the consummation in 2 Peter. See Hays, *When the Son of Man Didn't Come*, 87.

29. This is the main emphasis of Hendrickx which he chose as the title of his exegetical monograph on Luke 21. See Hendrickx, *The End Will Not Be At Once*, 28–29.

where the reader familiar with the older version of the story would expect to see an emphasis on the proclamation about *the nearness of God's kingdom* (cf. Mark 1:14–15). But surprisingly, that is not what we see in Luke. Instead of emphasizing the *nearness* of God's kingdom, Luke underscores the *Spirit-filled* nature of the ministry of Jesus, suggesting that the good news of God's kingdom is something that Jesus *lived out* – by bringing the good news to the poor, and working to release the captives, to heal the blind, and to emancipate the oppressed, which is the way forward to show the Lord's favor (Luke 4:18–19).

In Mark, Jesus began his ministry by proclaiming, with apocalyptic urgency, the *coming* of the mysterious kingdom. In Luke, Jesus surprisingly begins his ministry with the reading of Isaiah's scroll, where he says in effect: "As anointed by the *Spirit*, my vocation *now* is to proclaim an exodus for those whose lives are in bondage." The drama is enhanced further when he adds: "Today this scripture has been fulfilled in your hearing" (Luke 4:21). The advantage of reading Luke-Acts as a diptych is that it helps us see the connection of these words to his final message immediately before the ascension story. Shifting back to Acts 1:8, we now see Luke's reinvention of tradition when he has Jesus practically say: "My *Spirit-filled* vocation to proclaim freedom is now your vocation when the Spirit comes at Pentecost." Thus, Luke-Acts effectively moves beyond Mark by departing from the older apocalyptic speculations about the parousia and the imminent arrival of God's kingdom. While Luke's two-volume work retains the belief in the coming of the Lord, the overall emphasis shifts from *waiting* to one of *becoming* (like Luke's Jesus) *Spirit-filled witnesses*, demonstrating God's kingdom by working *daily* to release the captives, heal the blind, and emancipate the oppressed. In this sense, Luke-Acts resonates with Matthew's "ethical eschatology."

John's Poimaine *Eschatology*

Our exploration of the parousia is not yet over. We finally turn to the contribution of the Gospel of John (AD 90–100), which arguably offers the most surprising eschatology in the entire New Testament.[30] So far, we have learned that the Synoptic Gospels retained the parousia, but not without modifications. The parousia is central in Mark 13, and it appears again, albeit in modified forms, in Matthew 24–25 and Luke 21. But John surprisingly omits the so-called Olivet Discourse. Instead of the Olivet Discourse, what we find

---

30. My reading of John's gospel has immensely benefited from the sustained conversation I had with the Filipino theologian Professor Lorenzo Bautista.

in John is the Farewell Discourse (John 14–17). Why is this so? If the Synoptic Gospels saw it essential to retain "the coming of the Son of Man in power and glory," why is it absent from the Fourth Gospel?

The short answer is because John wrote in a different setting toward the end of the first century, addressing a fundamental question not discussed in the Synoptic Gospels. Instead of emphasizing the parousia "in power and glory," we notice that John identifies a different event he regards as "glorious." Instead of the typical glorious parousia, John *reinterprets* the death of Jesus as the "glorious" event. In Jesus's death, John sees a fundamental insight into the kind of life worth emulating:

> The hour has come for the Son of Man to be glorified.... Unless a grain of wheat falls into the earth and dies, it remains just a single grain; but if it dies, it bears much fruit. Those who love their life lose it, and those who hate their life in this world will keep it for eternal life. Whoever serves me must follow me, and where I am, there will my servant be also. (John 12:23–26)

Indeed, we see the Son of Man in John's gospel. But, unlike in the Synoptic Gospels, the Son of Man's "glory" in John is *not* in the context of the imminent parousia of the Olivet Discourse. Instead, Jesus's glorious *death* has now become the proper context of discipleship. Thus, rather than seeing the Son of Man's *glory* in the parousia, John redirects his readers to see the *glory* in Jesus's death, which is now a gospel invitation to a *death sentence*.

We can imagine that John's reinterpretation of the Son of Man's glory may not have satisfied the expectations of his early readers. The only thing that would satisfy them would be the chance to experience something more ethereal, like the coming of the Son of Man in power and the transcendental experience of seeing God face to face. This longing for God's intervention is what we find in Philip's question in John 14:8: "Philip said to him, 'Lord, show us the Father, and we will be satisfied.'"

Philip's request sounds like the dramatic *Maranatha eschatology*, a prayer and painful wish for God to intervene mightily. John's gospel seems to reveal that it was not apparent even for the early Christians to gain a fundamental insight into the meaning of Jesus's life and death. John portrays Philip as fundamentally clueless:

> Jesus said to him, "Have I been with you all this time, Philip, and you still do not know me? Whoever has seen me has seen the Father. How can you say, 'Show us the Father'? Do you not believe that I am in the Father and the Father is in me? The words that I

say to you I do not speak on my own; but the Father who dwells in me does his works. Believe me that I am in the Father and the Father is in me; but if you do not, then believe me because of the works themselves. Very truly, I tell you, the one who believes in me will also do the works that I do and, in fact, will do greater works than these, because I am going to the Father. (John 14:9–12)

By the end of the first century, John's audience had to confront a grim fact: How would they now come to terms with the painful *absence* of Jesus without any sign of his return? Instead of encouraging his readers to wait for the imminent parousia of the Olivet Discourse, John boldly replaced this with the Farewell Discourse (John 14–17). In the Farewell Discourse, the disciples' grief mirrors the grief of John's readers. Thus, to address this profound sorrow, John reinterprets the final days of Jesus together with his disciples. In this revision, Jesus leaves the disciples with a word of assurance: "I tell you the truth: it is to your advantage that I go away, for if I do not go away, the Advocate will not come to you; but if I go, I will send him to you" (John 16:7). For John, Jesus had to die, and he had to go (16:10). Nevertheless, this *absence* of Jesus is the essential condition for the Spirit to come. In this way, we may observe that John's reworking of the tradition, emphasizing the Spirit's coming, resonates with Luke's Pentecost but is told in a fundamentally different way.

The death and eventual absence of Jesus are central to John's understanding of the gospel. Jesus's death, which must have been more than a source of profound disorientation for the early Christians, has finally become a profound Johannine message of what it means to *believe* and *live* meaningfully as followers of Jesus. In John 17:4, Jesus prays to the Father: "I glorified you on earth by finishing the work that you gave me to do." Here, Jesus's life and death, implied in the phrase "I glorified you on earth," is the commitment to finish the work of God. Thus, before Jesus died on the cross, his final words, in John's version (but not in Mark, Matthew, or Luke), were: "It is finished" (John 19:30).

But where is the imminent parousia in John? Where is the Son of Man who comes in power and glory? It should be clear by now that John does not retain the apocalyptic language of the parousia. Instead of the Olivet Discourse, which he omits, we have seen that John spends more time developing the Farewell Discourse (John 14–17). Thus, one of the more crucial highlights for John is that Jesus had *finished* God's work. Now it is the disciples' turn to do the work of God and, likewise, to finish it. This commitment of taking up Jesus's burden, which is a vital point in John's gospel, is also found in the Synoptic Gospels. But John expands this tradition even further. In John's resurrection story, for example, Jesus appears to the disciples, saying: "'Peace be with you. As the Father has sent me, so I send you.' When he had said this, he breathed on them and said to them, 'Receive the Holy Spirit'" (John 20:21–22).

But the more dramatic example of this revision is found in the Johannine story of Peter. I propose that this story further brings out the meaning of the Farewell Discourse. In John 13:36–37, Peter says, "Lord, where are you going?" But Jesus enigmatically replies that Peter *cannot* follow him. To which Peter responds: "Lord, why can I not follow you now? I will lay down my life for you." But the embarrassing story handed down by the gospel tradition is that Peter denied Jesus three times.

In John's final chapter (John 21:15–17), the resurrected Jesus appears to Peter. And after all the embarrassing moments and painful events they have gone through together, Jesus three times categorically asks: "Do you love me?" Each time, Peter replies, "Yes, Lord, and you know it." And each time, Jesus responds with either *Boske* or *Poimaine*,[31] which in English is "feed" or "tend." What is the Fourth Gospel doing in developing this unique material, totally absent from the Synoptic Gospels? Why is Peter's love of Jesus linked to the popular pastoral image of *feeding* and *tending*? Why is there a firm emphasis on *Poimaine* instead of *Maranatha*?

John 10 offers a further clue. Here we find the story of Jesus as the good shepherd. Why would he not do the sheep's feeding, tending, and nurturing if he is the good shepherd? After all, that is his job! Why does he, in John 21, hand that burden over to Peter? The usual reading of John 10 restricts the good shepherd's image to Jesus. "I am the good shepherd" (John 10:11). It is Jesus who came to the world to enhance life. Therefore, the typical reading usually misses John's literary technique, making us unable to see that John 10 should enrich the overall sense of John 21. Once we observe this, we discover that the erratic disciple who denied Jesus three times is now, in John 21, called to exercise the love of the good shepherd. Thus, we may now see that the Fourth Gospel's final eschatological contribution is not so much about a powerless bunch of people waiting for a mighty God to deliver them from their powerlessness. Unlike Paul, Mark, Revelation, and Matthew, John's gospel is, surprisingly, *not a Maranatha eschatology*. Instead, John bequeaths an "empowering farewell eschatology," leading one to act like the good shepherd, the exact opposite of

---

31. The Greek text has two forms: *Boske, Poimaine*, and back to *Boske*. See Barbara Aland, Kurt Aland, Johannes Karavidopoulos, Carlo M. Martini, and Bruce Metzger, eds., *The Greek New Testament* (Stuttgart: Deutsche Bibelgesellschaft, 2001). *Boske ta arnia mou* (v. 15); *Poimaine ta probata mou* (v. 16); *Boske ta probata mou* (v. 17).

killing, stealing, and destroying lives (John 10:7–10). Thus, to love Jesus means to live dangerously in this world. John's readers must have realized that they would most likely find themselves standing against the destructive forces if they loved *as Jesus, the good shepherd, loves*. In short, Peter, who probably mirrors the many erratic disciples in the Johannine community, finally learns that following Christ is a death sentence (John 21:18–19). While there is a hint of the parousia in John 21:22, it is vague and abrupt, making it difficult to interpret with total confidence. In John's final chapter, what stands out are the words of the good shepherd, who says, "Follow me!" In other words: "Bear the burden of the good shepherd." Thus, we may now describe the eschatological transition in the gospels especially as a movement from *Maranatha* to one that we may term *Poimaine*, emphasizing the disciples' commitment and resolve to embody Jesus's ethic of love.

Were the New Testament Writers Wrong about Jesus's Parousia? Critical and Pastoral Remarks

I write this chapter within the evangelical tradition and thus I am fully aware that this study can be rather unsettling because the theological modifications we have observed above suggest that the biblical writers erred in their expectation of the coming of the Lord. Perhaps the uneasiness is partly caused by the way evangelicals generally regard the Bible as the word of God. If we are not careful, this commonly held belief can be rather misleading because it might inadvertently turn the Bible into a primarily "divine" document, as though it fell straight from the sky. Mainstream evangelicalism has resisted and continues to oppose this distorted view of the Bible by affirming that the Bible is God's word but qualifying it further that it is God's word in *human words*. In general, mainstream Christianity is not prepared to diminish the human agency involved in producing the biblical texts. It is certainly a mistake to claim that the biblical writers were either superhuman or subhuman. It is equally erroneous to claim that the Bible is divinely inspired and therefore there is nothing human about it. While evangelicals continue to believe in the notion of the divine inspiration of Scripture, they must come to terms with the fact that the Bible *remains* fully – not less or beyond – human.[32] And since this

---

32. For excellent discussions on biblical inspiration within the evangelical tradition, see I. H. Marshall, *Biblical Inspiration* (Vancouver: Regent College Publishing, 2004), and Paul J. Achtemeier, *The Inspiration of Scripture: Problems and Proposals* (Philadelphia: Westminster, 1981). For a Filipino attempt to propose a versatile approach to handling biblical inspiration and authority that takes into account the contribution of biblical criticism, see Lorenzo C.

is fundamental to the nature of Scripture, we are duty bound to respect this in the way we study and use the Bible today. Regardless of how one defines divine inspiration, it is unacceptable to subscribe to the notion that eradicates or downplays the fundamental human elements that shaped the Bible. In the first place, it is impossible to talk of divine inspiration without these human elements because, at its most basic level, the Bible itself does not have a "divine language" apart from human language. The biblical writers could only use the available languages of the day, notably Hebrew, Aramaic, and Greek, which are all human languages and should be respected and studied alongside their historical and cultural moorings. There is absolutely nothing new in restating this elementary observation about the nature of Scripture. Nevertheless, it is a sober reminder that in the production of the Bible, God *did not* bypass the limits of literature, culture, and history. Therefore, the discipline of critical hermeneutics employed here intuitively interacts with the sacred texts, moving only along the path hinted at by the biblical evidence.

However, it is possible that readers may still find the outcome of this chapter rather unsettling. Doesn't this chapter suggest that some of the biblical writers made a mistake concerning the expectation of the parousia? To be sure, we may generally assume that the New Testament writers were honest and sincere in their expectation of the imminence of the parousia. Yet, as observed above, there is a movement within the New Testament, from an initial expectation of an imminent return (Paul and Mark), to an approach where the apocalyptic urgency is noticeably less (Luke-Acts). While the results of scholarly research may not always sit well with Christian orthodoxy, the anxiety that this tension creates should not obscure the practical gains of the method. In particular, we should be encouraged to read the New Testament texts as part of the wider whole, which encourage us to live lives of faith, hope and love in eager anticipation of the coming kingdom, rather than reaching for isolated proof texts to justify our expectations of the timing.

I suggest two crucial pastoral implications arising from this study. The first is that, through the critical method, evangelicals can begin more fully to appreciate the mystery and ambiguity of the parousia. Evangelicals must come to terms with the fact that there is much that they cannot know for sure about the belief in the Lord's coming. This realization may be a good sign that evangelicals are serious about the importance of intellectual honesty when

---

Bautista, "The Bible: Servant in the Formation of Communities of Faith," in *Doing Theology in the Philippines*, ed. John D. Suk (Quezon City: Asian Theological Seminary; and Manila: OMF Literature, 2005).

dealing with the New Testament evidence. At the same time, it guards them against getting too excited and overconfident about their assumptions. The second and most crucial gain concerns the potential of this study to redirect evangelical readers back to the centrality of Jesus's ethic of love, as we have seen in our discussions on the Gospel of Matthew, Luke-Acts, and John. One can argue that even Paul's epistles, when carefully reviewed, may guide us back to Jesus's love command (cf. Gal 5:13–15; Rom 13:8–10), despite the strong emphasis on the imminent parousia. While evangelicals may not know the exact nature and timing of the parousia, they need not feel spiritually or theologically incapacitated. On the contrary, the outcome of this study can equip evangelicals to avoid the one-sided and otherworldly view of Felipe. This can be empowering because, regardless of their assumptions about the parousia, they might begin to realize that what matters most is for disciples to be like Jesus: living compassionately and aligning themselves courageously with God's will.

The *Pater Noster*, the prayer that Jesus taught his disciples, nicely sums up our present investigation of the New Testament's parousia by underscoring our nonnegotiable ethical duty as followers of Christ today. In this prayer (Matt 6:9–13), we can observe that the petition for God's reign to become a reality on earth proceeds to the line that says: "Your will be done, on earth as it is in heaven." As we conclude this study, we may need to re-emphasize the obvious but crucial point that the *Pater Noster* is the daily prayer of the earthly disciples of Jesus. By praying the *Pater Noster*, the disciples are offering their lives *each day* to do God's will on earth as it is in heaven. This remarkable commitment underscores a wholesome faith that seeks first the justice and righteousness inherent in the coming kingdom of God (Matt 6:33).

Bibliography

Achtemeier, Paul J. *The Inspiration of Scripture: Problems and Proposals*. Philadelphia: Westminster, 1981.

Adams, Edward. "The Coming of the Son of Man in Mark's Gospel." *Tyndale Bulletin* 56, no. 1 (2005): 39–61.

Aland, Barbara, Kurt Aland, Johannes Karavidopoulos, Carlo M. Martini, and Bruce Metzger, eds. *The Greek New Testament*. Stuttgart: Deutsche Bibelgesellschaft, 2001.

Bautista, Lorenzo C. "The Bible: Servant in the Formation of Communities of Faith." In *Doing Theology in the Philippines*, ed. John D. Suk, 51–64. Quezon City: Asian Theological Seminary; and Manila: OMF Literature, 2005.

Cross, Frank Moore. *Canaanite Myth and Hebrew Epic: Essays in the History of the Religion of Israel*. Cambridge, MA: Harvard University Press, [1973] 1997.

Hankins, Barry. *American Evangelicals: A Contemporary History of a Mainstream Religious Movement*. Plymouth: Rowman & Littlefield, 2008.

Harris, Stephen L. *The New Testament: A Student's Introduction*. 8th ed. New York: McGraw-Hill Education, 2015.

Hays, Christopher M. *When the Son of Man Didn't Come: A Constructive Proposal on the Delay of the Parousia*. Minneapolis: Fortress, 2016.

Hendrickx, Herman. *The End Will Not Be at Once*. Studies in the Synoptic Gospels. Makati: St. Paul's Publications, 1992.

Koester, Craig R. *Revelation: A New Translation with Introduction and Commentary*. Anchor Yale Bible. New Haven: Yale University Press, 2014.

Luz, Ulrich. *Matthew 1–7*. Hermeneia: A Critical and Historical Commentary on the Bible. Minneapolis: Fortress, 2007.

———. *Matthew 21–28*. Hermeneia: A Critical and Historical Commentary on the Bible. Minneapolis: Augsburg Fortress, 2005.

Marguerat, Daniel. *The First Christian Historian: Writing the "Acts of the Apostles."* Cambridge: Cambridge University Press, 2004.

Marshall, I. H. *Biblical Inspiration*. Vancouver: Regent College Publishing, 2004.

Schweitzer, Albert. *The Quest of the Historical Jesus: A Critical Study of Its Progress from Reimarus to Wrede*. Baltimore: Johns Hopkins University Press, 1998.

Wright, N. T. *Jesus and the Victory of God*. Vol. 2 of *Christian Origins and the Question of God*. Minneapolis: Fortress, 1996.

8

Shepherding a Coalition for Justice

Carlo Diño

Introduction

I was Convenor of the Coalition for Justice (CFJ), a broad multisectoral coalition that was formed to defend democracy and judicial independence. CFJ was actively involved in the public defense of the former Chief Justice Maria Lourdes Sereno during her impeachment[1] and quo warranto[2] cases between 2017 and 2018. My participation in CFJ was grounded on my convictions about the role of Christians in society, both as citizens of a democratic republic and as prophets to the nation.

This chapter aims to help our evangelical brothers and sisters appreciate that being a follower of Jesus brings us to direct engagement with critical issues in society. We need to be prepared to respond based on a more thoughtful consideration of what the Lord requires of us as his people.[3]

In this chapter, I will explain why I believe that the move to oust Chief Justice Sereno was not only a threat to democracy but a social and political evil, and why the church needed to perform its prophetic role in response. After this, I will recount how the CFJ was formed and how it exercised a prophetic

---

1. Impeachment is an expressed power of the Congress of the Philippines to formally charge impeachable government officials, including Members of the Supreme Court. See 1987 Philippine Constitution, Art. XI.

2. The special civil action of quo warranto is a writ of inquiry under the Rules of Court that determines whether an individual or an entity has a legal right to a public office, position, or franchise. See Rules of Court, Section 1, Rule 66.

3. Mic 6:8.

role during its time. I will close with the lessons I learned as we formed and shepherded the Coalition for Justice.

The Threat to Democracy and the Church's Prophetic Role

I believe in my heart that the Philippines is blessed by God to be a democracy. The country was liberated from a dictatorship and transitioned into a constitutional democracy more than thirty years ago. What could have been a bloody civil war after a failed coup attempt against the Marcos government became a bloodless revolution when an estimated 2 million Filipinos flocked to EDSA and forced the Marcos family to flee.[4] I believe this to have been a miracle, possible only by the grace of God. I consider the restoration of democracy and the freedom Filipinos enjoy today to be God's gifts to the Filipino people.

Democracy, however, is a fragile political system. Dr. Roberto Barredo, in chapter 5 of this book, "Duterte, Democracy, and Dissent," points out that because power "tends toward corruption and injustice," people in a democracy have a "tacit suspicion of power." The framers of the 1987 Philippine Constitution understood this and installed safeguards to preserve democracy. The Constitution clearly defined the responsibilities and limits of authority of elected government officials.[5] It delineated the division of powers and laid down a system of "checks and balances," for the purpose of exacting accountability from corrupt and abusive leaders. It was so designed to ensure that "no citizen, no authority, however exalted his official status in governance may be, is above the law."[6]

In his chapter, Dr. Barredo also correctly points out that the "primal burden and political obligation" to create what the Constitution aspires to be a more "just and humane society"[7] lies in the hands of the Filipino people. And yet, the majority of Filipinos are silent in the face of corruption and abuse of power. Democracy requires, and the Constitution expects, that the Filipino people be engaged in the affairs of all levels of government. Failure to do so is an

---

4. Monina Mercado, *People Power: An Eyewitness History – The Philippine Revolution of 1986* (Manila: J. B. Reuter, S. J. Foundation, 1986).

5. 1987 Constitution, Art. VI, VII, VIII, IX, X, XI, XII.

6. Felipe B. Miranda, "Conceptualizing and Measuring Modern Democracy," in *Chasing the Wind: Assessing Philippine Democracy*, eds. Felipe B. Miranda and Temario C. Rivera (Quezon City: Commission on Human Rights and United Nations Development Program, 2016), 9.

7. 1987 Constitution, Preamble.

abdication of a sacred responsibility. To me, it is like selling our democratic "birthright" for "a bowl of soup."[8]

We may look at civic participation as part of Christ's call for us to be salt and light in society, and to participate in the *missio Dei*, God's mission to restore all things to his will and establish justice in the world.[9] Christians are not meant to disengage from society. The presence of social evil requires vigilance and active engagement by Christians as citizens. As they do so, they can also exercise their prophetic role in society.

Dr. Annelle Sabanal confirms this in her chapter 2, "Perspectives on Power and Politics," where she explains that Old Testament prophets not only concerned themselves with religious matters, but also paid close attention to the social and political events of their time. It is the prophet's role to proclaim God's will to do justice and righteousness in society. This call goes out not only against the active commission of injustice, but also against a passive stance and silence in the face of such injustice.

Christians all over the world and throughout history have performed this role and have spoken out against the powers of their time.[10] We find faithful prophets even in Philippine history. From the time of the Spanish

---

8. Filipinos' abdication of civic responsibility is similar to Esau trading away to his brother Jacob his birthright as Isaac's firstborn in Gen 25:29–34.

9. Waldron Scott, *Bring Forth Justice* (Carlisle: Paternoster, 1997), xv–xvi.

10. See (1) Scott, *Bring Forth Justice*, 108, for an account of how early Christian leaders upheld the dignity of slaves and spoke out against unjust economic structures; (2) Eric Metaxas, *Amazing Grace: William Wilberforce and the Heroic Campaign to End Slavery* (New York: Harper Collins, 2007), for William Wilberforce's role in the abolition of slavery in the British Empire; (3) Heath W. Carter, *Union Made: Working People and the Rise of Social Christianity in Chicago* (Oxford: Oxford University Press, 2015), 31, for the work of Protestant ministers in the US Northern states against slavery before the US Civil War; (4) Eric Metaxas, *Bonhoeffer: Pastor, Martyr, Prophet, Spy – A Righteous Gentile vs. the Third Reich* (Nashville: Thomas Nelson, 2010) for Dietrich Bonhoeffer's opposition to the Nazi regime in Germany during World War II; (5) Mark A. Noll, *God and Race in American Politics: A Short History* (Princeton, NJ: Princeton University Press, 2008), 107, for Rev. Martin Luther King's role in the Civil Rights movement in the US during the 1950s and 1960s; (6) Anthony Balcomb, "From Apartheid to the New Dispensation: Evangelicals and the Democratization of South Africa," in *Evangelical Christianity and Democracy in Africa*, ed. Terence O. Ranger (Oxford: Oxford University Press, 2008), 204–17, for the role of South African Protestant and evangelical ministers in opposing apartheid.

colonization,[11] to the American occupation,[12] up to the Marcos regime,[13] and even following the EDSA revolution,[14] courageous members of the church have

---

11. See Kathy Nadeau, "Peasant Resistance and Religious Protests in Early Philippine Society: Turning Friars against the Grain," *Journal for the Scientific Study of Religion* 41, no. 1 (2002): 83, for the early Spanish friars' opposition to abuses by colonial officials in the late 1500s. It can be argued that some of our national heroes were prophets of their time, drawing on their faith in God to speak out against the abuses of the Spanish colonizers. See Andres Bonifacio, "Decalogue of the Duties of the Sons of the People" (1896). The "Decalogue" served as a manifesto of what the "Katipunan," the revolutionary movement started by Andres Bonifacio stood for. It was a list of duties and responsibilities to be followed by every Filipino who joined the movement. Bonifacio's decalogue reminds people of the biblical Ten Commandments. At the top of the list is "Love God full-heartedly." The second in the list is about the love of country: "Bear always in mind that the true love of God is love of Country, love which is also true love of man." This provides a justification to liberate the country rooted in the love for God, love for country and for its people. A copy of a translation of the decalogue can be found in Jim Richardson, "Andres Bonifacio, 'Katungkulang gagawin ng mga Z. Ll. B.' (The Decalogue), c. 1896," (http://www.kasaysayan-kkk.info/membership-documents/andres-bonifacio). See also, Apolinario Mabini, "The True Decalogue" (1898) and José Rizal, *El Filibusterismo* (Ghent, 1891). Apolinario Mabini served as one of the key advisers of Emilio Aguinaldo, the president of the revolutionary government that declared independence from Spanish rule. Mabini had the reputation of being the "brains of the Philippine revolution." He wrote "The True Decalogue" as an introduction to the Malolos Constitution of 1898. His decalogue articulated the ideals that Mabini believed the Philippine revolution should embody. The English translation of "The True Decalogue" can be found in Napoleon Jr., Mahinay Mabaquiao, "Mabini's 'true decalogue' and the morality of nationalism," Asia-Pacific Social Science Review 17(3) (2018), p.17-18. Available online at https://www.researchgate.net/publication/327688783_Mabini%27s_true_decalogue_and_the_morality_of_nationalism.

12. See Kenton J. Clymer, "Religion and American Imperialism: Methodist Missionaries in the Philippine Islands, 1899–1913," *Pacific Historical Review* 49, no. 1 (1980): 44–45, 50, for accounts of how the Protestant church served as a check against abuses by the American administrators during the American occupation of the Philippines. See also Robert Youngblood, "Church Opposition to Martial Law in the Philippines," *Asian Survey* 18, no. 5 (1978): 508, for how the Roman Catholic Church became deeply involved in the plight of the poor after World War II.

13. See the following: (1) Youngblood, "Church Opposition," 506, for accounts of how the Catholic Church remained the only institution to challenge the Marcos government after the declaration of martial law; (2) Al Tizon, *Transformation after Lausanne: Radical Evangelical Mission in Global-Local Perspective* (Oxford: Regnum, 2008), 197, for resistance efforts of Protestants under the NCCP; and (3) David Lim, "Consolidating Democracy: Filipino Evangelicals between People Power Events, 1986–2001," in *Evangelical Christianity and Democracy in Asia*, ed. David H. Lumsdaine (New York: Oxford University Press, 2009), 254–56, for resistance efforts by evangelical Christians.

14. See the following: (1) Tizon, *Transformation*, 172, for the church's opposition to the renewal of the US bases agreement; (2) also Antonio Moreno, "Engaged Citizenship: The Catholic Bishops' Conference of the Philippines (CBCP) in the Post-Authoritarian Philippines," in *Development, Civil Society and Faith-Based Organizations Bridging the Sacred and the Secular*, eds. Gerard Clarke and Michael Jennings (New York: Palgrave Macmillan, 2008), 129, on the church's opposition to Charter Change under the Ramos and Estrada administrations; (3) Lim, "Consolidating Democracy," 263, for the church's opposition to the corruption of the Estrada administration; and (4) Cesar Vicente P. Punzalan, *PCEC @50 (1965–2015): One Master, One Message, One Mission* (Makati City: Church Strengthening Ministry, 2016), 131–32, for how evangelical churches became involved in various social issues.

spoken truth to power and expressed opposition to their oppressive policies. For the former chair of the Philippine Council of Evangelical Churches (PCEC) Bishop Cesar Punzalan, "truth-telling" is an integral part of the ministry of the church. It involves "intersecting the truth claims of the gospel [with] current truth claims of the public square," and "[speaking] the mind of God in the public square, in the marketplace, in the media."[15]

It is through this lens that we need to look at the move to oust the former Chief Justice Maria Lourdes Sereno. An independent judiciary is a key institution of a democratic system. The constitutional mandate of the judicial branch of government is to uphold justice for all, most especially the poor. However, by the time Sereno was appointed Chief Justice in 2012, the institution was already in serious need of reform.[16]

A devout evangelical Christian, Chief Justice Sereno prioritized the implementation of the Judiciary Reforms Program,[17] to give the poor and marginalized sectors better access to justice. I speculate that these reforms had adverse effects on certain interest groups within and outside the judiciary and made Chief Justice Sereno politically vulnerable under the Duterte administration.

When President Rodrigo Duterte began issuing public threats against Chief Justice Sereno, and the Solicitor General initiated the process to remove her from office through quo warranto, it sent a "chilling message" to members of

---

15. Punzalan, *PCEC @50*, 40–41.

16. Various studies have assessed that the rule of law and judicial independence are relatively weak in the Philippines. The judiciary is tainted with politicization and corruption. Not only is there failure to give the poor access to justice, but there is also failure to guarantee due process. Arbitrary detention, disappearances, kidnappings, and abuse of suspects have become common. Lawyers and prosecutors have even been assassinated for simply doing their jobs. See Eric Vincent C. Batalla, Michelle Sta. Romana, and Karen Rodrigo, "The Judiciary under Threat," in *Routledge Handbook of the Contemporary Philippines*, eds. Mark R. Thompson and Eric Vincent C. Batalla (New York: Routledge, 2018), 141. See also Freedom House, "Freedom in the World 2020: Philippines," accessed 22 November 2020, https://freedomhouse.org/country/philippines/freedom-world/2020.

17. Chief Justice Sereno's Judiciary Reforms Program reduced the average duration of cases to three years, reduced the backlog of court cases, and gave the poor and marginalized groups better access to justice. The program facilitated the release of over five thousand Filipinos languishing in jail for petty crimes, computerized judicial processes and made them run more efficiently, and brought down the cost of filing small cases. See Asian Development Bank, *Philippines: Governance in Justice Sector Reform Program* (Mandaluyong City: Asian Development Bank, 2017), 2–5.

the judiciary and posed a threat to judicial independence.[18] This was a direct attack on a key pillar of democracy, and called for a prophetic response.

The Constitution itself provided us with "a whole range of political freedoms"[19] which serve as the platform for the church to perform its prophetic ministry.[20] If democracy is indeed a gift of God to the Filipino people, and a key pillar of democracy is under attack, then I believe Christians need to utilize these "political freedoms" to exercise their prophetic responsibility to call to task those behind this attack.

Coalition for Justice as Prophetic Expression

This was the context of my participation in the Coalition for Justice (CFJ). It was an expression of my prophetic role in society as a Christian. CFJ marched under the banner of "Katotohanan, Katarungan, Katuwiran" (Truth, Justice, Righteousness), values which Psalm 89:14 declares to be the foundation of God's rule.[21]

The broad objective of the CFJ was to put up a defense for democratic institutions. The specific objective of the campaign, however, given the vulnerability of the Chief Justice at that time, was to make it politically costly to remove her from office. This required a show of force.

Initially, my main task was to seek support for Chief Justice Sereno's cause from our evangelical brothers and sisters. Initial support came from a group of evangelical leaders that convened under Palawan 5.[22] But the majority of evangelical pastors were reluctant to be engaged. I found this unfortunate

---

18. Diego García-Sayán, "Judicial Independence in Philippines Is under Threat, Says UN Human Rights Expert," United Nations Human Rights, 1 June 2018, accessed 23 November 2020, https://www.ohchr.org/EN/NewsEvents/Pages/DisplayNews.aspx?NewsID=23163&LangID=E.

19. Miranda, "Measuring Modern Democracy," 7.

20. The Constitution provides the people with the right to file complaints against any public official, office, or agency in Art. XI, Sec. 13, and against human rights violations in Art. XIII, Sec. 18. More importantly, it provided the people with the avenue to call on erring officials to "repent" and "turn from their evil ways" through the right of free speech, to peaceful assembly, and to petition government for redress of grievances, in Art. II, Sec. 4.

21. "*Righteousness* and *justice* are the foundation of Your throne; Mercy and *truth* go before Your face" (Ps 89:14 NKJV; emphasis added).

22. Signatories to the Palawan 5 statement were Bishop Noel Pantoja of the Philippine Council of Evangelical Churches (PCEC), Bishop Dan Balais of Intercessors for the Philippines (IFP), Bishop Leo Alconga of Free Mission Churches, Philippines (FMCP), and Bro. Wyden King of NFS Ministries. They made a strong call "on our fellow citizens to stand with Chief Justice Sereno in the face of this partisan attack on judicial independence. We ask our people to echo her call to come to the defense of the Rule of Law."

because the person under attack was a "sister in the Lord," the same person whom the evangelical community had lauded when she was appointed Chief Justice in 2012. At a critical time when her position was under threat, most of the evangelical leaders were suddenly silent, and could not give her their support in public.

We had to look for other groups that were willing to stand alongside us. So, we reached out to our Protestant brothers and sisters, who gave full support to the call to defend judicial independence. We also reached out to influential groups in the Catholic Church, and they too gave their active support.

But our numbers were not great enough. For the campaign to be effective, we needed a show of force. The only way we could do this was to link up with other groups with a similar agenda.[23] Many groups from various ideological perspectives responded to our call. What we had in common was our shared commitment to democracy, and the belief that judicial independence had to be defended.

I have been asked many times why we associated with activists. My answer is that the gospel requires us to be "activists" as well. An activist is simply someone who campaigns to bring about change in society. That is what the gospel requires us to do. The good news is that people who work for justice are not far from God's kingdom, because they too are working with the poor, giving voice to the voiceless, fighting against injustice, and resisting forces that oppress the poor.

We need to accept that we live in a pluralistic society[24] with people who embrace all kinds of beliefs and ideologies. We are called to live in peace with them. As we proclaim the lordship of Jesus, we need to interact with them on crucial issues of common concern. On certain occasions it is appropriate to use biblical language to express our views. But in most cases, we discuss issues with them using language and arguments that can be generally understood, without straying from our convictions.

Dr. Thomas Johnson of the World Evangelical Alliance said it best:

> The biblical message pushes us to be radicals, deeply dissatisfied with our societies as they currently exist. The biblical message

---

23. Ronald D. Holmes, "Local Governments, Civil Society, Democratization, and Development," in *Chasing the Wind: Assessing Philippine Democracy*, eds. Felipe B. Miranda and Temario C. Rivera (Quezon City: Commission on Human Rights and United Nations Development Program, 2016), 115.

24. Ronald J. Sider, *The Scandal of Evangelical Politics: Why Are Christians Missing the Chance to Really Change the World?* (Grand Rapids, MI: Baker, 2008), 39.

is much more than a message of protest against the deep-seated evils of our world, but it should not be less. Similarly, although it should also be many more things, the Christian community should not be less than a community of dissidents, talking about what is wrong with our world and offering solutions. And we should especially be offering a message of reconciliation with God and with our neighbours to our fellow dissidents who do not yet believe in Christ.[25]

Christians who seek to serve the poor, and who seek to address the injustice and corruption of the powerful, cannot help but find themselves on the same side of the fence as most political activists. We differ in our foundational beliefs, but we share the same platforms where we seek to be heard.

There is nothing illegal or immoral about this. We are all citizens of the Philippines. We are supposed to take advantage of the democratic space that the Constitution provides. If we fail to do this, people who do not know Christ will dominate that space, and we will be eased out of the public conversation. If we abdicate from this responsibility, we may find that the proclamation "Jesus the Messiah is Lord" will no longer be tolerated in the public sphere.

We had these things in mind when we organized the Coalition for Justice. At its height, CFJ was composed of more than eighty churches, faith-based organizations, and civil society groups. It brought together what I believe to be the most diverse collection of organizations, representing the broadest range of political and ideological positions – the Left, Left of Center, a variety of groups at the Center, and even the Right. It brought together Filipinos from a wide range of beliefs and religious traditions – Roman Catholics, Protestants, evangelicals, Muslims, and even atheists.

Within a period of seven months, the CFJ grew from an initial group of three hundred people who held a prayer rally at the Quezon Memorial Circle on 4 December 2017, to a large coalition that at its height mobilized as many as five thousand people protesting in front of the Supreme Court building.

Between March and July 2018, the CFJ led a sustained campaign to defend Chief Justice Sereno, judicial independence, and the rule of law. It organized at least twelve major protest activities in several locations within a span of four

---

25. Thomas K. Johnson, "The Protester, the Dissident and the Christian," *Evangelical Review of Theology* 44, no. 4 (2020): 295, accessed 5 November 2020, https://theology.worldea.org/evangelical-review-of-theology/.

months, from March to June 2018.²⁶ That was practically one protest activity per week. It gathered signatures of hundreds of prominent Filipinos for a statement of support for the beleaguered Chief Justice that was published in two major newspapers.²⁷ It mobilized high-profile lobby groups at the Senate.²⁸ It organized a month-long *lamay* or wake for the "death of democracy" in front of the Supreme Court Building from 1 to 31 May.²⁹ This was participated in by Roman Catholics, Protestants, and evangelicals. It held prayer vigils, candlelight vigils, prayer walks, a Jericho march, Catholic masses, and evangelical praise and worship services in the streets.³⁰

The campaign culminated on 19 June 2018, when the Supreme Court's quo warranto decision became final, and "Champion of Justice" Sereno was welcomed by the Coalition of Justice to its fold.³¹

Lessons Learned from Shepherding the CFJ

After a seven-month-long campaign in coalition-building and mobilizing, the CFJ failed to prevent the removal of Chief Justice Sereno. I believe the institution of judicial independence was seriously compromised as a result. But in hindsight, we in the CFJ realized that it had not been a complete failure.

---

26. The Coalition for Justice organized twelve protest events within a span of four months: "Martsang Bayan: March for CJ" (Batasan Road QC, 6 March 2018); "CJS Press Conference" (UP Bahay Kalinaw, 12 March 2018); "Quo Warranto Ibasura" (Padre Faura, Manila, 20 March 2018); "Bantay Supreme Court, Biyaheng Baguio" (Baguio City, 9–10 April 2018); "Hustisya Para Kay CJ, Hustisya Para sa Lahat" (Padre Faura, Manila, 17 April 2018); "Hustisya Para Kay CJ, Hustisya Para sa Lahat" (Baguio City, 17 April 2018); "Hustisya Para Kay CJ, Hustisya Para sa Lahat" (SC Compound, Baguio City, 24 April 2018); QW Ibasura press conference (PRRM Quezon City, 9 May 2018); indignation rallies (Padre Faura, Katipunan, LB, Cebu, 11 May 2018); "Black Friday Protest" (Padre Faura, Timog, Katipunan, 18 May 2018); "Ipaglaban ang Katarungan" (Padre Faura, Manila, 5 June 2018); filing of opposition to candidacy of Justice Martirez for Ombudsman (18 June 2018).

27. "A Betrayal of Democracy," *Philippine Daily Inquirer*, 2 May 2018; *Philippine Star*, 7 May 2018.

28. CFJ leaders lobbied for support for Chief Justice Sereno's cause at the Philippine Senate on three occasions: 2 May 2018; 15 May 2018; and 30 May 2018.

29. "Dasal at Ayuno, Lamay sa Katarungan," Padre Faura, Manila, 1–31 May 2018.

30. "Stand with CJ Prayer Rally" (Quezon Memorial Circle, 4 December 2017); "Light for Justice" (Baguio City, 2–3 April 2018); "Prayer Walk @Merville" (Merville Subd., Paranaque City, 21 April 2018); "Wall of Light" (Padre Faura, Manila, 10 May 2018); "Jericho March for Justice" (Padre Faura, Manila, 11 May 2018).

31. "Kasama Ko Si CJ" (UP Bahay ng Alumni, 19 June 2018).

Through our sustained action during that period, we achieved our objective of making the removal of Chief Justice Sereno politically costly.[32]

Regardless of the results, putting together and shepherding the Coalition for Justice was an extremely rich and deeply moving experience. The following are a few lessons I learned from it.

1. Varied Emotions Drive Social Engagement

My experience in CFJ made me appreciate the value of emotions in civic engagement.[33] For many of our colleagues in the CFJ, anger and indignation were the dominant emotions. The CFJ attracted many people with deep resentments toward the present administration. For others, it was fear that the political situation would worsen if we failed to act. Some felt moral outrage at the efforts of administration allies to undermine judicial independence.

But I was neither angry nor fearful. What I felt was grief. Given my biblical understanding of sin, I know too well that corruption and abuse of power in government are irresistible. The sinful tendency is in every government official, the opportunities for corruption and abuse are ever present, and the systemic failure of accountability mechanisms in government is so pervasive that corruption and abuse of power become inevitable. And my heart grieves because of this.

What disturbs me deeply is the great chasm between the kind of human society God desires and the evil structures I see at work in government. I feel anguish, a longing for righteous rule to be established. It was this anguish and longing – and not anger – that motivated me to be involved in CFJ.

I did feel outrage whenever disturbing news about the impeachment and quo warranto cases came up. But the anger never lasted long, even as a feeling of abhorrence against the injustice of it all remained. Being surrounded by people who were in a prolonged state of deep anger evoked a sense of compassion and compelled me and other evangelicals in CFJ to focus on ministering to them spiritually.

---

32. During the period of the CFJ campaign, congressional allies of the Duterte administration ran out of time to push for the approval of Charter Change. Elections in 2019 proceeded as scheduled. It was also costly for the Speaker Pantaleon Alvarez, as he lost the speakership to former President Gloria Macapagal Arroyo in July 2018.

33. Jeff Goodwin, James M. Jasper, and Francesca Polletta, "Why Emotions Matter," in *Passionate Politics: Emotions and Social Movements*, eds. Jeff Goodwin, James M. Jasper, and Francesca Polletta (Chicago: University of Chicago Press, 2001), 5–10.

Beyond anger, fear, and grief, there was also love and genuine concern for one another. There was deep respect for one another in the context of shared experiences, even in shared suffering. There was joy in the shared struggle that bound us together and kept us going.

2. Creative Expressions of Prophetic Engagement

CFJ was not just about political rallies; it utilized other forms of prophetic engagement. We strived to integrate faith elements in our protest activities. We had prayer rallies, and we had ecumenical liturgy during rallies. Catholic masses were heard in the streets, as well as evangelical praise and worship celebrations. We held candlelit vigils. We had a Jericho march around the Supreme Court area. A group within CFJ staged a "wake" or *lamay* for the death of democracy. *Lamay* ran for one whole month in Padre Faura. It was the most creative form of prophetic expression carried out during our seven-month campaign.

Prophetic expressions are meant to be heard, and we were able to attract the attention of the media because of the varied forms of expression implemented by the CFJ.

3. Integrity of Shepherds

Holding together a coalition of various organizations with clashing political perspectives was difficult and nearly impossible. But the coalition held together because the CFJ Convenors were perceived by the CFJ member organizations to be "honest brokers."

As one of the Convenors of CFJ, I always had to be an impartial mediator. I had to make sure I did not favor one group over another. Years of pastoring a church with a diverse constituency prepared me for that role. The coalition members were willing to work together because we were perceived as fair in our dealings with each group, and that we did not have any political agenda other than what we officially declared.

4. Upholding Democratic Principles and Christian Values

CFJ was founded on the principles of justice and democracy. Our partners in the coalition might not have been motivated by the Christian faith, but they, too, recognized the rights and dignity of every person, and were willing to defend those rights. Shepherding the coalition required the Convenors to uphold the same values. We served the God of justice, so we needed to be just in our dealings. We had to recognize the right of each represented group to be heard. The opinion of one group, no matter how small, had to be given the same opportunity to be heard as that of the biggest group in the coalition.

Democracy is about citizen participation in decision-making. Decision-making requires informed citizens. Truth, therefore, is vital in an effective democracy. Because we serve Jesus who is the "truth" in the flesh, shepherding the coalition required us to be truthful in everything. Even when we had to speak painful truth to our colleagues in the CFJ, we spoke the truth in love.

We made decisions by consensus as much as possible, and by majority vote when necessary. Our decisions were binding on the group. At times I disagreed with the decisions of the group, but as long as these decisions did not impinge on my faith convictions I submitted to them and implemented them on behalf of the group.

5. Conflict Resolution and Peacemaking

Differences of opinion were bound to arise and discussions sometimes turned into heated arguments. This was the unavoidable consequence of leading a very broad coalition. CFJ was composed of major groups with deep, longstanding conflict with each other, and some with histories of hostile relations. We were always careful not to allow any argument to escalate. We had to ensure no group could hijack the overall agenda. We were careful to maintain the balance of power among the groups.

Because we served the Prince of Peace, Convenors had to be instruments of peace. We tried to sort out differences as best we could, striving as far as possible to be fair and impartial.

6. Proclaiming Jesus Christ to Secular Activists

It was challenging to bring the message of the gospel in a coalition representing a diversity of beliefs and ideological positions. Initially, the Christian message was drowned out by the clashing agendas of the various groups. What we did was to collaborate with other Christian groups to bring God's agenda to the table. We integrated prayer in all activities. We sought opportunities to point people to Christ. We made it clear to everyone that the reason why evangelicals were there was because Jesus is Lord, and his agenda of justice and righteousness in society was our agenda. And we always consciously sought to live up to what we proclaimed.

Dr. Maggay explains that evangelism is proclaimed within a certain context. It requires "a setting in which the things we say about Jesus become truly incarnate. The Word must take flesh."[34] Thus, whatever we proclaimed we needed to demonstrate. We advanced God's justice, and that meant we stood alongside them in the struggle against injustice.

7. Christian Citizenship

The most common objection to Christian participation in rallies is that political activism represents rebellion and disorder and is therefore sin. I believe this is a serious misappreciation of democracy and what is required of citizens in a republic.

Very few Christians, if ever, have read the Philippine Constitution, so many have no knowledge of our rights as citizens. Many do not understand that democracy requires active engagement by citizens to work. Some Christians even choose to ignore, and even tolerate, everything that is wrong with government, and incorrectly invoke the "separation of church and state."

I am personally disturbed by church leaders who associate closely with corrupt politicians. I am deeply ashamed of church leaders who receive money from politicians, as though they are too naive not to be aware that their loyalty is being bought. This is one of the reasons why these church leaders are silent when politicians commit illegal acts.

The church has a unique role of proclaiming the kingdom of God in Christ Jesus. That entails teaching society what is wrong and what is right in human affairs. Many churches and faith-based organizations have taken concrete steps to address the ills of society and have demonstrated the will of God by setting up institutions that provide services directly to the people.[35] But Christian social involvement does not end there. When the survival of the country's democratic institutions is at stake, Christians should not hesitate to use the freedoms provided by the Constitution. Filipino Christians are citizens of the Philippine Republic. We can and should go out into the streets, assemble in a peaceful and nonviolent manner, and speak out when the situation so requires.

---

34. Melba Maggay, *Transforming Society: Reflections on the Kingdom and Politics* (Quezon City: Institute for Studies in Asian Church and Culture, 2004), 27.

35. Nancy J. Davis and Robert V. Robinson, *Claiming Society for God: Religious Movements and Social Welfare in Egypt, Israel, Italy, and the United States* (Bloomington, IN: Indiana University Press, 2012), 1.

A growing number of churches have started to do this. They are willing to hold rallies to speak out about their favorite moral issues. Examples include mobilization in opposition to legislation on sexual orientation and identity, on abortion, and on gambling. What I find unusual is their silence when it comes to other moral issues such as extra-judicial executions, or graft and corruption. I urge my fellow Christians to broaden their definitions of social sins to include the unjust killing of poor Filipinos, graft and corruption by civil servants, and plunder by officials at the very top.

I also ask, in view of God's gift of democracy and our birthright, to include as social sin the abuse of power by public servants, especially as their acts weaken our democratic institutions. This is a sin against the Filipino people, and we must speak on their behalf.

Discipleship for Integral Mission

The failed effort to rally support for Chief Justice Sereno from among the evangelical community opened my eyes to the need for a more holistic perspective on discipleship.[36] The Great Commission to "go and make disciples" needs to be viewed in light of the larger mission, the *missio Dei*, of establishing justice in the world.[37] We need to mentor followers of Jesus who view the gospel in the Philippine context, who appreciate God's gifts to and birthright of the Filipino people, who understand the rights and freedoms guaranteed in the Constitution, and who are ready and willing to nurture and defend them.

Evangelicalism has witnessed tremendous growth in the last twenty years,[38] and a growing number of evangelicals have become politically involved since 1986.[39] But we still have a long way to go. The good news is that social and political transformation is possible[40] through the efforts of even just a small but

---

36. The Lausanne Movement, "The Cape Town Commitment," 2011, https://www.lausanne.org/content/ctc/ctcommitment.

37. Scott, *Bring Forth Justice*, xv.

38. From 2.8 percent of the population (based on the 2000 census), the percentage of evangelicals in the population has grown to between 12.3 percent (Operation World, "Pray for: Philippines," accessed 23 November 2020, https://www.operationworld.org/country/phil/owtext.html) and 14 percent (Joshua Project, "Country: Philippines," accessed 23 November 2020, https://joshuaproject.net/countries/RP).

39. Lim, "Consolidating Democracy," 241–65.

40. Erica Chenoweth and Maria J. Stephan, *Why Civil Resistance Works: The Strategic Logic of Nonviolent Conflict* (New York: Columbia University Press, 2012), 21–25.

committed group of people.[41] A just and humane Filipino society is possible and within reach. Intentional discipleship is key. In the words of Ron Sider, "if even a modest fraction of that rapidly growing number of . . . evangelicals and Pentecostals would develop a commonly embraced, biblically grounded framework for doing politics, they would change the world."[42]

Bibliography

Asian Development Bank. *Philippines: Governance in Justice Sector Reform Program.* Mandaluyong City: Asian Development Bank, 2017.

Balcomb, Anthony. "From Apartheid to the New Dispensation: Evangelicals and the Democratization of South Africa." In *Evangelical Christianity and Democracy in Africa*, edited by Terence O. Ranger, 191–224. Oxford: Oxford University Press, 2008.

Batalla, Eric Vincent C., Michelle Sta. Romana, and Karen Rodrigo. "The Judiciary under Threat." In *Routledge Handbook of the Contemporary Philippines*, edited by Mark R. Thompson and Eric Vincent C. Batalla, 130–43. New York: Routledge, 2018.

Bonifacio, Andres. "Decalogue of the Duties of the Sons of the People." 1896. In Richardson, Jim, "Andres Bonifacio, 'Katungkulang gagawin ng mga Z. Ll. B.' (The Decalogue), c. 1896, available from http://www.kasaysayan-kkk.info/membership-documents/andres-bonifacio-katungkulang-gagawin-ng-mga-z-ll-b-the-decalogue-c-1896

Carter, Heath W. *Union Made: Working People and the Rise of Social Christianity in Chicago.* Oxford: Oxford University Press, 2015.

Chenoweth, Erica, and Maria J. Stephan. *Why Civil Resistance Works: The Strategic Logic of Nonviolent Conflict.* New York: Columbia University Press, 2012.

Clymer, Kenton J. "Religion and American Imperialism: Methodist Missionaries in the Philippine Islands, 1899–1913." *Pacific Historical Review* 49, no. 1 (1980): 29–50.

Davis, Nancy J., and Robert V. Robinson. *Claiming Society for God: Religious Movements and Social Welfare in Egypt, Israel, Italy, and the United States.* Bloomington, IN: Indiana University Press, 2012.

Freedom House. "Freedom in the World 2020: Philippines." Accessed 22 November 2020. https://freedomhouse.org/country/philippines/freedom-world/2020.

García-Sayán, Diego. "Judicial Independence in Philippines Is under Threat, Says UN Human Rights Expert." United Nations Human Rights, 1 June 2018. Accessed 23

---

41. David Robson, "The '3.5% Rule'": How a Small Minority Can Change the World," BBC Future, 14 May 2019, accessed 23 November 2020, https://www.bbc.com/future/article/20190513-it-only-takes-35-of-people-to-change-the-world.

42. Sider, *Scandal of Evangelical Politics*, 23.

November 2020. https://www.ohchr.org/EN/NewsEvents/Pages/DisplayNews.aspx?NewsID=23163&LangID=E.

Goodwin, Jeff, James M. Jasper, and Francesca Polletta. "Why Emotions Matter." In *Passionate Politics: Emotions and Social Movements*, edited by Jeff Goodwin, James M. Jasper and Francesca Polletta, 1–26. Chicago: University of Chicago Press, 2001.

Holmes, Ronald D. "Local Governments, Civil Society, Democratization, and Development." In *Chasing the Wind: Assessing Philippine Democracy*, edited by Felipe B. Miranda and Temario C. Rivera, 107–41. Quezon City: Commission on Human Rights and United Nations Development Program, 2016.

Johnson, Thomas K. "The Protester, the Dissident and the Christian." *Evangelical Review of Theology* 44, no. 4 (2020): 294–301. Accessed 5 November 2020. https://theology.worldea.org/evangelical-review-of-theology/.

Joshua Project. "Country: Philippines." Accessed 23 November 2020. https://joshuaproject.net/countries/RP.

The Lausanne Movement. "The Cape Town Commitment." 2011. https://www.lausanne.org/content/ctc/ctcommitment.

Lim, David. "Consolidating Democracy: Filipino Evangelicals between People Power Events, 1986–2001." In *Evangelical Christianity and Democracy in Asia*, edited by David H. Lumsdaine, 235–84. New York: Oxford University Press, 2009.

Mabini, Apolinario. "The True Decalogue." 1898. In Mabaquiao, Jr., Napoleon Mahinay., "Mabini's 'true decalogue' and the morality of nationalism," Asia-Pacific Social Science Review 17(3) (2018): 15-29. Available from https://www.researchgate.net/publication/327688783_Mabini%27s_true_decalogue_and_the_morality_of_nationalism.

Maggay, Melba. *Transforming Society: Reflections on the Kingdom and Politics*. Quezon City: Institute for Studies in Asian Church and Culture, 2004.

Mercado, Monina. *People Power: An Eyewitness History – The Philippine Revolution of 1986*. Manila: J. B. Reuter, S. J. Foundation, 1986.

Metaxas, Eric. *Amazing Grace: William Wilberforce and the Heroic Campaign to End Slavery*. New York: HarperCollins, 2007.

———. *Bonhoeffer: Pastor, Martyr, Prophet, Spy – A Righteous Gentile vs. the Third Reich*. Nashville: Thomas Nelson, 2010.

Miranda, Felipe B. "Conceptualizing and Measuring Modern Democracy." In *Chasing the Wind: Assessing Philippine Democracy*, edited by Felipe B. Miranda and Temario C. Rivera, 1–42. Quezon City: Commission on Human Rights and United Nations Development Program, 2016.

Moreno, Antonio F. "Engaged Citizenship: The Catholic Bishops' Conference of the Philippines (CBCP) in the Post-Authoritarian Philippines." In *Development, Civil Society and Faith-Based Organizations Bridging the Sacred and the Secular*, edited by Gerard Clarke and Michael Jennings, 117–44. New York: Palgrave Macmillan, 2008.

Nadeau, Kathy. "Peasant Resistance and Religious Protests in Early Philippine Society: Turning Friars against the Grain." *Journal for the Scientific Study of Religion* 41, no. 1 (2002): 75–85.

Noll, Mark A. *God and Race in American Politics: A Short History.* Princeton, NJ: Princeton University Press, 2008.

Operation World. "Pray for: Philippines." Accessed 23 November 2020. https://www.operationworld.org/country/phil/owtext.html.

Punzalan, Cesar Vicente P. *PCEC @50 (1965–2015): One Master, One Message, One Mission.* Makati City: Church Strengthening Ministry, 2016.

Rizal, José. *El Filibusterismo.* Ghent, 1891.

Robson, David. "The '3.5% Rule'": How a Small Minority Can Change the World." BBC Future, 14 May 2019. Accessed 23 November 2020. https://www.bbc.com/future/article/20190513-it-only-takes-35-of-people-to-change-the-world.

Scott, Waldron. *Bring Forth Justice.* Carlisle: Paternoster, 1997.

Sider, Ronald J. *The Scandal of Evangelical Politics: Why Are Christians Missing the Chance to Really Change the World?* Grand Rapids, MI: Baker, 2008.

Tizon, Al. *Transformation after Lausanne: Radical Evangelical Mission in Global-Local Perspective.* Oxford: Regnum, 2008.

Youngblood, Robert. "Church Opposition to Martial Law in the Philippines." *Asian Survey* 18, no. 5 (1978): 505–20.

Epilogue

As we end this book, we could not help but ask the following questions in light of what is now happening to our bayan: Will our bayan be continually led by – and persistently support – wayward and evil rulers? What if, after all our efforts, the murderers, thieves, and oppressive leaders continue to rule our *Inang Bayan* (Motherland)? What if, after all our engagement and attempts, injustice still gets the upper hand? Those who are concerned about our bayan may be asking similar questions.

Admittedly, we still have a long way to go. "Malayo pa ang umaga" (Morning is still a long way away). This line from one of our Tagalog songs captures how we feel. Given our recent experience wherein a significant number of our fellow Christians were either apathetic toward or – whether openly or silently – actually supportive of the current administration's disregard for justice and human rights abuses as exemplified by its brutal and inhumane "war on drugs," the future looks bleak. The current administration's march against justice, peace, and righteousness has become familiar to us. We witnessed how President Duterte pushed for the ouster of the country's Chief Justice, the enactment of the dangerous Anti-Terror Act, the shutting down of a major broadcasting network, the scuttling of promising peace negotiations with communist rebels, and the defense of widespread corruption in government agencies especially during this pandemic, all the while spilling the blood of alleged "drug addicts."

We have to admit that there are times when we feel helpless and powerless before this "Leviathan," which in our current Philippine context has not been a source and upholder of peace and order as Thomas Hobbes conceived it to be.[1] Indeed, while some affectionately call President Duterte *Tatay* (Father), to many Filipinos his position as the "father of the nation" has become fictitious and hypocritical for its being deadly and despotic, similar to the Titan Cronus of Greek mythology, who as a father killed and swallowed his own children.

---

1. According to Thomas Hobbes, the Leviathan, a figure taken from the book of Job, represents the ideal commonwealth headed by an all-powerful sovereign who brings about peace by means of the social contract. See Hobbes, *Leviathan*, ed. Edwin Curley (Cambridge: Hackett, 1994), 109.

In the face of such power before which any form of social action by well-meaning citizens often proves inadequate or ineffective, what can we do? As we mentioned in the introduction, this book is about the relationship between "faith and bayan." How do we engage with our bayan? Here we share some suggestions as we reflect on the chapters of this book and their potential contribution to our engagement with our bayan.

Admission

We think that, first and foremost, there should be an admission, a somber acknowledgment, of the seriousness of our situation. Florante's description of our bayan as "bayan kong sawi" (my defeated bayan) is very true to our situation today. Unfortunately, we are not good at confronting our situation. We tend to deny, even laugh at, our problems. As one of our songs puts it, "Tawanan mo ang iyong problema" (Laugh at your problem). But as we have learned in this book, complaining, lament, dissent – all these play an important part in the Christian faith. If we want to move forward, we have to look back. Unless we admit the gravity of our situation, there is no reason for moving on. Admitting that we feel helpless and powerless in the face of our current situation is not a sign of cowardice. On the contrary, it is those who are able to admit their weakness who are courageous, for it takes courage to face the reality.

But while we may feel helpless and powerless, we are not without hope.

Hope

Hope is embodied in the community who have the courage to speak the truth even in the face of danger. The reason we do not speak is because we have lost our voice. As Pilosopo Tasyo, one of the characters in the novel *Noli Me Tangere*, expresses it: "Hindi dumaraing ang bayan sapagkat walang tinig. Hindi kumikilos sapagkat nanghihina"[2] (The nation does not plea because it has no voice. It does not act because it is weak). Some Christians prefer to be silent than to speak out, for various reasons. Some want to maintain unity. But unity in what? Others are silent because they may simply be afraid. According to a survey, 45 percent of Filipinos are afraid to publish anything against the Duterte

---

2. José Rizal, *Noli Me Tangere*, trans. Virgilio S. Almario (Quezon City: Adarna House, 1999), 162–63.

administration.³ But as we have seen in this book, it is part of the Christian's responsibility to engage with society.

Discipleship

In its most important sense, this book is about discipleship. But not discipleship in the individualistic kind of way; rather, a discipleship where faith is actively engaged with our *bayan*. Discipleship in our own context is about following Jesus in the Philippine social-political realities of our time. It is about announcing to our bayan the good news that Jesus proclaimed – freedom for the prisoners, recovery of sight for the blind, freedom for the oppressed, and the proclamation of the year of the Lord's favor (Luke 4:18–19; Isa 61:1–2). Jesus's ministry concerns the whole of human reality, not just the spiritual.

Unfortunately, the Christianity that we have inherited has tended to limit the Christian life to spiritual matters, heavenly things. But at the heart of the gospel is the command to love God and neighbor. Our "neighbor" includes the victims of extra-judicial killings and their families. The son or daughter, or father or mother, who has been killed is part of our own family. How can we say we love our neighbors, our *kababayan*, if we are not concerned about what is happening to them? Would we be silent if it was our own son or daughter who was killed in the "war on drugs"? Would we do nothing if it was our loved one who lost her or his job just because the government closed down her or his company in the midst of the pandemic? It was painful to hear some pastors even rejoicing when ABS-CBN was closed down. But we choose to mourn with those who mourn.

Pagmamalasakit

Pagmamalasakit (deep concern) is what we need to exemplify at this time. In the Old Testament, God demonstrated his deep concern for the Israelites who were experiencing an unjust social-political situation. He told Moses: "I have indeed seen the misery of my people in Egypt. I have heard them crying out because of their slave drivers, and I am concerned about their suffering" (Exod 3:7).⁴ Do we "see the misery" of our many *kababayan*? Do we hear their cries?

---

3. Philstar.com, "SWS: 45% of Filipinos Say 'Dangerous' to Publish Criticism of Government," 14 October 2021, accessed 9 November 2021, https://www.philstar.com/headlines/2021/10/14/2134138/sws-45-filipinos-say-dangerous-publish-criticism-government.

4. All Scripture quotations in this chapter are from NIV.

Jesus himself cried for his bayan as he lamented, "Jerusalem, Jerusalem, you who kill the prophets and stone those sent to you, how often I have longed to gather your children together, as a hen gathers her chicks under her wings, and you were not willing" (Matt 23:37).[5] Becoming like Jesus means also being concerned for our bayan. We believe Jesus loves our bayan and other bayan in the same way that he loves Jerusalem. A modern example of a Christian who loved his bayan is the German martyr Dietrich Bonhoeffer, whom Hitler killed. Loving one's nation includes not tolerating the wrong. Based on his Christian convictions, Bonhoeffer opposed the evil authorities who were leading his nation. He did not wish his people success and victory in war, but rather, as he said in an ecumenical gathering in 1941, "I am praying for the defeat of my nation. Only in and through defeat can it expiate the grievous wrong which it has done Europe and the world."[6]

Although we are taught to be "peacemakers," there are times when, like Bonhoeffer, we cannot avoid struggling against those whose primary aim is to kill, steal, and destroy (John 10:10a). In the Philippines, such resistance to tyranny was shown by the "theologians of struggle"[7] against the Marcos dictatorship. Through struggle they recognized more deeply the concrete and this-worldly dimension of salvation and God's kingdom, as Rebecca Asedillo insightfully remarks:

> It took living under Martial Law and the popular struggles which I supported and in which I participated, for me to realize that salvation really had much to do with the here and now, with the reign of God on earth, with the concrete material and historical concerns of people as they struggle for land, for food, for shelter, for the most basic stuff of life which are denied them.[8]

---

5. God's caring love for Israel is also well illustrated in Hos 11 where the relationship is described in terms of a father tenderly leading his child.

6. Quoted by Reinhold Niebuhr in "Death of a Martyr," *Christianity and Crisis*, 25 June 1945, reproduced at "Political Questions Are Not Irrelevant to Faith: A Reflection on Dietrich Bonhoeffer's Martyrdom," *Providence*, 4 August 2020, https://providencemag.com/2020/08/political-questions-irrelevant-faith-reflection-dietrich-bonhoeffer-martyrdom/.

7. The origin of the term "Theology of Struggle" is attributed to Fr. Louie Hechanova. It finds affinity with Latin America's liberation theology. See the excellent work of Eleazar S. Fernandez, *Toward a Theology of Struggle* (Eugene, OR: Wipf & Stock, 2008).

8. Rebecca Asedillo, "A Protestant Woman's Emerging Spirituality," *In God's Image* 12, no. 3 (1993): 16, quoted in Lisa Asedillo, "The Theology of Struggle," *Indonesian Journal of Theology* 9, no. 1 (July 2021): 76–77.

Theology of Struggle

The theology of struggle remains relevant as it maintains incisively that the Christian faith provides much-needed resources and guidance in fighting and advocating for the "felt needs" and the common good of the people, which are often frustrated by unjust and corrupt political systems, people, and practices. Those who think that getting involved in the struggle in the political sphere is outside the church's concern need to be reminded that discipleship is a "political responsibility"[9] which is brought about by the believer's *union* or *participation in Christ*.

Participation in Christ

Participation in Christ is of course the essence of what we evangelicals call having a "personal relationship" with God through Jesus Christ. Such personal relationship is also described by the apostle Paul in terms of our membership of God's family. For through what Christ did on the cross, we have become God's adopted children (Rom 8:14–17; Gal 3:26; Eph 1:5) by grace through faith *in Christ*. This means we participate and become God's children because of God's decisive action in reaching out to us through Jesus's life, death, and resurrection, not because of what we have done. It is this divine action which makes possible the experience of being God's adopted children through the Spirit (Rom 8:15).[10] This grace-filled relationship is therefore one of "divine gift-giving," which is fulfilled in Christ as a gift.[11] In this relationship of gift-giving on the part of God and gift-receiving on the part of sinful human beings, God's agency which is primary for transformation is not the result of a person's previous worth or action, but is due to the "unconditioned gift of God-in-Christ."[12]

But God's unconditional gift does not mean we no longer have a part to play. The divine action does not diminish or delete human agency. Believers participate in Christ's ethical ways uniquely, as children and coheirs who

---

9. John Howard Yoder, *Discipleship as Political Responsibility* (Scottdale, PA: Herald Press, 2003).

10. Grant Macaskill, "Incarnational Ontology and the Theology of Participation in Paul," in *"In Christ" in Paul: Explorations in Paul's Theology of Union and Participation*, eds. Michael J. Thate, Kevin J. Vanhoozer, and Constantine R. Campbell (Tübingen: Mohr Siebeck, 2014), 98.

11. John M. G. Barclay, *Paul and the Gift* (Grand Rapids, MI: Eerdmans, 2015), 4, 361. Barclay incisively argues that the term "grace" as used by Paul and his contemporaries is related to the ancient and broad anthropological category of "gift."

12. Barclay, *Paul and the Gift*, 360.

imitate Christ not merely in a formal sense, but by real participation even in "the mind of Christ." For according to the apostle Paul, "believing" has an intrinsic ethical dimension – that is to say, there is no real dichotomy between *act* and *being* or between the confessional faith and its ethical outworking. As one of our sayings wisely puts it: "Nasa Diyos ang awa, nasa tao ang gawa" (With God belongs mercy, but action is expected from humans). Christian faith or belief is therefore an *act* of *believing*. It means participating in the mind of Christ which enables us to genuinely engender and not merely imitate Christlike *actions*, foremost of which is the commitment to love God and others. As we learn from Galatians 5:6, "the only thing that counts is faith expressing itself through love."[13] Good action then expresses the *subjective root* or the inner impulses of the human agent, and the *objective ground* of agency which is God's own action.[14] Said another way, from an evangelical perspective human action as participation is responsive action to God's action in Christ.

Pananagutan

Participation in Christ, then, is about Christian responsibility. It seeks to answer the interrelated questions "To whom, and for what, am I responsible?" This image of the responsible self requires the subordination of other images of the human person, such as "man-the maker," which mainly seeks to actualize rational ideas, and "man-as-self-legislator," which understands personhood in light of obedience to society's laws.[15] While to a certain extent these images are helpful, the image of the person as *response-able*, someone who is accountable and has *pananagutan* (accountability), conforms more closely to Scripture.

We participate in God's actions because we have a *pananagutan* (responsibility) to our bayan. We need to hear once again the message of the song "Pananagutan": "walang sinuman ang nabubuhay para sa sarili lamang (no one lives for one's own alone). We all have responsibility to our *kababayan*. This means not just those inside the church. For we are called to be the salt and light of the earth, not just of the church. Just as the biblical faith rejects dividing belief from action, the biblical proclamation of God's lordship through Christ (1 Cor 15:24–28) also rejects the dichotomization of reality into categories

---

13. Douglas A. Campbell, "Participation and Faith in Paul," in Thate, Vanhoozer, and Campbell, *"In Christ,"* 39–41, 48–51.

14. Oliver O'Donovan, *Self, World and Time*, vol. 1 of *Ethics as Theology* (Cambridge: Eerdmans, 2013), 109.

15. Helmut Richard Niebuhr, *The Responsible Self: An Essay in Christian Moral Philosophy* (Louisville, KY: Westminster, 1963), 69–71.

such as sacred/secular or spiritual/political, which has led to the withdrawal or noninvolvement of believers in the political realm. Bonhoeffer's incisive view on this is that there is only one reality and only one way through which reality can truly be known – in and through Christ. This means that the political as well as other spheres in society are all part of the single reality over which God reigns. Christian responsible action is therefore action that conforms to this reality in Christ,[16] which the Old Testament pointed to.

From this perspective, it becomes more comprehensible to see Jesus's actions and decision as genuinely "political." While Jesus did reject the kind of political messiah the people expected, the option he took was no less political. Jesus did not say no to political involvement itself. It was the political options such as glory and worldly power that were being offered to him, as signified by the temptations he faced right after his baptism, that he rejected. In rejecting worldly power, Jesus shows us very clearly that "'political' does not always mean 'governmental.'"[17] His crucifixion at Golgotha could not make this point any clearer.

Christian political involvement does not draw its energy from, nor is it sustained by, the possibilities and promises of attaining power or victorious outcomes. As his disciples, we participate in Christ in opposing injustice, oppression, and unrighteousness because God calls us to a life of faithfulness and participation in Christ as his witnesses and agents of transformation in the groaning political spaces of creation. As Romans 8:22 says, "We know that the whole creation has been groaning as in the pains of childbirth right up to the present time."

The Silence of God

Like the rest of creation, we too are groaning over our bayan. We groan not only because of our pitiful situation, but, even more agonizingly, because God does not seem to care. One of the striking questions that was asked by one of the participants on our "Faith and Bayan" webinars was this: "God heard the complaints and suffering of the Israelites . . . and acted . . . by delivering them. We are aware of some of the sufferings of the people of God these days when they fight against the oppressors and aggressors of our society. . . . Why then does it seem that God is silent in response to their cries today?"

---

16. Dietrich Bonhoeffer, *Dietrich Bonhoeffer Works*, vol. 6, *Ethics*, ed. Clifford Green (Minneapolis: Fortress, 2005), 222–24.

17. John H. Yoder, *The Christian Witness to the State* (Scottdale, PA: Herald, 2002), 54–57.

In the face of God's silence, how do we respond? Not by giving up. Interestingly, the absence of God in the Bible, far from weakening the resolve of God's people, strengthens it all the more. In their many complaints, laments, and cries for justice in society the prophets of old show us that feeling helpless and powerless is not the end. We can use our situation creatively to become strengthened. Likewise in the New Testament, we have seen that the delay to the second coming made the early church believers more creative and persistent. Rather than giving up, they made their situation a means to emphasize the need for human participation. God's silence and absence engendered active engagement. In one of our Revolutionary writings, we read the following prayer:

> Mahabaging langit, iyong natitiis, pinanununghan mo kaming nasa hapis
> Kaya nga sa antak ng maraming sakit ay kusang nagbalak ng panghihimagsik.
>
> (Merciful heaven, you can bear to look at us who are in a terrible mess
> That is why because of so much pain we have initiated a revolt.)

We know that our Lord Jesus himself prayed something similar when he cried out on the cross, "My God, my God, why have you forsaken me?" (Matt 27:46; Ps 22:1). In both the gospels of Mark and Matthew, this is the last cry of our Lord. It's a cry of divine abandonment. And yet, why is it that in that cry of abandonment we feel we are not alone? Because, with so many of us today continuing to grapple with questions of God's hiddenness and abandonment, we realize we are not alone. Jesus's cry is the answer to the question raised by our webinar listener. It is also his cry which gives us the courage to rise up and speak against the powers that be. For our cry is at one with the cries of our bayan and of our Lord.

Bibliography

Asedillo, Lisa. "The Theology of Struggle." *Indonesian Journal of Theology* 9, no. 1 (July 2021): 62–92.

Barclay, John M. G. *Paul and the Gift*. Grand Rapids, MI: Eerdmans, 2015.

Bonhoeffer, Dietrich. *Dietrich Bonhoeffer Works*. Vol. 6, *Ethics*. Edited by Clifford Green. Minneapolis: Fortress, 2005.

Campbell, Douglas A. "Participation and Faith in Paul." In *"In Christ" in Paul: Explorations in Paul's Theology of Union and Participation*, eds. Michael J. Thate,

Kevin J. Vanhoozer, and Constantine R. Campbell, 37–60. Tübingen: Mohr Siebeck, 2014.

Fernandez, Eleazar S. *Toward a Theology of Struggle*. Eugene, OR: Wipf & Stock, 2008.

Hobbes, Thomas. *Leviathan*. Edited by Edwin Curley. Cambridge: Hackett, 1994.

Macaskill, Grant. "Incarnational Ontology and the Theology of Participation in Paul." In *"In Christ" in Paul: Explorations in Paul's Theology of Union and Participation*, eds. Michael J. Thate, Kevin J. Vanhoozer, and Constantine R. Campbell, 87–101. Tübingen: Mohr Siebeck, 2014.

Niebuhr, Helmut Richard. *The Responsible Self: An Essay in Christian Moral Philosophy*. Louisville, KY: Westminster, 1963.

Niebuhr, Reinhold. "Death of a Martyr." *Christianity and Crisis*, 25 June 1945. Reproduced at "Political Questions Are Not Irrelevant to Faith: A Reflection on Dietrich Bonhoeffer's Martyrdom." *Providence*, 4 August 2020. https://providencemag.com/2020/08/political-questions-irrelevant-faith-reflection-dietrich-bonhoeffer-martyrdom/.

O'Donovan, Oliver. *Self, World and Time*. Vol. 1 of *Ethics as Theology*. Cambridge: Eerdmans, 2013.

Philstar.com. "SWS: 45% of Filipinos Say 'Dangerous' to Publish Criticism of Government." 14 October 2021. Accessed 9 November 2021. https://www.philstar.com/headlines/2021/10/14/2134138/sws-45-filipinos-say-dangerous-publish-criticism-government.

Rizal, José. *Noli Me Tangere*. Translated by Virgilio S. Almario. Quezon City: Adarna House, 1999.

Yoder, John H. *The Christian Witness to the State*. Scottdale, PA: Herald, 2002.

———. *Discipleship as Political Responsibility*. Scottdale, PA: Herald Press, 2003.

Langham Literature and its imprints are a ministry of Langham Partnership.

Langham Partnership is a global fellowship working in pursuit of the vision God entrusted to its founder John Stott –

> *to facilitate the growth of the church in maturity and Christ-likeness through raising the standards of biblical preaching and teaching.*

Our vision is to see churches in the Majority World equipped for mission and growing to maturity in Christ through the ministry of pastors and leaders who believe, teach and live by the word of God.

Our mission is to strengthen the ministry of the word of God through:
- nurturing national movements for biblical preaching
- fostering the creation and distribution of evangelical literature
- enhancing evangelical theological education

especially in countries where churches are under-resourced.

Our ministry

Langham Preaching partners with national leaders to nurture indigenous biblical preaching movements for pastors and lay preachers all around the world. With the support of a team of trainers from many countries, a multi-level programme of seminars provides practical training, and is followed by a programme for training local facilitators. Local preachers' groups and national and regional networks ensure continuity and ongoing development, seeking to build vigorous movements committed to Bible exposition.

Langham Literature provides Majority World preachers, scholars and seminary libraries with evangelical books and electronic resources through publishing and distribution, grants and discounts. The programme also fosters the creation of indigenous evangelical books in many languages, through writer's grants, strengthening local evangelical publishing houses, and investment in major regional literature projects, such as one volume Bible commentaries like *The Africa Bible Commentary* and *The South Asia Bible Commentary*.

Langham Scholars provides financial support for evangelical doctoral students from the Majority World so that, when they return home, they may train pastors and other Christian leaders with sound, biblical and theological teaching. This programme equips those who equip others. Langham Scholars also works in partnership with Majority World seminaries in strengthening evangelical theological education. A growing number of Langham Scholars study in high quality doctoral programmes in the Majority World itself. As well as teaching the next generation of pastors, graduated Langham Scholars exercise significant influence through their writing and leadership.

To learn more about Langham Partnership and the work we do visit **langham.org**

www.ingramcontent.com/pod-product-compliance
Lightning Source LLC
Chambersburg PA
CBHW070536170426
43200CB00011B/2445